Biopolitics and Resistance in Legal Education

Taking up the study of legal education in distinctly biopolitical terms, this book provides a critical and political analysis of resistance in the law school.

Legal education concerns the complex pathways by which an individual becomes a lawyer, making the journey from lay-person to expert, from student to practitioner. To pose the idea of a biopolitics of legal education is not only to recognise the tensions surrounding this journey but also to recognise that legal education is a key site in which the subject engages, and is engaged by, a particular structure—and here the particular structure of the law school. This book explores the resistance to that structure, including: different ways in which law's pedagogic structures might be incomplete, or are being fought against; the use of less conventional elements of cultural discourse to resist the abstraction of the lawyer in students' subject formation; the centralisation of queer and feminist discourses to disrupt the hierarchies of the legal curriculum; the use of digital technologies; the place of embodiment in legal education settings; and the impacts of posthuman knowledges and contexts on legal learning.

Assembling original, field-defining essays by both leading international scholars and emerging researchers, this book constitutes an indispensable resource in legal education research and scholarship that will appeal to legal academics everywhere.

Thomas Giddens is Chair of Jurisprudence at the University of Dundee, UK.

Luca Siliquini-Cinelli is Reader in Law at Cardiff University, UK.

Biopolitics and Resistance in Legal Education

Edited by Thomas Giddens
and Luca Siliquini-Cinelli

Routledge
Taylor & Francis Group
a GlassHouse Book

First published 2023
by Routledge
4 Park Square, Milton Park, Abingdon, Oxon OX14 4RN

and by Routledge
605 Third Avenue, New York, NY 10158

Routledge is an imprint of the Taylor & Francis Group, an informa business

a Glasshouse book

British Library Cataloguing-in-Publication Data
A catalogue record for this book is available from the British Library

ISBN: 978-0-367-77524-7 (hbk)
ISBN: 978-1-032-01604-7 (pbk)
ISBN: 978-1-003-17928-3 (ebk)

DOI: 10.4324/9781003179283

Typeset in Bembo
by Deanta Global Publishing Services, Chennai, India

Contents

Contributors

Foluke I Adebisi is Associate Professor of Law at the University of Bristol, UK.

Chris Ashford is Professor of Law and Society at Northumbria University, UK.

Karen Crawley is Senior Lecturer in Law at Griffith University, Australia.

Daury Fabriz is Professor of Law at the Faculdade de Direito de Vitória, Brazil.

Francesco Forzani is Postgraduate Researcher in Law at the University of Westminster, UK.

Julia Ávila Franzoni is Adjunct Professor of Legal Theory at the Universidade Federal do Rio de Janeiro, Brazil.

Kate Galloway is Associate Professor of Law at Griffith University, Australia.

Thomas Giddens is Chair of Jurisprudence at the University of Dundee, UK.

Peter Goodrich is Professor of Law at Cardozo School of Law, USA, and Visiting Professor in the School of Social Science, New York University Abu Dhabi.

Laura Graham is Senior Lecturer in Law at Northumbria University, UK.

Katherine Langley is Senior Lecturer in Law at the University of Sunderland, UK.

Kryss Macleod is Principal Lecturer in Law at Manchester Metropolitan University, UK.

Timothy D Peters is Associate Professor of Law at the University of the Sunshine Coast, Australia.

Samantha Rasiah is Lecturer in Policing at Staffordshire University, Australia.

Iván Darío Vargas Roncancio is Associate Director at the Centre for Indigenous Conservation and Development Alternatives (CICADA) at McGill University, Canada.

Cassandra Sharp is Associate Professor of Law at the University of Wollongong, Australia.

Luca Siliquini-Cinelli is Reader in Law at Cardiff University, UK.

Prue Vines is Professor of Law at the University of New South Wales, Sydney, Australia.

Juliana Zaganelli is an Independent Researcher, Brazil.

Introduction

Thomas Giddens

Resisting the Law School

Following a course of legal education means becoming with power. To be a student of the law is to be—to grow, change, develop, unfold—within the structures of the law school and the legal tradition in which it provides training. These structures govern the learning subject and condition the forms of life that such education produces or enables, both with respect to individual students and the wider social contexts they go on to populate. But law, and its study, is an area of human and intellectual endeavour oriented around the legitimate exercise of authority—querying not only the structure of legal regulation but the manner in which it can be deployed and administered to produce justice in the governance of community. In many renditions, law is not merely about the promulgation of power (although that is something law can enable) and thus its education is not merely the memorisation of rules as the expression of static forms of authority. More fundamentally, law is—or, perhaps, should be—about questioning and seeking to ensure the legitimacy of the way power is exercised, and its education about developing the tools required for such conduct.

Law governs through structure, delineating the multifarious ways in which life takes shape, facilitating the formation, maintenance, and variation of lawful relations. Law is thus often a question of the relationship between the structures of power and the conduct of individuals—as either subjects or agents of power, or both. To learn the law is doubly concerned with power: if we accept—in line with critical pedagogies such as those of Paulo Freire or Jacques Derrida—that pedagogy is always an exercise of power in itself, then to teach is to control or direct, or at least influence, the intellectual exposure and journey of learners (including teachers). It is to manage the backgrounding and foregrounding of knowledge and experience, and the concomitant patterning of the learning subject into certain habits of mind and ways of working with legal and other materials, as well as into different institutional structures and modes of (lawyerly) life.

DOI: 10.4324/9781003179283-1

Legal education is not about memorising regulations, but about training for governance—for the care of the social, economic, cultural, and political effects of the positions taken up by law students as they move through their subsequent careers, within and beyond the expressly legal institution. Legal education is also a form of governance, a relation of power in itself—a governance of the minds and development of students (and teachers-as-students). As such, legal education—like other areas of pedagogy—is always in tension with those that are governed. As Foucault frames it, power always operates through agonistic relations:

> At the very heart of the power relationship, and constantly provoking it, are the recalcitrance of the will and the intransigence of freedom. Rather than speaking of an essential freedom [against which power defines itself], it would be better to speak of an 'agonism'—of a relationship which is at the same time reciprocal incitation and struggle, less of a face-to-face confrontation which paralyzes both sides than a permanent provocation.[1]

To study law, then, is not simply to be subjected to legal knowledge as a docile student body. Students are not blank canvasses waiting for pre-determined legal knowledge to be inscribed upon them. To follow a course of legal education is to be exposed to the pedagogic power of the law school—and to become in an agonistic relation to it. To be a law student is to *resist* the law school. And law teachers, too, dwell in resistance to the structures that govern academic endeavour, including the resistant power of law students and other governmental and managerial technologies that surround, hold, delimit, and structure experience and condition the agency of teachers, scholars, and students alike.

The question that this volume begins to map, however, is not merely whether there is or can be resistance to these structures of power (indeed, the vision outlined above would hold that resistance is a necessary feature in the very operation of power itself). Working within a broadly biopolitical frame—investigating the ways in which different forms of life are produced or enabled, or the broad relations between individual forms of life and the operations or structures of power—the question that engages this volume, rather, is how such resistance unfolds or takes form in the context of legal education, broadly understood.[2] And across its chapters, a variety of perspectives and articulations of this concern can be witnessed. The chapters in this collection are not divided into sections, but are instead arranged in a way that they move through

1 Foucault (1982) p 790.

2 This volume is part of a two-volume project on the biopolitics of legal education. The other volume is focused on mapping the broadly biopolitical structures implicated by, in, and through the law school: see Siliquini-Cinelli and Giddens (2023).

a range of possibilities and perspectives. Together, they tell a story of resistance to the dominant forms and assumptions of the traditional, Western law school.

Overview of Chapters

The volume is organised into three rough parts, each collecting chapters that focus on a different quality of resistance within the biopolitics of legal education: Normative Resistance, Internal Resistance, and Posthuman Resistance. Part 1, 'Normative Resistance', encompasses Chapters 1–5 which each consider resistance that can be understood as based upon a normative engagement—from the embedded racialised and sexualised norms of Western law, through the norms of engaged citizenship, to the different ways in which technology intervenes in various normative assumptions. Our story in Part 1 begins with the necropolitical qualities of modern Western law. Focused on the governance of death rather than the production and protection of earthly life, Foluke I Adebisi unpacks the radically unsettling project of decolonisation in legal education that goes far beyond mere surface tweaks to the curriculum, aiming instead to excavate and reform the deeply rooted assumptions of a legal knowledge that remains wedded to the necropolitical logics of colonialism. From here, Chris Ashford, Laura Graham, and Samantha Rasiah examine how alternative forms of legal knowledge—in their case, zines—can facilitate a decentring of dominant ideologies and stagnating pedagogies in law schools. Through an empirical case study, which uses the production of feminist and queer zines by law students, their work aims to give presence and voice to a range of traditionally excluded identities and subject positions within the structures of legal education.

The scale of concern then expands, as Juliana Zanganelli and Daury Fabriz take up the role of legal education with respect to the production of subject positions capable of engaging in the wider political milieu. By undertaking legal education on the level of citizenship, they claim, deeper and more meaningful participation in democratic processes, reform, and dialogue in the context of collective life can be achieved. Katherine Langley then continues the theme of community participation, but zeroes back in on the experience of legal education itself. She undertakes a reflective analysis of the role that Twitter and other forms of social media can play in legal education and the production and maintenance of a community that supplements or undermines the 'dehumanising' effects that can be seen to come with online and distanced learning, especially since the COVID-19 pandemic. As life becomes increasingly mediated through electronic environments, perhaps the sophistication of these kinds of social media platforms can offer a mode of relation that traditional law school structures and technologies struggle to provide. And, of course, technological changes also affect the legal profession. Kryss Macleod accordingly takes up this theme, querying how legal education can be harnessed as an active force for arming students (i.e. future practitioners) with the expertise to use advancing technologies and develop innovative and adaptable ways of working that have the potential to resist and reformulate dominant paradigms and orthodoxies in a legal profession riven with inequalities. What is imagined is the production of modes of lawyerly life that embrace the technological landscape and its implications for mixing up the heavy sediment of a patriarchal and classist profession.

Part 2, 'Internal Resistance', takes up the narrative by shifting focus to modes of resistance internal to legal pedagogic practice. Prue Vines opens this section by transitioning from one form of technology to another, applying the techniques of poetic composition and interpretation to the problem of lawyerly subject formation. Framing the law teacher as a poet, the linguistic sophistication and techniques of poetic expression—which can capture and articulate human experience, meaning, relation, and valuation in a way often impossible for mainstream legal forms—are able to enhance the emotional education of students and, perhaps, unsettle the model of both law and lawyers as mechanical entities for governance and technocratic regulation.

Indeed, how we frame and narrate law, legal education, and legal ideas can have a profound effect on the kind of lawyers and legal system—and wider social and cultural structures and forms—that emerge. Julia Ávila Franzoni's contribution works on this foundational level, examining a project from a Brazilian law school that seeks to undertake collective storytelling around the way legal pedagogy is imagined. Engaging through critical pedagogies, feminism, legal geography, and critical materialism, she highlights a potential pathway to reformulating primary assumptions towards an increasingly situated and inclusive legal mode.

Furthering consideration of a situated legality, of one's corporeal presence within a system or tradition of law and its institutional forms, Peter Goodrich points out the embodied humour that is involved in legal education and praxis. For Goodrich, law school captures and restrains the body in chains of decorum and reverence—a restraint that can meaningfully and explosively be resisted through a practice of comedy that unlocks a way of knowing and mode of engagement with law and its training that is overtly sensitive to its affective dimensions and the limitations of its traditionally staid forms. But legal decorum, of course, can be resisted in less hilarious ways—as demonstrated by Timothy D Peters and Karen Crawley in their analysis of teaching cultural legal studies, an undergraduate module and disciplinary endeavour that counterposes the seriousness of institutional law and legal knowledge with the seeming delights and vagaries of popular and artistic culture. Expanding the legal apparatus beyond state forms, cultural legal studies hones the sensitivities of law students to the law found within and through the reading of cultural texts, thus enabling the production of lawyerly life forms more reflexively capable and responsible for their own interpretive practice.

Merging this kind of cultural understanding with the questions of legal poetry and how we narrate legal forms and ideas, Cassandra Sharp advocates for the self-conscious participation by students in conversation and storytelling.

Story consumption, she demonstrates, engages with biopolitical concerns of subject formation and the construction of reality. Employing storytelling techniques and reflections in legal pedagogy thus unlocks a powerful potential for law schools to develop ethically reflexive and politically self-aware individuals to go out and occupy lawyerly and professional workplaces.

In the final section, the context is shifted again—this time to 'Posthuman Resistance'. Continuing the concern with the subjectivity enabled by epistemic forms, Luca Siliquini-Cinelli interrogates Rosi Braidotti's posthuman work for modes of subjecthood that might help resist or challenge problematic features of Western legal education. Focused on the distinction between knowledge and experience, he shows how Braidotti's work can reinvigorate sensitivity towards the relational finitude of life often overlooked by dominant legal-pedagogic paradigms, but how, at the same time, it remains limited within the domains of knowledge itself. We must aim, Siliquini-Cinelli says, to escape the strictures of epistemic form and open to the immanence of factual alterity. Yet the turn to the posthuman also signals an awareness of the distinctly anthropocentric qualities of law and legal education, focused always on the human subject and the human world: imagining human subjects as rights-holders with dominion over the non-human. Legal curricula side-line or overlook posthuman perspectives, despite the radical challenges posed, for example, by the climate emergency. Kate Galloway rejects such backgrounding, demonstrating the way biopolitics brings into focus law's anthropocentric priorities. But to regulate effectively, legal education needs to acknowledge and embrace the complex and irresolute entanglement of human and non-human worlds, and craft lawyers sensitive to their planetary place.

On which note, Iván Darío Vargas Roncancio works to begin reimagining legal systems within the context of the Anthropocene. Roncancio's contribution does this by considering the deep-rooted ontological and epistemic assumptions that shape a standard comparative law textbook, and placing them alongside radically alternative conceptions of legal as found in indigenous and ecological jurisprudence. Working on the assumption of the co-emergence of human and non-human, rather than the dominant assumption of their separation in Western law, Roncancio highlights the potential to develop truly relational models of legality and legal education.

Rounding off the gestural narrative of the collection, Francesco Forzani considers the resistant effects of legal study itself. Through the work of Giorgio Agamben, Forzani highlights the questioning of legal power and its biopolitical processing of 'life' into political form that active legal study entails. In contrast to passive learners, who are disciplined into docile bodies, students continually and endlessly question and challenge the law and its claim to decide the contours of community.

Across this collection, we move through a number of different modes of resistance to dominant traditions and assumptions in legal knowledge, education, and form. From decolonisation, through queering, political empowerment, technological appropriation and occupation, poetic training, embodiment, comedy, interpretive sensitivity, storytelling and narration, to a posthuman and indigenous resistance to Western epistemic form, the pedagogic embracing of non-human alterity, and legal study as the endless critique of legal claims to political adjudication. The ways in which resistance permeates and runs through legal education—understood in its broadest sense—are manifold, and the diversity of the gestures articulated in this collection are testament to the rich potential of framing legal education in a way that acknowledges its biopolitical qualities: as an area of life that trains for governance and is thus inherently embroiled in the complex political processes of knowledge-making and subject-formation, concomitantly enabling the forms of communal life.

References

Michel Foucault (1982) 'The Subject and Power' 8 *Critical Inquiry* 777.

Luca Siliquini-Cinelli and Thomas Giddens (eds) (2023) *Biopolitics and Structure in Legal Education*, Routledge.

Part I

Normative Resistance

Chapter 1

Educating for the End of a Necropolitical World

What Happens Beyond Decolonisation in Legal Education?

Foluke I Adebisi

Introduction or How We Can No Longer Breathe

While writing this essay, three overarching global 'events' demonstrated the perdition in which the earth and humanity exists. The first is the global pandemic which has had a devastating effect on individual and collective ways of living. Yet, within the general impact, lines of inequality are exacerbated, and government responses [including heightened criminalisation and border surveillance, as well the emerging 'vaccine apartheid'] have increased the vulnerability of those already living in proximity to premature death.[1] The filming of the killing of George Floyd led to a global outcry that highlighted continuing structural and direct racism as a significant harm to people racialised 'below the line of the human'. This resulted in many institutional promises to change and repair historically and contemporarily unjust systems. The convergence of these two issues led the American Medical Association, in November 2020, to recognise racism—systemic, cultural, and interpersonal—as a 'public health threat'.[2] Finally, the danger of climate change has become increasingly evident in environmental devastation and unusual weather patterns around the world. These three global challenges are intertwined through the restriction of breath—the very essence of life. COVID-19 attacks the lungs' ability to breathe; George Floyd could not breathe as Derek Chauvin placed a knee on Floyd's neck for approximately nine minutes. Many cannot breathe in rising temperatures and waters. These three issues are also entangled in how they have been produced and who they most affect, as well as those whose voices and experiences are most silenced.

Yet, many Indigenous people, people from colonised states, and people from underrepresented populations choose to enter into the field of law because they seek liberation within it. This sadly often turns out to be an

1 Adebisi and Jivraj (2021) 65; Adebisi (2021a).

2 American Medical Association (2020) Press Release, 16 November, www.ama-assn.org/press-center/press-releases/new-ama-policy-recognizes-racism-public-health-threat.

DOI: 10.4324/9781003179283-3

empty promise because law and legal education are implicated in historic and systemic reproduction or maintenance of the challenges listed above, especially in leftovers of colonisation and/or in the colonial logics preceding and surviving administrative/territorial control of colonies. It should be noted that 'race', a social construct, was a key technology deployed in colonisation to determine a hierarchy of valuable bodies, as well as spaces for exploitation. This has resulted in current racial states.[3] In other words, Euro-modern law, as a tool of global and local order is implicated in creating and maintaining a world system that produces unequal pain and death. The hierarchy it governs protects systems and structures over humanity … corporality over corporeality. Legal education thus serves the interests of the powerful at the expense of humanity and the earth on which we currently survive. The registers of hierarchisation determine the proximity to 'premature death' of the bodies thus hierarchised. This system is evidenced not only in temporalised practices of racialised enslavement and direct administration of colonies, but also in the world that is produced therefrom, exemplified by anthropocentricism, diverse technologies of racialisation and borderisation, continuing colonial logics, all backed by legal knowledge. So, legal education, in a world driven by these logics thought of as normative and natural, preserves the permanence of dehumanising biopower. We do not have to live like this, but we think there is no other way. Consequently, academic disciplining within law operates more as a system of restrictive regulation than a system of possibility … of knowledge as a practice of freedom.[4] There is currently limited capacity within legal education for imagining and thinking radically different ways of being in the world. Therefore, this chapter argues that legal education is a field of pain and death,[5] because through its adherence to Eurocentric method it unequally protects not the presence of life [humans] but the presence of structures [persons]. So, while 'decolonisation of the curriculum' may provide a way for the field to operate more biocentredly, what matters more than performative decolonisation is that the field of law be able to offer a means for students and staff to together imagine, craft and bring to life, worlds beyond this necropolitical one. I begin this chapter with an examination of the nexus of legal thought, biopolitics and necropolitics, explaining how the permanence of colonialism ties them together in the production of particular visions of the world and the human subject. Next, I explore how decadence manifests in legal knowledge. The chapter concludes with a short reflection on ways legal education can imagine within itself, hope of a world in which large swathes of humanity are not destined for immediate and slow death.

3 Goldberg (2008) pp 233–58.

4 Freire (2005) p 34.

5 'Legal interpretation takes place in a field of pain and death'. In Cover (1985) p 1601.

On Law, Racialised Bodies, Coloniality, and This Necropolitical Space

Euro-modern legal knowledge plays a pivotal role in producing and sustaining the current world structure. Darian-Smith describes this type of law as law which began in Europe, but also arose out of colonial activities in the Americas, Africa, Asia, and Oceania, whose ontology places Euro-America at the centre of the world and is intimately tied to these origins and uses.[6] This type of law is recognised as integral to undergirding coercive power and interests and desires of capital—what Thornton calls 'technocentrism'.[7] The process of universalising and globalising Euro-modern law solidifies its complicity with the market and the emergence and normalisation of ways of living that underpin global challenges such as inequality and climate change.[8] In other words, this uncovers the futility of attempts to use law to change the world, that do not include a re-examination of the nature of legal knowledge itself and its complicity in creating the unequal world we are attempting to change. Legal education finds itself drawn into these processes of reproduction through its role in transmitting incomplete and distorted knowledge about law and society.

One major marker that has influenced the emergence of this unequal world is the hierarchisation of humanity. This is often exemplified by actually indivisible [un]protected characteristics such as class, race, gender, sexuality, etc., which are imbricated with colonialism—especially within 'coloniality of gender'.[9] Quijano connects the creation of these characteristics in the establishment of what he calls the 'colonial matrix of power'.[10] This matrix, whose inception is dated to 1492, is operationalised in the intractable globalised control of the rest of the world by Euro-America through four spheres: economy; authority; gender and sexuality; subjectivity and knowledge.[11] 'Race' [or gendered-race] emerges most strongly through these histories and processes as a key technology of control. Classification into 'scientific races' was manufactured as 'the constitutive, founding element of the relations of domination that the conquest imposed'.[12] Therefore, whose labour could be coerced or who could be dispossessed of land and liberty was determined by where a person fit into a nebulous system of racialisation. Such dispossession along artificed racial lines served the purpose of accumulation of capital. So, the intertwining of colonial spheres of control emphasises the centrality of capital to this matrix—the scalation of humanity functions to ensure wealth accretion for a few. Thus

6 Darian-Smith (2013) pp 247–64; Darian-Smith (2015) pp 647–51.
7 Thornton (1998) pp 369–98.
8 Adebisi (2021b) pp 428–49.
9 See: Lugones (2013) pp 379–400; Icaza and Vázquez (2016) pp 62–73; Oyěwùmí (2005) pp 3–21.
10 Quijano and Ennis (2000) pp 544–5.
11 Mignolo (2007) p 156.
12 Quijano and Ennis (2000) pp 533, 544–5.

'class' and 'race' do not materially exist as separate legitimate categorisations of humanity. Instead, they 'are two, compatible ways of explaining how society is split into strata of material security'.[13] Add to this gender, ability, and sexuality, etc., and we see how the externalised capacity of a body to contribute to capital also determines how much value is placed on that body. Thus, I call these characteristics 'unprotected'. However, racialisation of peoples into categories, specifically and particularly, was and is enacted on a major global scale and so remains a primary determinant of global division of power. This main mode of control relies on normativising an epistemically artificed division of humanity into 'below and above the line of the human'.[14] Thus Euro-modern law maintains this line through: defining land as property when its becomes held in Eurocentric ways; defining the boundaries of liberty and freedom within racialised enslavement and exploitative colonisation; and ensuring [through governing borders] that the chains of succession of dispossession and accumulation are unbroken in the continuities between colony and state.

Thus, it is argued that the very existence/creation of racial-gender categories, for example, but also particularly, produce the life-death dichotomy that marks the necropolitics of a world perpetually suffused in colonial logics and praxis. Gilmore thus defines racism as 'the state-sanctioned or extralegal production and exploitation of group-differentiated vulnerability to premature death'.[15] This definition recognises the structural effects of racialisation as well as the entrenchment of state-power and thus law in race's emergence as category and reproduction as harm/privilege. In other words, being artificially drafted into a contrived but materially effective lower scale of humanity systemically places those so drafted closer to death. The counterpoint is also true—those drafted into the higher scale of humanity are placed further away from vulnerability to premature death. In the constitution of the human-subject in law—and the subject's relationship to bordered space—legal knowledge reproduces differential proximities to death. So, it is suggested that the colonial difference in conceptualisation of, for example, Wynter's 'Man',[16] may attempt to be diluted by inclusive representation, but unless directly dismantled, this colonial difference is structurally self-reproductive. This is because the legal concept of the human is already contingent on artificed categorisation, thus representation still operates on the norms of the system—new norms are needed for new systems.[17]

In other words, as legal education is ultimately the study of the human subject in relation to society, closer attention should be paid within it to the actual social-historical construction of this human subject beyond its presumption as

13 Táíwò (2021).
14 Grosfoguel (2016) pp 11–2.
15 Gilmore (2007) p 28.
16 Wynter (2003) pp 257–337.
17 Gordon (2020) p 47.

a biological organism. Within legal education and practice, the enfoldment of unprotected characteristics is not central to our understanding of the human and the relation between law and society. In contrast with the legal person, the human and the human body are thus under-theorised as legal agents within the main corpus of law itself, though there is some attention paid to the body within areas of law that focus on health, such as medical law.[18] Thus, there is a jurisprudential gap here which arises from the fact that Euro-modern law's premises about who can be considered the ideal law's human subject, have remained set and largely unchanged since the dawn of colonialism—1492.[19] In other words, within legal knowledge, the [un]protected characteristics are mostly still considered to be legitimate, neutral, and divisible categorisations of humanity and not carriers of inequality. To undo this presumption is to reconceptualise our understanding of society. Therefore, we must also consider how Euro-modern law's code is entangled in producing vulnerability in certain bodies, the society that proceeds therefrom, and thus the emergence of a necropolitical world.

Foucault, in his reflections on the concept of biopolitics, was concerned with the functional and legitimated power of the sovereign to regulate the life of the legitimate population.[20] So, he describes the population as to the sovereign a political, scientific, and biological problem.[21] Thus, questions of law and governance manifest themselves in multidisciplinary modes of control. The law is necessary to control all spheres of life—housing, education, health, work, order, etc. Foucault recognises this as an extension of logics from the battlefield into the domestic sphere—an effective reduction of human interaction to appearing only in the starkness of either death or life.[22] There is no liminal space. On the battlefield, the living soldier is fighting for the sovereign; the dead/wounded soldier has no impact on the war. By extending this death/life frame to civil 'peacetime', the concern of the sovereign in the domestic sphere is reduced to only the same concerns that pervade the warscape—some will live, and some will die. Bodies become merely functional. The civil warscape is the economy—the accumulation of capital. Citizens either contribute to the economy or they are dead/dying. There is no in-between space. Expanding on Foucault's biopolitical thesis, Mbembé introduces 'necropolitics'—sovereign death-power. He asserts, 'the ultimate expression of sovereignty largely resides in the power and capacity to dictate who is able to live and who must die'.[23] Mbembé's treatise recognises the limits of a biopolitical analysis that fails to account for extreme situations that arise therein where 'life was not so much

18 Naffine (2009) p 6; Travis (2014) pp 526–47; Dietz *et al.* (2020) p 7.
19 Dussel (1995).
20 Davies et al. (2017) p 1267.
21 Foucault and Ewald (2013) p 66.
22 Foucault and Ewald (2013) p 75.
23 Mbembé (2019) p 66.

being governed, as much as death itself was being sanctioned'.[24] The survival of necropolitical spheres as such is contingent on death being, not just a possible outcome, but the definite outcome for certain members of its population. The logics of Foucauldian biopolitics are not divorced from necropolitical orders but exacerbated within them. Thus, the biopolis and the necropolis are described as co-constitutive near counterpoints of each other—zones of life and death respectively.[25] The biopolis is constructed so the state—the sovereign—survives at all costs [some will die]; the necropolis is comprised of variously located zones of exclusion containing populations whose lives point only to death [some must die].[26] Put differently, in the biopolis, for survival of the sovereign-economy, the death of some is possible, while in the necropolis, the death of some is inevitable. Mbembé describes the necropolis as emerging through 'the generalized instrumentalization of human existence and the material destruction of human bodies and populations'.[27] Thus, this unfolding destruction began with identifying populations who are marked 'must die', and can be found in the colonial matrix of power's appropriation-led creation of 'zones of non-being' predicated on gendered racialisation.[28] In regulation in response to the global pandemic, in enduring racial injustice, in disproportionate vulnerability to the violence of climate change—some have been labelled 'must die' for the survival of colonialism's power. And so, this process continues with the overexploitation of appropriated and commodified land as well as the enclosure of unfree labour, the untrammelled extraction of resources, and their entrapment behind and within colonially devised borders.[29]

Thus, both Foucault and Mbembé recognise structural or state-sanctioned racism as not just one example of sovereign death-power, but *the* example; they also recognise the role of imperial control in the emergence of the biopolis and the necropolis.[30] Mbembé pays closer attention to the contemporary extension and evolution of colonial ideology, unsurprisingly, as his thesis relies more heavily and overtly on the scholarship of Fanon.[31] The limits of Foucault's analysis reveal themselves in how he, similar to Marx before him, does not engage with how action below the abyssal line,[32] [designated the Global South and sphere of indigenous life] not only has effect on zones above the abyssal line, but is also contingent on conditions above the abyssal line. Thus, Foucault only finds racism significant when it occurs above

24 Davies et al. (2017) pp 1267–8.
25 McIntyre and Nast (2011) p 1467; Braidotti (2013) p 122.
26 McIntyre and Nast (2011) p 1467.
27 Mbembé (2019) p 68.
28 Grosfoguel (2016) pp 11–2; Fanon (2008) p 2; Weheliye (2014) pp 41–2, 96.
29 El-Enany (2020).
30 Foucault and Ewald (2013) pp 74–7; Mbembé (2019) pp 1–5, 38.
31 Mbembé (2019) especially chapters 4 and 5.
32 de Sousa Santos (2015) pp 117–18.

the abyssal line.[33] This absence in Foucault's thesis on biopolitics causes an analytical schism, splitting the historical-colonial from the colonial-present. It also splits geographically contingent zones from each other. Such a parochial analysis fails to note how the logics of being and space, that constitute the soul of colonialism, survive direct political colonial control and physical presence. Hence, Maldonado-Torres distinguishes colonisation [spatial-temporal bound event] from colonialism/coloniality [continually evolving logics and praxis]. According to him, the latter describes 'long-standing patterns of power that emerged … that define culture, labor, intersubjective relations, and knowledge production well beyond the strict limits of colonial administrations'.[34] Colonialism precedes and outlasts colonisation, 'maintained alive in books, in the criteria for academic performance, in cultural patterns, in common sense, in the self-image of peoples, in aspirations of self'.[35] Thus, colonialism is the very breath of 'modernity'.[36] It operates as contiguous extractive and dehumanising ideologies and practices working in tandem, creating contingent zones of accumulation and dispossession, along fault-lines produced by racial marking of bodies 'may live/must die'. Race, or more accurately racialisation, thus unveils itself as having a particular significance beyond being a neutral method of categorisation, but rather a producer of racial disparities.[37] As Van den Berghe notes, 'without racism, physical characteristics are devoid of social significance … it is not the presence of objective physical differences between groups that creates race, but the social recognition of such differences as socially significant or relevant'.[38]

Consequently, Weheliye contends that the biopolitical function of race is racism.[39] One could argue, based on the foregoing, that the function of racialisation, especially below the line, is ultimately necropolitical. Put differently, the division of humans into racial [and other overlapping] categories, functions to identify populations structurally coded for death—slow or immediate. Legal education failing to note this morphology, and the attendant requirements of law's complicity in the process, ensures the survival of colonialism, the consequent destruction of populations necropolitically marked for death, as well as environmental catastrophe. Law and legal education dedicate themselves to regulating/maintaining the social order, therefore, legal knowledge, without a rethink, of necessity reproduces the world that produces bodies coded for death. This legitimation by law can be identified in many ways, in the dictates of law and order and crime, in normalising what is of value in the eyes of the

33 Weheliye (2014) p 61.
34 Maldonado-Torres (2007) p 243.
35 Maldonado-Torres (2007) p 243.
36 Maldonado-Torres (2007) p 243; also Mignolo (2011) pp 2–3.
37 Kendi (2017).
38 Van den Berghe (1967) p 11.
39 Weheliye (2014) pp 55–6.

law, in creating legal ontologies about land or whose work and what work has value, etc. Two main modes of legitimation are of interest in this chapter. The first, discussed above, is the production of bodies permanently vulnerable to premature death. The second—related to the first—is the creation of contingent spaces of destruction through 'borderisation' which, according to Mbembé, is 'the process by which world powers permanently transform certain spaces into impassable places for certain classes of populations'.[40] Thus, it is argued that the late 20th century emergence of state borders is a manifestation of hyper-legitimation of selected bodies and de-legitimation of othered bodies, granting certain bodies an overabundance of the natural human ability to move, and an attendant over-restriction of movement on other bodies. Borderisation is aided by the appearance of land as private property which is itself deeply embedded in the roots of colonialism. These roots conceptualise borderisation that requires the identification of law's legitimate subject, enables amassing of capital [value], but is also underwritten by de-legitimation of human subjects [commodification], and de-legitimatising ways of being, as well as the emergence of unfree labour.[41] Thus, d'Aspremont argues[42] that current theories of statehood actually arose as a recent reaction to Western anxieties at the emergence of new postcolonial states and thus granted 'an aura of historical legality to the expropriation of the lands of indigenous peoples'.[43] The creation of contemporary borders and the rules that regulate them, serve to stem the ascendency of peoples and states that had been subject to colonial rule. These borders 'control access to the spoils of empire which are located in Britain … colonialism is thus an ongoing project, sustained via the structure of law'.[44] By withholding recognition of new states and imposing stringent conditions on the movement of people from and in newly independent states, what is often called 'decolonisation' [that is, flag-independence], in actual fact proceeds as a continuity and expansion of the logics and praxes of colonialism.[45] So, Mbembé names borders as producing a very specific type of death-politics in 'dead spaces of nonconnection which deny the very idea of a shared humanity, of a planet, the only one we have, that we share together, and to which we are linked by the ephemerality of our common condition'.[46] Extending Foucault's metaphor of war, Mbembé describes borderisation as a 'battle, waged against certain undesirables, reducing them to mounds of human flesh'.[47] Borders and

40 Mbembé (2019) p 99.
41 Mignolo (2013) pp 334, 364; Bhandar (2018) pp 3–5; Harris (1993) pp 1715–16, 1721–4; Keenan (2010) p 428.
42 d'Aspremont (2018) pp 15–28.
43 Reisman (1995) p 352.
44 El-Enany (2020) p 1.
45 d'Aspremont (2018) pp 15–28.
46 Mbembé (2019) p 99.
47 Mbembé (2019) p 100.

the laws that govern them are necropolitical, marking bodies 'must die'. Thus, it is argued that borders carry on the work of the colonial in their redefinition of the human and space: 'A border is a dividing line, a narrow strip along a steep edge. A borderland is a vague and undetermined place created by the emotional residue of an unnatural boundary … The prohibited and forbidden are its inhabitants'.[48]

This attritional, out-of-sight borderised violence, also finds resonance in the overexploitation of the earth and in 'long dyings—the staggered and staggeringly discounted casualties, both human and ecological that result'.[49] The appropriation of land from Indigenous peoples was key to success and prosperity of imperial projects. Appropriation required epistemologies of law that were able to translate indigenous lands and bodies as naturally alienable and disposable, respectively. Thus, property law is described as 'a settler colonial technology'[50] that separates indigenous life from the land and makes both exploitable. This contributes to an overuse of land, not for the benefit of life [human and non-human], but for the benefit of capital, by decomplicating the meanings that land has for colonised and Indigenous peoples.[51] Consequently, our current age is described as the Anthropocene—an age in which a particular vision of Man is made paramount, to the detriment to all other life … human, non-human, and planetary.[52]

A Decadent Discipline and Reinventing Possibility: To Decolonise or to Build 'Worlds Otherwise'?

Yet, despite how fundamental the foregoing continuing process is to the production of the current socio-political-ecological order, attention to it hardly ever appears within legal education. So, legal education, in its silence, ensures the reproduction of this order. Thus, Euro-modern law continually reveals itself as a corpus that operates through legal orientalism and the superiorisation of certain bodies of law over others.[53] Nevertheless, Euro-modern law does not emerge on the other side of this epistemicide unscathed. Saturated as it is with Eurocentrism and methodological whiteness, the discipline itself becomes self-destructive. Desperate to preserve itself, it preserves nothing. Unwilling to adapt, it decays. Therefore, though it may never die, it may never bring life.

This decadence is exemplified in what is absent and present in our analysis of the human and global condition. Bhambra describes 'methodological whiteness' as a study of the world that ignores the role played by racialisation and

48 Anzaldúa (1987) p 3.
49 Nixon (2011) p 2.
50 la paperson (2017) p 27.
51 Liboiron (2021) p 40.
52 Jackson (2017) p 23.
53 Darian-Smith (2015) pp 647–51; de Sousa Santos (2018) p 8.

attempts to universalise Euro-modern knowledge.[54] This pretence of universality renders any analysis incomplete and unable to respond to global injustice, massive inequality, and environmental devastation. By placing Europe at the centre of analysis, law's ability to address past and present global challenges to build a better future world is curtailed. Thus, Maeso and Araújo indict Euro-modern law in their definition of Eurocentrism as a linear interpretation of the world that deifies European achievement and the rule of law.[55] This leaves us with a discipline—and profession and world systemiser—that has failed to come to grips with its own nature and history. The cautionary note sounded by Gordon in his conceptualisation of disciplinary decadence in the global academy asks [legal] scholars to consider how to reconfigure disciplines that create death worlds. Disciplinary decadence, according to Gordon, arises when a discipline, rooted in colonial practices, considers itself complete, self-created, method-obsessed, immortal, and omniscient about all other disciplines.[56] One could argue that disciplinary decadence is itself necropolitical—the discipline, to survive at all costs, deifies its own methods, refusing to recognise its complicity in consigning sections of humanity to slow and immediate death, and the planet to perdition. Rather than question the discipline itself, through a deficit model, we question the legitimacy of people whose 'problems' fall outside the sacred method of our discipline—we attempt to squeeze them in, but they just cannot fit.[57] Thus the accurate application of Euro-modern legal method results in legal knowledge treating such people as 'problems, instead of people who face problems'.[58] The discipline struggles to be bio-centred.

'Decolonisation' therefore, sounds like a fitting remedy for colonialism's death-production. But decolonisation must primarily be understood as a specific long-standing political project of Indigenous peoples, racialised peoples, and colonised peoples, also born in the cauldron of colonialism. It is an immediate, continuing, and stubborn refusal of colonial conditions of domination, dispossession, and dehumanisation, as well as the epistemologies that keep colonial logics eternally re-emergent. Decolonisation is a repudiation of all aspects of our necropolitical world. It is not curricula redesign or innovation. What decolonisation suggests for those of us within academia, who wish to adopt its logics and praxis in our work, is a means to redesign our work, so that it redesigns the world. For example, some scholars favour an approach that decentres dominant ideologies, encouraging a pluriversity of knowledges, and a complete rethinking of the structure of the current world. In other words, they strongly encourage us to use a diversity of epistemologies to produce

54 Bhambra (2017).

55 Maeso and Araújo (2015) p 1.

56 Gordon (2015) pp 4–5; Gordon (2014) p 86; Gordon (2011) p 98; Gordon (2018) p 241.

57 Gordon (2014) p 87.

58 Gordon (2014) p 84.

'worlds otherwise'—a world that is not a deathscape.[59] Other scholars focus their writings on the reversal of the fruits of colonialism, specifically the return of the meanings and substance of stolen indigenous land and life.[60] Yet others, writing from postcolonial contexts, where physical presence is currently absent, but neo-colonial control remains, focus on disruption or dislocation of the epistemic, political, and economic continuities of colonisation.[61] This scholarship almost always converges on the complete repudiation of colonialism and its products ... 'an endless fracturing of the world colonialism created'.[62] This scholarship extends beyond numbers-diversity, beyond representation that does not acknowledge structural propensity to exclude, and beyond equality that does not reckon with the creation of law's human and his normativity, in our quest for equality.

Thus, deployment of decolonisation in legal education goes beyond a sprinkling of non-white scholars and topics in the curriculum. It asks for 'dismantling of relations of power and conceptions of knowledge'[63] that produce immiseration and slow violence. This requires us to engage in our teaching and research with how law's complicity with slow violence shows up in macro and micro ways in legal education. For example, in how legal epistemologies enable acquired capital to be retained through abstractions from time, and spatial and temporal entanglements in the legal continuum. We can go so far as to question whether law's main concepts such as 'justice' can be universalised. Justice for the settler is not the same as justice for the dispossessed ... 'the claim of the universal translatability of the English word "justice" is an extraordinarily presumptive one'.[64] Furthermore, legal knowledge obscures the colonial continuities in human rights—detaching the right to education and development from dispossession and the destruction of non-European epistemologies.[65] The reproduction of colonialism's concern with commodification is also evident in the predominance of private law subjects in the core of the legal curriculum. These subjects rely on conceptualisation of the normative human as standard and the preservation of the borderisation, social orders and power relations that result from the colonial rupture. Even public law units that form part of the core, including Criminal Law, proceed from these presumptions. Ultimately, while rethinking legal knowledge may start with individual units, it must extend beyond that to the content, nature, and purposes of legal education and law schools. Decolonial thinking within legal education requires radically transgressive pedagogical practices of reimagination of

59 Mignolo (2007) pp 155–67.
60 Tuck and Yang (2012); Smith (2021).
61 Fanon (2007); Fanon (2008) p 2.
62 Modiri (2020) p 172.
63 Maldonado-Torres (2006) p 117.
64 Gordon (2013) p 70.
65 Abdulrahman et al. (2021) pp 47–75.

possibility in service of a very different world,[66] where the law's subject and the future world made around this subject are conceived in life-giving ways. This sort of thinking is 'a pluriversal epistemology of the future—a redemptive and liberatory epistemology'.[67] It allows us to imagine an end to 'state-sanctioned or extralegal production and exploitation of group-differentiated vulnerability to premature death'.[68] It allows us to imagine the end of a necropolitical world.

Conclusion

This chapter has argued that Euro-modern legal education in its dedication to preserving social order, allies itself with political and economic power and thus contributes to the emergence of a necropolitical world. This is evidenced not just in the structure of the world, but also in the discipline's rigid adherence to its own method. Colonialism, [here described as the primary structure of global domination in the present], then, is the major obstacle in reversing our necropolis. Decolonisation is, seemingly, the most suitable response to colonialism. However, it must be understood beyond curricular innovation, as an epistemology for a world in which humanity and the earth may be preserved. Therefore, imagining the end of necropolis requires multifaceted academic action which 'offers the paradox of loving, by virtue of action, anonymous generations to come'.[69] And so, in our teaching, together with our students, we can seek to imagine new worlds in whose fabric the injustices of the past and present will not be persistently interwoven and recreated. This radical imagination reminds us to 'imagine and craft the worlds all of us cannot live without, just as we imagine the undoing of the world many on this planet, cannot move, cannot live, cannot breathe, within'.[70]

References

Hadiza Kere Abdulrahman et al (2021) 'Revisiting (Inclusive) Education in the Postcolony' 9 *Journal of the British Academy* 47.

Foluke Adebisi (2021a) 'The "Vaccine Apartheid": A Long History in the Making' *Foluke's African Skies*, https://folukeafrica.com/the-vaccine-apartheid-a-long-history-in-the-making/.

Foluke Adebisi (2021b) 'Should We Rethink the Purposes of The Law School? A Case for Decolonial Thought in Legal Pedagogy' 2 *The Journal of the Society for Advanced Legal Studies* 428.

66 Freire (2005) 34; hooks (1994) p 207.
67 Mignolo (2007) p 159.
68 Gilmore (2007) p 28.
69 Gordon (2020) p 47.
70 Paraphrased from Benjamin (2019) p 14.

Foluke Adebisi and Suhraiya Jivraj (2021) 'Racism as Legal Pandemic: Thoughts on Critical Legal Pedagogies' in D Cowan and A Mumford (eds) *Pandemic Legalities: Legal Responses to COVID-19–Justice and Social Responsibility*, Bristol University Press.

Ruha Benjamin (2019) *Captivating Technology: Race, Carceral Technoscience, and Liberatory Imagination in Everyday Life*, Duke University Press.

Pierre Van den Berghe (1967) *Race and Racism: A Comparative Perspective*, Wiley.

Gurminder Bhambra (2017) 'Why are the White Working Classes Still Being Held Responsible for Brexit and Trump?' *LSE Blog*, https://blogs.lse.ac.uk/brexit/2017/11/10/why-are-the-white-working-classes-still-being-held-responsible-for-brexit-and-trump/.

Brenna Bhandar (2018) *Colonial Lives of Property: Law, Land, and Racial Regimes of Ownership*, Duke University Press.

Rosi Braidotti (2013) *The Posthuman*, Polity.

Robert M Cover (1985) 'Violence and the Word' 95 *Yale Law Journal* 1601.

Eve Darian-Smith (2013) 'Postcolonial Theories of Law' in R Banakar and M Travers (eds) *Law and Social Theory*, Hart Publishing.

Eve Darian-Smith (2015) 'Postcolonial Law' in JD Wright (ed) *International Encyclopedia of the Social and Behavioral Sciences*, Elsevier.

Jean D'Aspremont (2018) 'The International Law of Statehood and Recognition: A Post-Colonial Invention' in T Garcia (ed) *La Reconnaissance Du Statut d'Etat À Des Entités Contestées: Approches De Droits International, Régional Et Interne*, Editions A. Pedone.

Thom Davies et al (2017) 'Violent Inaction: The Necropolitical Experience of Refugees in Europe' 49 *Antipode* 1263.

Chris Dietz et al (2020) 'Nobody, Anybody, Somebody, Everybody: A Jurisprudence of the Body' in C Dietz et al (eds) *A Jurisprudence of the Body*, Palgrave-Macmillan.

Enrique Dussel (1995) *The Invention of the Americas: Eclipse of "the Other" and the Myth of Modernity* (Translation Barber Michael D), Continuum.

Nadine El-Enany (2020) *(B)ordering Britain: Law, Race and Empire*, Manchester University Press.

Frantz Fanon (2007) *The Wretched of The Earth*, Grove/Atlantic.

Frantz Fanon (2008) *Black Skin, White Masks*, Pluto Books.

Michel Foucault and François Ewald (2013) '"Society Must Be Defended": Lectures at the Collège de France, 1975–1976' in TC Timothy and A Sitze (eds) *Biopolitics: A Reader*, Duke University Press.

Paulo Freire (2005) *Pedagogy of the Oppressed*, Continuum.

Ruth Wilson Gilmore (2007) *Golden Gulag: Prisons, Surplus, Crisis, and Opposition in Globalizing*, University of California Press.

David Theo Goldberg (2008) 'Racial States' in DT Goldberg and J Solomos (eds) *A Companion to Racial and Ethnic Studies*, Wiley.

Lewis R Gordon (2011) 'Shifting the Geography of Reason in An Age of Disciplinary Decadence' 1 *Transmodernity: Journal of Peripheral Cultural Production of the Luso-Hispanic World* 95.

Lewis R Gordon (2013) 'Thoughts on Dussel's "Anti-Cartesian Meditations"' 11 *Human Architecture: Journal of the Sociology of Self-Knowledge* 67.

Lewis R Gordon (2014) 'Disciplinary Decadence and the Decolonisation of Knowledge' 39 *Africa Development* 81.

Lewis R Gordon (2015) *Disciplinary Decadence: Living Thought in Trying Times*, Routledge.

Lewis R Gordon (2018) 'Disciplining as a Human Science' in M Gržinić and A Stojnić (eds) *Shifting Corporealities in Contemporary Performance*, Palgrave-Macmillan.

Lewis R Gordon (2020) *Freedom, Justice, and Decolonization*, Routledge.
Ramon Grosfoguel (2016) 'What is Racism?' 22 *Journal of World-Systems Research* 9.
Cheryl Harris (1993) 'Whiteness as Property' 106 *Harvard Law Review* 1707.
bell hooks (1994) *Teaching to Transgress*, Routledge.
Rosalba Icaza and Rolando Vázquez (2016) 'The Coloniality of Gender as a Radical Critique of Developmentalism' in W Harcourt (ed) *The Palgrave Handbook of Gender and Development*, Palgrave-Macmillan.
Mark Jackson (2017) 'For New Ecologies of Thought: Towards Decolonising Critique' in M Jackson (ed) *Coloniality, Ontology, and the Question of the Posthuman*, Routledge.
Sarah Keenan (2010) 'Subversive Property: Reshaping Malleable Spaces of Belonging' 19 *Social and Legal Studies* 423.
Ibram X Kendi (2017) *Stamped from the Beginning: The Definitive History of Racist Ideas in America*, Random House.
Max Liboiron (2021) *Pollution is Colonialism*, Duke University Press.
Maria Lugones (2013) 'The Coloniality of Gender' In WD Mignolo and A Escobar, (eds) *Globalization and the Decolonial Option*, Routledge.
Silvia Rodríguez Maeso and Marta Araújo (2015) 'Eurocentrism, Political Struggles and the Entrenched Will-To-Ignorance: An Introduction' in SR Maeso and M Araújo (eds) *Eurocentrism, Racism and Knowledge*, Palgrave-Macmillan.
Nelson Maldonado-Torres (2006) 'Cesaire's Gift and the Decolonial Turn' 9 *Radical Philosophy Review* 111.
Nelson Maldonado-Torres (2007) 'On the Coloniality of Being: Contributions to the Development of a Concept' 21 *Cultural Studies* 240.
Achille Mbembé (2019) *Necropolitics*, Duke University Press.
Michael McIntyre and Heidi J Nast (2011) 'Bio (Necro) Polis: Marx, Surplus Populations, and the Spatial Dialectics of Reproduction and "Race"' 43 *Antipode* 1465.
Walter D Mignolo (2007) 'Introduction: Coloniality of Power and De-Colonial Thinking' 21 *Cultural Studies* 155.
Walter Mignolo (2011) *The Darker Side of Western Modernity: Global Futures, Decolonial Options*, Duke University Press.
Walter D Mignolo (2013) 'Delinking: The Rhetoric of Modernity, the Logic of Coloniality and the Grammar of De-Coloniality' in WD Mignolo and A Escobar (eds) *Globalization and the Decolonial Option*, Routledge.
Joel Modiri (2020) 'The Aporias of Decolonisation in the South African Academy' in O Tella and S Motala (eds), *From Ivory Towers to Ebony Towers: Transforming Humanities Curricula in South Africa, Africa and African-American Studies*, Jacana.
Ngaire Naffine (2009) *Law's Meaning of Life: Philosophy, Religion, Darwin and the Legal Person*, Bloomsbury.
Rob Nixon (2011) *Slow Violence and the Environmentalism of the Poor*, Harvard University Press.
Oyèrónké Oyěwùmí (2005) 'Visualizing the Body: Western Theories and African Subjects' in O Oyěwùmí (ed) *African Gender Studies: A Reader*, Palgrave-Macmillan.
la paperson (2017) *A Third University Is Possible*, University of Minnesota Press.
Anibal Quijano and Michael Ennis (2000) 'Coloniality of Power, Eurocentrism, and Latin America' 1 *Nepantla: Views from South* 533.
Michael Reisman (1995) 'Protecting Indigenous Rights in International Adjudication' 89 *American Journal of International Law* 350.
Boaventura de Sousa Santos (2015) *Epistemologies of the South: Justice against Epistemicide*, Routledge.

Boaventura de Sousa Santos (2018) *The End of the Cognitive Empire: The Coming of Age of Epistemologies of the South*, Duke University Press.

Linda Tuhiwai Smith (2021) *Decolonizing Methodologies: Research and Indigenous Peoples*, Zed Books.

Olúfẹ́mi O Táíwò (2021) 'A Unified Story for a Divided World', https://www.dissentmagazine.org/article/a-unified-story-for-a-divided-world.

Margaret Thornton (1998) 'Technocentrism in the Law School: Why the Gender and Colour of Law Remain the Same' 36 *Osgoode Hall Law Journal* 369.

Mitchell Travis (2014) 'Non-normative Bodies, Rationality, and Legal Personhood' 22 *Medical Law Review* 526.

Eve Tuck and K Wayne Yang (2012) 'Decolonization is not a Metaphor' 1 *Decolonization: Indigeneity, Education and Society* 1.

Alexander G Weheliye (2014) *Habeas Viscus: Racializing Assemblages, Biopolitics, and Black Feminist Theories of the Human*, Duke University Press.

Sylvia Wynter (2003) 'Unsettling the Coloniality of Being/Power/Truth/Freedom: Towards the Human, After Man, Its Overrepresentation—An Argument' 3 *CR: The New Centennial Review* 257.

Chapter 2

Centring Feminist and Queer Experiences in the Law School

Legal Zines as a Humanising Pedagogy

Chris Ashford, Laura Graham, and Samantha Rasiah

Introduction

Brooks and Parkes have asked 'is it possible to teach law in a way that leaves us feeling like full human beings?'[1] Their question was rooted in a queering of legal education but also built upon outsider pedagogy and sought to offer a radical intervention in pedagogy.[2] Their question was the latest in a line of similar iterations offered by educators and theorists. Freire in his landmark text *Pedagogy of the Oppressed* explored the challenge of humanisation (and noted that the mere question highlights the presence of dehumanisation)[3] and argued for the importance of transforming the relationship between the academic and student in disrupting our assumptions about who 'knows things' and the nature of 'knowing'.[4] To challenge ourselves and ask these questions of the human in pedagogy is, therefore, an ongoing radical intervention, with this chapter offering a further attempt to respond to this challenge in a project that blends teaching and research.

The synthesis of teaching and research, relatively well-established within the broader social sciences, is a more recent development for law schools.[5] For legal education research, there is an opportunity to both explore the impact of law research on substantive law subjects and the impact that our research, and the perspectives it brings, can have on the broader law school experience. For an area like gender, sexuality, and law,[6] the theoretical interventions of feminist and queer theory provide not only a significant catalyst for an evolution in legal research, but also in law school pedagogy, in turn challenging the orthodoxies

1 Brooks and Parkes (2004) p 424.
2 Brooks and Parkes (2004).
3 Freire (1993) p 17.
4 Freire (1993) p 37.
5 See more generally: Birks (1994a) and Oliver (1996).
6 See: Ashford (2021).

DOI: 10.4324/9781003179283-4

and hierarchies[7] of legal education, and a history of legal education[8] that has at times sought to reject theory.[9]

This more critical intervention moves us beyond well-rehearsed debates about the formal legal curriculum content,[10] and contributes to our understanding of the role of law teachers, and our relationship with students in a shared human-focused endeavour. Moreover, this contributes to the liberal model of legal education in which the role of the law school provides a broader role in equipping students for active roles in society and shaping change, as well as preparation for the professions.[11]

One way to provide context and a broader impact in legal education is through the inclusion of 'outsider pedagogy'. Bakht et al. define outsider pedagogy as courses that 'focus on the law as it applies to historically under-represented and/or marginalised groups such as women, racialized peoples, people with disabilities, Aboriginal peoples, and people who identify as queer'.[12] Engaging with outsider pedagogy allows students to challenge law's claims to neutrality, 'explore the disproportionate impact of legal rules and regimes, highlight the differential experience of the law for those with outsider status, and expose the ways in which the law (and legal education) has supported the privilege of dominant groups'.[13]

This chapter documents how we sought to apply an outsider pedagogy that consciously sought to re-centre female, Lesbian, Gay, Bisexual, and Trans experiences through the introduction of a Feminist and Queer Zine Project, to 'humanise' the law school experience. It provided opportunities for students to explore intersectional issues that also engaged with themes of race and class. The project created moments of shared endeavour between students, but also for students with Faculty as co-creators, contributing to a broader notion of law teaching as a 'sacred' vocation in which we share in the intellectual and spiritual growth of our students.[14] Moreover, we believe our project goes some way to answering Guth's call to law schools 'to find a way to channel our students' curiosity; we need to allow them to follow it in the same way that we seek to follow our own'.[15]

7 Kennedy (1982).
8 This also contributes to viewing the law school as a 'liberal legal education'. See more generally: Guth and Ashford (2014) and Twining (1995).
9 Wilson (1987); Bradney (1999) p 21.
10 See for example: Birks (1994b). This curriculum focus has deep roots; see for example: Wade (1951).
11 See: Kahn-Freund (1966) and more generally: Guth and Ashford (2014).
12 Bakht et al. (2007) p 669.
13 Bakht et al. (2007) p 684.
14 hooks (1994) p 13.
15 Guth (2016) p 251. This also reflects the argument of Brownsword (1999) who suggested that the role of the law school is to produce 'really good citizens' and law for the public through a process of continuing to ask questions and probe, rather than always being about finding the answers.

We provide what we believe to be the first documenting of zine use in law school as an extra-curricular activity, drawing on our original empirical findings from focus group data and reflective accounts to explore the impact and value of utilising feminist and queer zine-making as part of a humanising pedagogy. The study is rooted in an English law school and whilst there are arguably jurisdiction-specific aspects of character and structure that are distinct to the law schools of England,[16] we believe the queer and feminist elements of this project are applicable to other jurisdictions.

Feminist and Queer Theories and the Law School

For decades, feminist legal scholars have challenged the traditional framing of law and have instead positioned women and their experiences as central to understanding law and its norms.[17] Women have long been outsiders in legal education and practice,[18] while law has been framed as genderless and neutral. While feminist legal theory is not a monolith, feminist legal scholars have in common the aim of exposing 'law's role in disadvantaging women with a view to bringing about transformative social and political change'.[19]

Reflecting the growing closeness of research and teaching, the development of feminist legal theory is mirrored by an increasing focus on feminism in legal education. Early feminism in legal education focused on the lack of women's voices and the penalties faced by being a woman in the law school.[20] While arguments for women entering the academy were based on sameness, feminism legal education has since sought to teach 'how women's distinctive experiences, concerns, and values are marginalized under existing institutional structures'.[21] Like other forms of outsider pedagogy in legal education, the student is challenged to pay attention to the relationship between law and marginalised groups, to critique the supposed neutrality of law, and to identify with law from the subject's perspective.[22]

Much feminist legal education has been delivered on outsider pedagogy courses—there has been a rapid growth of courses on 'gender and the law' or 'women in the law' in the UK and internationally.[23] Yet, by focusing on these specialist courses, as MacKinnon argues, feminism's role in legal teaching can often be misunderstood as narrow or biased: 'when vast ranges of materials are

16 See: Twining (1997).
17 Graycar and Morgan (2002) p 2.
18 Conaghan (2013) p 3.
19 Conaghan (2000) p 359.
20 Worden (1985).
21 Rhodes (1993) p 1548.
22 Bakht et al. (2007) pp 675, 676, 682.
23 Graycar and Morgan (2002) p 1.

scrutinized and reconfigured through a gendered lens, it seems only the lens is seen'.[24]

A similar picture can be seen with sexuality in the law school. We have arguably moved some way from a time when to even research 'the status of gay persons' is viewed as subversive,[25] yet sexuality remains a key aspect of outsider identities and pedagogy in the law school, and wider university environment. The campus has been acknowledged for some decades—at least in the Global North—as a popular space in which students 'come out'. How Faculty might be part of that experience, specifically as one that is a shared human experience, has historically been an important aspect of the discussion, particularly in the late 1970s.[26] In the context of the modern campus and the commercial marketised encounters between students and Faculty, the emphasis has arguably shifted alongside broader shifts in law, policy, and attitudes relating to sex and sexuality.

In almost five decades of developing literature relating to sexuality in the education setting, there have been subtle shifts in what this means and increasingly a debate about the form it takes, for example the question of visibility of sexualities. Does visibility constitute a married same-sex partner, or might it involve a 'more queer' lifestyle embracing non-monogamy, for example.[27] Similarly, the presence of queer politics and the long-standing equality/liberation tension creates additional questions for how gender, sex, and sexuality is presented and analysed in the classroom.

Queer theory has also become more influential in the law school in this time. Queer theory emerged in the 1990s offering an approach to gender and sexuality that acknowledged fluidity and less certainty in identity, one that challenged the assimilation of LGBTQ people into the 'mainstream' structures of normativity—heteronormativity—in which the cultural distinctiveness and historic challenges to institutions such as marriage are sacrificed for acceptance.[28] As such, it offers an important tool of analysis—particularly for law students—seeking to make sense of the law's contemporary relationship with people based on gender and sexuality. Queer theory can also be regarded as an 'emancipatory' teaching and learning practice[29] and is also one that has provided a means to challenge the oppression of homosexual identities.[30]

This emancipatory practice also has potential implications for the ways that queer educationalists situate and present their identity in the Academy and

24 MacKinnon (2003) p 200.
25 Crew (1978) p 3.
26 Lehman (1978).
27 See more generally: Skelton (2020).
28 See more generally: Barker and Scheele (2016).
29 See: Luhmann (1998).
30 See: Sedgwick (1993).

appear 'out'.[31] Rofes has previously noted the dual identities of the teacher and the 'lover' is a constant presence, yet even where teachers are out—notably in relation to gay men—that identity can become de-sexed.[32] To be out is to reveal something of our intimate desires and sex lives—and to know that of our students.[33]

Feminism and queer theory have both been criticised for focusing predominantly on the experiences and needs of white people. Hill Collins has argued that the omission of other groups, particularly Black women, from mainstream feminism has 'promoted the notion of a generic woman who is White and middle class'.[34] Failing to reflect on the intersectional, complex identities of women offers a picture of the law almost as lacking as one assuming a universal gender-neutral experience. Queer theory has also often been located within a liberal narrative of whiteness and wealth, although this privilege is being challenged by some queer theorists who have argued for a queer theory that does not merely speak of challenging 'the system' and positions itself as antinormativity (whilst still privileging white male experiences), but which places class, poverty, and race at the centre of its thinking.[35] Similarly, several feminist legal scholars have challenged the dominance of one subsection of women, both in their own writings and in their pedagogy, highlighting the role of race[36] and sexuality,[37] among other factors. This intersectional approach, Crenshaw argues, is necessary to challenge the alienation and objectification of minority students, for whom legal abstraction requires segregation and denial of their embodied identities.[38]

Feminist and queer teaching has also brought theory into the law school through alternative, more embodied, pedagogy. Bouclin et al.'s use of a silent card game challenges the disembodied textual approach to teaching law.[39] By playing a card game without words, and in which different rules have been delivered to different students, students 'feel' the power imbalances between 'insiders' and 'outsiders', rather than just being told about them.[40] The Zine Project similarly developed along this project approach, using an extra-curricular activity to bring intersectional feminist and queer legal theory into legal education beyond the classroom, and push students to feel as well as think.

31 See: Robson (1998) p 220.
32 Rofes (2000). Rofes also reflects in this article on his earlier de-sexing of his identity in what was a landmark text in Rofes (1985). See more generally: Garber (1994), (1982), and Kissen (1996).
33 See more generally: Rofes (2000).
34 Hill Collins (2000) p 8.
35 Brim (2020).
36 Crenshaw (1988).
37 Robson (1998).
38 Crenshaw (1988) p 3.
39 Bouclin et al. (2013).
40 Bouclin et al. (2013).

The Feminist and Queer Zine Project

The Feminist and Queer Zine Project first operated in the 2018–19 academic year as an extra-curricular activity open to all students at Northumbria Law School. The project offered a pedagogical space for students to develop their understanding of feminist and queer legal (and non-legal) issues within a non-assessed framework. Zines were chosen because of their history within feminist and queer communities of providing radical spaces in which ideas and concepts that counter normative assumptions can be expressed, communities can mobilise, and agendas of dignity and fair treatment can advance.

Zines have been defined as 'cheaply made printed forms of expression on any subject. They are like mini-magazines or homemade comic books'.[41] They have cultural and social value that extends beyond their physical description of being akin to a DIY arts and crafts project, providing an outlet for unfettered expression and a connection to a larger underground world of publishers doing the same.[42] Independent and free from external processes such as review and funding, zines are rooted in dialogue that is collaborative in nature and not censored by the dominant ideology.[43] As a result, zines have been said to 'possess some of the most intelligent, political and outrageous writing today'.[44] The Zine Project at Northumbria Law School builds on the limited but growing research on zine use, notably in a feminist context,[45] as a radical space to re-appraise gender and authority, as a transformative learning tool,[46] to promote classroom participation,[47] and to promote student voice.[48]

Through the academic year, 12–15 students took part in the project to varying degrees. Fewer students contributed content to the final zine, producing content that featured original poetry, collages of printed photos, screenshots of Instagram profiles and YouTube videos, articles, and drawings. The students decided not to make digital copies of the zine for online distribution, opting—in keeping with zine tradition—to limit it to a physical artefact. The zines were printed and made available to the students, their networks, and placed in the law school community.

41 Todd and Watson (2006).
42 Duncombe (2017).
43 Desyllas and Sinclair (2014).
44 Green and Taormino (1997).
45 Piepmeier (2009).
46 Desyllas and Sinclair (2014).
47 Potter and Sellie (2016).
48 deGravelles (2011).

The Focus Group and Reflective Data

Data on the project was gathered from a final focus group session and project leads' reflective research notes. Although only three students participated in the final focus group, limiting the generalisability of any findings, the combined data provides an interesting picture of the impact of this particular project.

The student focus group opted for four open questions[49] that were shared with the students at the start of the session and that formed the structure of the focus group discussion:

1. What led to you being involved in the project?
2. How did you become aware of feminism?
3. Discuss your experience on this Zine Project.
4. How has this project impacted you?

Student voice was invaluable, as students' experiences shaped and led the project. Our analysis of the data produced by the focus group seeks to prioritise the knowledge created by the students, in line with queer and feminist commitment to challenging hierarchies. This approach, as described by Kolb, allows for better socio-emotional development in students, and it allowed students to challenge the hierarchy between educator-student, and transform knowledge based on their experiences.[50] Analysis of the data identified three themes that emerged across the student experiences.

a) Emotional Development and Embodiment in Zine Making

In exploring 'lawyering skills', Jones notes that there is insufficient opportunity created for law students to develop their emotional intelligence in law schools.[51] Referring to Gardner,[52] she describes this as 'access to one's own feeling', and the 'ability to notice and make distinctions among other individuals'.[53] In Tsaoussi's exploration of this idea, he argues that legal pedagogy today focuses disproportionately on the model of the 'thinking lawyer', when it should equally empower students to develop the skills of a 'feeling lawyer'.[54] He suggests that legal education which empowers students to 'feel' would: promote crucial pedagogical goals such as imparting to students the social values of tolerance, solidarity, and respect for students who are members of minorities

49 As commonly used in focus group methods. See: Creswell (2009) p 181. Ethical approval for the project was given by Northumbria University.
50 Kolb (2014).
51 Jones (2017).
52 Gardner (2006).
53 Jones (2017).
54 Tsaoussi (2020).

or students with disabilities; encourage students to engage in a genuine democratic dialogue with each other and with their professors; and help students to evaluate and appreciate the law as a living, evolving social institution that can act as a powerful instrument of social change.[55]

One aspect of humanising pedagogy is the creation of 'safe zones' in which different perspectives and controversial topics are able to be expressed and explored, often drawing on the perspectives of faculty.[56] In exploring themes such as sexuality, race, and marginalised communities' relationships with the law, a 'safe zone' can allow students to not only think about the social justice elements of these issues, but can enable them to immerse themselves in the exploration of these topics and 'feel' the law from different perspectives. What exactly makes a 'safe zone' is dependant of various socio-cultural factors; however, participants of the Zine Project gave insight on some of these potential factors. The Zine Project was repeatedly framed as a 'safe' space in both the focus group and in the reflective accounts of project leads. During the focus group, students referred to the project discussions as '*a place of no judgment*', '*an open space*', '*a safe space*', '*no pressure*'. Participants noted that the project offered a comfortable space in which they had a common interest and could explore issues in a way they felt they would be unable to do so ordinarily. One participant described losing friends when she had posted about feminist issues on social networks, while another shared that in other contexts people often rolled their eyes or were uncomfortable with discussions associated with the term 'feminism'; this project conversely allowed them to explore provocative issues without fear of judgment and rejection.

Students also expressed that they felt a sense of community and belonging in the project, which allowed them to feel '*vulnerable*' in the discussion sessions. Participants reflected on their own positionality and how this impacted their experiences of law and legal education. This type of experience described by the students also aligns with the experiences of many from the marginalised communities which were the focus of this project. Through participation in this project, they experienced ostracisation to some degree from their personal social circles, allowing them to engage with and feel marginalisation.

Intersectionality, as an increasingly prioritised feature of feminist and queer education,[57] was a further theme that emerged from the project. Intersectionality was relevant in this project in relation to the material considered, representation within the space, and how participants understood themselves and each other. Participants in the project were from a range of cultural backgrounds and the project was a space where participants were actively encouraged to reconsider social constructions and view social justice issues through their unique lenses

55 Tsaoussi (2020).
56 Schwartz et al. (2013) p 249.
57 hooks (1994) chapter 2.

as informed by their intersecting identities.[58] By the second workshop, these reflections were also shared by the academics leading the project with the one cis male academic noting:

> *'I was glad that it was a female led workshop. I say this as I was acutely aware of my gender in this space and I felt at times my presence maybe contributed to a limiting of what the students said. Is this just gender, power differentials or some combination'.*

The issue of intersectionality also proved significant for another academic, noting:

> *'I could relate to many issues which the student spoke about regarding being a woman of colour … I felt very comfortable in this workshop although we've had a long break'.*

The project appeared, therefore, to encourage participants' self-awareness and allow a broader understanding of positionality of subgroups within the law school and beyond, as well as power hierarchies within society.[59] Such critical reflections are often something law students are said to lack, with them placing little, if any, focus on reflectivity and reflexivity. Reflection on one's own positionality is in itself a method of examining and challenging hierarchies which exist within the law school and in the law that is taught. Through their critical reflections of their personal experiences of legal education as well as engagement with queer and feminist ideas, students became more conscious of their positionality and intersectional identity within the complex socio-cultural dynamics of the law school and the law.

The Zine Project experience was described by students as '*positive*', '*uplifting*', '*interesting*', and '*purposeful*'. In particular, the zine allowed participants to engage with and showcase their preferred creative expression. Students noted that this creative outlet provided a healthy break from the daily experiences of law school, stating it helped them '*get out of the headspace of uni*' and that '*time went by really quickly when doing things for the zine … wish uni work was that way*'. The Zine Project provided a contrast with legal education's purported common emphasis on being objective and impartial, which Carter and Burke argue may stifle and strangle creativity.[60] Gardner refers to creativity as forms of intelligence.[61] He argues that producing music, poetry, or art is expression of knowledge in unconventional forms, and he opines that the creation of cultural

58 Desyllas and Sinclair (2014).
59 Desyllas and Sinclair (2014).
60 Carter and Burke (2002).
61 Gardner (2006).

products allows one to capture and transmit knowledge, or to express one's conclusions, beliefs, or feelings.[62] Here, the tools long associated with feminist and queer activism, to provide a means for expression and dialogue, provided an important creative space that is 'out of' the law school and yet ultimately remains a reconstructed key element of it.

Acknowledging diverse expressions of knowledge and creating a safe space for these expressions pluralises the traditional concept of knowledge and intelligence within law schools. These reflections from both staff and students highlight the significance of challenging conventional knowledge production and allowing spaces for students to reflect on their creations and rewrite their experiences and culture in dynamic, local spaces.[63] This adds to the growing body of literature suggesting the need to encourage development of softer skills in law school.

b) Social Development and Challenging Hierarchies

For feminists, some of the more problematic aspects of legal education come from the 'hierarchical, authoritarian relationship between students and professors'.[64] The didactic approach to teaching, which assumes that education is a unidirectional process, is at odds with feminist and queer approaches that seek to deconstruct and dismantle hierarchies and power relations. Feminist theory has long recognised the situated nature of knowledge[65] and that knowledge is always partial.[66] Pedagogy framed solely around the lecturer passing knowledge to the student fails to recognise the partial nature of the academics' knowledge. Instead, a more dialogical relationship between students and teachers in legal education can give space to multiple knowledges and shared ownership of the space. Similarly, breaking down binaries and challenging norms is key to queer theory. If pedagogy can sometimes be regarded as dogmatic, queer's disruptive antinormative agenda can be seen as a powerful challenge, forcing us to re-cast pedagogy[67] in a more fluid and evolving light.

This challenge to hierarchies and normative classroom relationships was a key finding in our project. Students described a sense of self-motivation and ownership of the project. Lonsdale describes, as one of the many advantages of zines for student education, the offering to students of a sense of ownership that other types of writing, especially classroom writing, do not provide.[68] Zines, by providing a variety of vehicles for meaning-making, can challenge

62 Gardner (2006).
63 Finlay (2008).
64 Rhodes (1993) p 1555.
65 Haraway (1988).
66 Tanesini (1999) p 10.
67 See: Luhmann (1998).
68 Lonsdale (2015).

the status quo in terms of authority, revealing the process by which a writer attains credibility on a particular topic.[69] Our participants' experiences of ownership support assertions that artistic methods are a powerful tool that have proven to provoke reflective dialogue and meaningful participatory action to change society.[70]

This was reflected in student accounts of the project. In the focus group, participants shared that they were highly motivated to carry out their own research and to share what they had found with the rest of the group, with one stating '*it was a nice way to get it off my chest and clear it out of my head*'. Participants also expressed a sense of pride and ownership:

> '*the things that I've contributed towards it, I'm proud of. It'll stick with me*'
>
> '*having a finished zine, I think that will be something that will remain with me that I'd list, other than my degree, as something I've achieved*'.

The assertion of student control was also noted by the academic leads, with one commenting early in the project that:

> '*After each student had talked about their item, we considered timing. I suggested working in the next session to write, but the students were keen to write in their own time and use the sessions for feedback*'.

This student comment reflects the students' comfort in rejecting suggestions made by the academic leads, and thus challenging normative power relations. Moreover, the students' decision to work away from the workshop reflects a dismantling of the boundaries of the classroom, allowing learning and reflection to take place beyond the barriers of the traditional educational setting. This highlights the influence of feminist and queer approaches on the management of the project as well as the content.

The second aspect of social development relates to the development of knowledge about social justice issues. Through the project, there were many discussions around the law school and the law curriculum still being whitewashed and reinforcing male as being the 'default gender', for example, through the use of 'he' in legislation and law textbooks. Participants expressed their interest in '*finding out more about feminism*' and gaining a '*better understanding of the various sexualities*' through this project. Again, relatively early in the project, the academic leads also noted that this ownership and enthusiasm—particularly in relation to feminist theory—was becoming pervasive beyond the confines of the workshop interactions:

69 Lonsdale (2015).
70 Desyllas and Sinclair (2014).

> *'The topics raised were as expected but the passion of the students was impressive and perhaps surprising. They were clearly engaging with feminist ideas outside of the workshop as an everyday activity that supports identity and well-being'.*

One participant noted:

> *'I didn't even realise I was typing for 5 hours ... because it's conversations that need to be had but aren't had. I like to discuss difficult topics and things that shouldn't be taboo or hidden away ... there's not a lot of people you can talk to about things like this so it's a way to get it out'.*

Students' engagement with feminist and queer topics and theory beyond the confines of the project demonstrates the capacity of individual projects to influence students' thinking across their legal education. By thinking about feminist and queer ideas in their everyday activities, they may be able to mainstream these ideas into their understanding of other legal topics, where they focus on substantive rules, but may reflect on ways that, even where the rules are formally equal, they may subject women and minorities to 'a range of harmful and discriminatory practices'.[71]

Students expressed that they had learnt about issues that they had not been aware of prior to the project. The project had an impact beyond the confines of the workshops, for example, one participant shared that the project had been a starting point to talk about gender and sexuality which led to further constructive discussions with their friends who were not involved in the project. In sharing with each other their thoughts and the tools that they used to be informed—for example feminist podcasts—the students were fostering learning and development that disrupted traditional boundaries between the 'classroom' and 'outside', queering the idea of education.

c) Towards Liberation and the Law Graduate

Ideas of liberation also form part of debates about the nature and form of legal education, particularly from feminist and critical thinkers. For example, Duncan Kennedy's 1983 polemic on the reproduction of hierarchy in legal education was a self-published critique of US-based legal education but quickly became an influential text in the United States of America and beyond, challenging the intellectual content and structures of legal education for the ways that they preserve and re-enforce existing systems and hierarchies.[72] As we noted in the previous section, this disruption of traditional hierarchies was one that produced positive results for our students. Menkel-Meadow noted in 1988 the shared

71 Auchmuty (2012) p 227.
72 Kennedy (2004). Also see Kennedy (1982).

focus on 'the hierarchy, passivity, depersonalization, and decontextualization of present-day legal education' but suggested that the feminist critique of legal education 'offers greater promise for the task of reconstruction'.[73] These ideas were later joined by queer theory and together provide a framework for reflecting upon and reconstructing pedagogy and knowledge within legal education, providing a freedom to think differently and construct what we teach and learn and how we teach it differently to existing paradigms.

Our project arguably provided such a site of reconstruction. Participants in the Zine Project felt that they had developed skills that would be important in their professional careers, for example the ability to work independently, to express ideas, and to learn from one another. This arguably reflects the hierarchical and structural power of law noted by Kennedy and the entrenched pedagogy that Mertz[74] has described as 'thinking like a lawyer'. Through this creative expression of ideas, students are able to challenge the norms of what it is to be a law student and lawyer. Yet, our participants also identified the themes of independence and liberation as a key aspect of the project. Participants stated that the Zine Project had:

> '*Given me a set of wings to express myself as clearly as I could*', and
> '*Just did it how you wanted to do it ... a freeing way of doing it*'.

They collectively suggested that this was in part because the project was not tutor-led, indicating that the disruption of established hierarchies in our pedagogy can—as feminist, critical, and queer theorists have argued—be liberating. The absence of a student-teacher dynamic in these sessions allowed for a form of outsider pedagogy which invites experimentation in teaching and scholarship.[75] Although the Zine Project did not entail any formalised 'teaching' as understood in a traditional paradigm, the sessions enabled students involved to learn from each other and from their own research and experiences. Students brought and discussed materials from a range of media—for example, television, podcasts, blogs, music videos, social media—that were relevant to the broad themes of gender, sexuality, and law. By drawing on unconventional sources (for a law school), students were able, in their discussions, to decentre dominant voices and demarginalise outsiders.

Moreover, the student-led dynamic had an impact on the relationship between academic staff and students in this environment. Rather than being taught didactically, students had conversations with academic staff in a way they usually would not have in a classroom setting, co-producing knowledge through a dialogical approach. This supports Giroux's claim that zine

73 Menkel-Meadow (1988).
74 Mertz (2007).
75 Bakht et al. (2007).

use can be an effective tool to equalise power relations between students-teachers, institutions-communities, researchers-subjects,[76] and also reflects the libationary potential of feminist and queer thinking. Moreover, this provided a moment of reflection during the focus group for the academic participants too, one of whom noted:

> *This focus group has made me realise how important it is to have activities like this in Law School.*

Finally, students noted the impact of their greater understanding of marginalisation on their potential future careers. One student shared that they realised they wanted to work with LGBTQ people as there is important work to be done there from a social justice perspective. Another noted that it was important for them to challenge any misconceptions they held: '*if I have any prejudices, I want to identify them as soon as possible*'. The development of students' ability to engage with the experiences of different groups will allow students to better identify the reality and effects of their work with outsider clients,[77] should they wish to practice in future, holding out the potential for feminist and queer legal education to transform legal practice. hooks has suggested that commitment to engaged pedagogy can be an expression of political activism,[78] and here we see the power of feminist and queer pedagogy to not only transform legal education, but to also transform law—as a key locus of power—and society.

Conclusion

Freire has argued that our 'efforts must coincide with those of the students to engage in critical thinking and the quest for mutual humanization'[79] and for all involved in the project, it did prove to be a powerful and humanising experience. In the student focus group data and the reflective accounts produced by academic staff, the three themes of emotional development and embodiment, social development and challenging hierarchies, and liberation and the law graduate emerged in response to our use of outsider pedagogy and the application of feminist and queer theories. Through both the students' responses and their creative work, we saw mission and criticality—arguably the foundation of much activism—given a safe space in which to thrive.

Moreover, zine creation as an artistic tool allowed students a more embodied educational experience, exploring emotions, experiences and identities and their entanglements with the law, in contrast to abstract (and, as noted, often

76 Giroux (1994).
77 Bakht et al. (2007).
78 hooks (1994) p 203.
79 Freire (1993) p 48.

alienating[80]), problem-solving approaches. Combining this approach with an explicit feminist and queer prism added a richness to this humanising effect; students used their contributions to reflect on larger societal hierarchies, and the relationship between law, marginalisation, and power. These insightful and humanised approaches to the law and legal teaching will be significant to the development of students' personal and professional identities.

Enriching though the experience proved to be, there is value in considering how activities such as these can be incorporated into the 'core' of the legal curriculum[81] to develop all law students' personal and professional identities within society. A holistic curriculum should emphasise reflection and encourage dialogue with others.[82] Reflection, as set out by Dewey,[83] is an important aspect of personal and professional development. By providing students with a conducive environment in which to reflect on and share their experiences and observations with others, transformative learning[84] can be promoted, and together with the feminist and queer focus described above, a more radical humanising pedagogy adopted.

Ethics Statement

Ethical approval for this research was granted by Northumbria University.

References

Chris Ashford (2021) 'Gender, Sexuality and the Law School: (Re)thinking Blackstone's Tower with Queer and Feminist Theory', 2(3) *Amicus Curiae* 450.

Rosemary Auchmuty (2012) 'Using Feminist Judgments in the Property Law Classroom' 46(3) *The Law Teacher* 277.

Natasha Bakht, Kim Brooks, Gillian Calder, Jennifer Koshan, Sonia Lawrence, Carissima Mathen and Debra Parkes (2007) 'Counting Outsiders: A Critical Exploration of Outsider Course Enrolment in Canadian Legal Education' 45(4) *Osgoode Hall LJ* 667.

Meg-John Barker and Jules Scheele (2016) *Queer: A Graphic History*, Icon Books.

Peter Birks (1994a) 'The Historical Context' in Peter Birks (ed) *Reviewing Legal Education*, Oxford University Press.

Peter Birks (1994b) 'Short-Cuts' in Peter Birks (ed) *Reviewing Legal Education*, Oxford University Press.

Suzanne Bouclin, Sharon Cowan and Gillian Calder (2013) 'Playing Games with Law' in Z Bankowski, M Del Mar and P Maharg (eds) *The Arts and the Legal Academy*, Ashgate.

Anthony Bradney (1999) 'Liberalising Legal Education' in Fiona Cownie (ed) *The Law School: Global Issues, Local Questions*, Ashgate.

80 Crenshawe (1988).

81 Savage and Watt (1996) p 50.

82 Hamilton et al. (2012).

83 Dewey (1933).

84 Mezirow (1990).

Matt Brim (2020) *Poor Queer Studies: Confronting Elitism in the University*, Duke University Press.

Kim Brooks and Debra Parkes (2004) 'Queering Legal Education: A Project of Theoretical Discovery' 27 *Harvard Women's LJ* 89.

Roger Brownsword (1999) 'Law Schools for Lawyers, Citizens, and People', in Fiona Cownie (ed) *The Law School: Global Issues, Local Questions*, Ashgate.

Lief H Carter and Thomas F Burke (2002) *Reason in Law*, 6th Edition, Longman.

Patricia Hill Collins (2000) *Black Feminist Thought*, Routledge.

Joanne Conaghan (2000) 'Reassessing the Feminist Theoretical Project in Law' 27 *Journal of Law and Society* 351.

Joanne Conaghan (2013) *Law and Gender*, Oxford University Press.

Kimberlé Crenshaw (1988) 'Towards a Race Conscious Pedagogy in Legal Education' 11 *National Black Law Journal* 1.

John W Creswell (2009) *Research Design: Qualitative, Quantitative and Mixed Methods Approaches*, 3rd Edition, SAGE Publications.

Louie Crew (1978) 'Before Emancipation: Gay Persons as Viewed by Chairpersons in English', in Louie Crew (ed) *The Gay Academic*, ETC Publications.

Karin H deGravelles (2011) 'You Be Othello: Interrogating Identification in the Classroom' 11(1) *Pedagogy* 153.

Moshoula Capous Desyllas and Allison Sinclair (2014) 'Zine-Making as a Pedagogical Tool for Transformative Learning in Social Work Education'33(3) *Social Work Education* 296.

John Dewey (1933) *How We Think: A Restatement of the Relation of Reflective Thinking to the Educative Process*, DC Heath.

Stephen Duncombe (2017) *Notes From Underground: Zines and the Politics of Alternative Culture*, 3rd Edition, Microcosm Publishing.

Linda Finlay (2008) *Reflecting on 'Reflective Practice'*. Practice-based Professional Learning Paper 52, The Open University.

Paulo Freire (1993) *Pedagogy of the Oppressed*, Penguin.

Linda Garber (ed) (1994) *Tilting the Tower: Lesbians Teaching Queer Subjects*, Routledge.

Howard Gardner (2006) *Multiple Intelligences: New Horizons*, Basic Books.

Henry Giroux (1994) 'Doing Cultural Studies: Youth and the Challenge of Pedagogy' 64(3) *Harvard Educational Review* 278.

Regina Graycar and Jenny Morgan (2002) *The Hidden Gender of Law*, 2nd Edition, Federation Press.

Karen Green and Tristan Taormino (1997) *A Girl's Guide to Taking Over the World: Writings from the Girl Zine Revolution*, St Martin's Press.

Jessica Guth and Chris Ashford (2014) 'The Legal Education and Training Review: Regulating Socio-Legal and Liberal Legal Education?' 48(1) *The Law Teacher* 5.

Jessica Guth (2016) 'Fostering Curiosity: The Importance of Research and Teaching in Law Schools' in Chris Ashford, Nigel Duncan and Jessica Guth (eds) *Perspectives on Legal Education: Contemporary Responses to the Lord Upjohn Lectures*, Routledge.

Neil W Hamilton, Verna E Monson and Jerome M Organ (2012) 'Empirical Evidence that Legal Education can Foster Student Professionalism/Professional Formation to become an Effective Lawyer' 10 *University of St Thomas Law Journal* 11.

Donna Haraway (1988) 'Situated Knowledges: The Science Question in Feminism and the Privilege of Partial Perspective' 14 (3) *Feminist Studies* 575.

bell hooks (1994) *Teaching to Transgress: Education as the Practice of Freedom*, Routledge.

Emma Jones (2017) 'One Size Fits All? Multiple Intelligences and Legal Education' 51 *The Law Teacher* 56.

Otto Kahn-Freund (1966) 'Reflections on Legal Education' 29(2) *Modern Law Review* 121.

Duncan Kennedy (1982) 'Legal Education and the Reproduction of Hierarchy' 32 *Journal of Legal Education* 591.

Duncan Kennedy (2004) *Legal Education and the Reproduction of Hierarchy: A Polemic Against the System*, New York University Press.

Rita Kissen (1996) *The Last Closet: The Real Lives of Lesbian and Gay Teachers*, Heinemann.

David A Kolb (2014) *Experiential Learning: Experience as the Source of Learning and Development*, Pearson Education.

J Lee Lehman, 'Gay Students' in Louise Crew (ed) *The Gay Academic*, ETC Publications.

Chelsea Lonsdale (2015) 'Engaging the "Othered": Using Zines to Support Student Identities' 30(2) *Language Arts Journal of Michigan* 8.

Susanne Luhmann (1998) 'Queering/Querying Pedagogy? Or, Pedagogy Is a Pretty Queer Thing', in William F Pinar (ed) *Queer Theory in Education*, Lawrence Erlbaum Associates.

Catharine MacKinnon (2003) 'Mainstreaming Feminism in Legal Education' 53 *Journal of Legal Education* 199.

Carrie Menkel-Meadow (1988) 'Feminist Legal Theory, Critical Legal Studies, and Legal Education or "The Fem-Crits Go to Law School"' 38(1/2) *Journal of Legal Education* 61.

Elizabeth Mertz (2007) *The Language of Law School: Learning to "Think Like a Lawyer"*, Oxford University Press.

Jack Mezirow (1990) 'How Critical Reflection Triggers Transformative Learning' in Jack Mezirow and Associates (eds) *Fostering Critical Reflection in Adulthood: A Guide to Transformative and Emancipatory Learning*, Jossey-Bass.

Dawn Oliver (1996) 'The Integration of Teaching and Research in the Law Department' 30(2) *The Law Teacher* 133.

Alison Piepmeier (2009) *Girl Zines: Making Media, Doing Feminism*, New York University Press.

Robin Potter and Alycia Sellie (2016) 'Zines in the Classroom: Critical Librarianship and Participatory Collections' in Nicole Pagowsky and Kelly McElroy (eds) *Critical Library Pedagogy Handbook Lesson Plans*, Volume 2, Association of College and Research Libraries.

Deborah Rhodes (1993) 'Missing Questions: Feminist Perspectives on Legal Education' 45 *Stanford Law Review* 1547.

Ruthann Robson (1998) *Sappho Goes to Law School*, Columbia University Press.

Eric Rofes (1985) *Socrates, Plato and Guys Like Me: Confessions of a Gay Schoolteacher*, Alyson.

Eric Rofes (2000) 'Bound and Gagged: Sexual Silences, Gender Conformity and the Gay Male Teacher' 3 *Sexualities* 439.

Nigel Savage and Gary Watt (1996) 'A "House of Intellect" for the Profession' in Peter Birks (ed), *Pressing Problems in the Law: What Are Law Schools For?*, Volume 2, Oxford University Press.

Michael Hunter Schwartz, Gerald F Hees and Sophie M Sparrow (2013) *What the Best Law Teachers Do*, Harvard University Press.

Eve Kosofsky Sedgwick (1993) 'How to Bring Your Kids Up Gay' in Michael Warner (ed) *Fear of a Queer Planet: Queer Politics and Social Theory*, University of Minnesota Press.

Tracey Skelton (2020) 'Teaching Sexuality Across Time, Space, and Political Contexts' 44(2) *Journal of Geography in Higher Education* 188.

Allesandra Tanesini (1999) *An Introduction to Feminist Epistemologies*, Blackwell.

Mark Todd and Esther Pearl Watson (2006) *Whatchamean, What's a Zine?: The Art of Making Zines and Mini-comics*, Clarion Books.
Aspasia I Tsaoussi (2020) 'Using Soft Skills Courses to Inspire Law Teachers: A New Methodology for a More Humanistic Legal Education' 54(1) *The Law Teacher* 1.
William Twining (1995) 'What Are Law Schools For?' 46(3/4) *Northern Ireland Legal Quarterly* 291.
William Twining (1997) 'Rethinking Law Schools' 21 *Law and Social Inquiry* 1007.
ECS Wade (1951) 'Legal Education; The Changing Scene' 1(6) *The Journal of the Society of Public Teachers of Law* 415.
Geoffrey Wilson (1987) 'English Legal Scholarship' 50 *Modern Law Review* 818.
KC Worden (1985) 'Overshooting the Target: A Feminist Deconstruction of Legal Education' 34 *American University Law Review* 1141.

Chapter 3

School and Fundamental Rights

An Active Responsible Citizenship

Juliana Zanganelli and Daury Fabriz

Introduction

Citizenship includes, among other constitutionally guaranteed rights, freedom, participation, solidarity, tolerance, and democracy. In this sense, this work aims to analyse whether awareness of fundamental rights and duties enhances democratic participatory processes and, as a result, the full exercise of citizenship, to promote actions aimed at solving and/or reducing social demands, whether in relationship to discrimination, incarceration, security, or corruption.

In this respect, to review the intersections between the effective application of citizenship education in schools, the exercise of responsible citizenship, acting in the democratic participatory process and the reduction and/or resolution of social demands, among other authors, Werneck Vianna, Fábio Konder Comparato, Ramón Pérez Juste, Dalmo Dallari, Maria Victória Benevides, Jaime Pinsky, Carlos Nelson Coutinho, Vera Telles, Maria Alice Rezende de Carvalho, Mercedes Oraisón, Ana María Pérez, and Nelson Luiz Guarinello.

At first, the concept of active and responsible citizenship was analysed to clarify all the nuances regarding the term. Subsequently, in order to demonstrate a global perception of social demands, the indices and surveys of the following institutes were examined: 'International Association for the Evaluation of Educational Achievement' (IEA), 'Transparency International', 'Secretary of Mexico's Security, Justice and Peace', 'Institute for Economics and Peace', 'Social Progress Imperative', 'World Health Organization' (WHO), 'World Economic Forum', 'Institute for Economic Research Foundation', 'National Council of Justice' (CNJ), 'Institute for Criminal Policy Research' (ICPR), 'Carceraria Pastoral', and 'Department of Economic and Social Affairs' (UNDESA). For this reason, there was a need to select analytical categories to analyse social demands, among which were: i) corruption; ii) violence; iii) security; iv) homicide; v) tolerance; vi) incarceration; vii) democracy; and viii) e-government.

Furthermore, the selection among the countries to be compared with Brazil was also crucial; they were chosen based on research systematically elaborated by the International Civic and Citizenship Study (ICCS), regarding civic

DOI: 10.4324/9781003179283-5

engagement in schools of 24 countries, undertaken by the IEA. This is because we sought to explore countries that permeated all the research data collected, thus, considering that the study prepared by the ICCS–IEA provided information about civic education, its use was essential. Thus, the analysis comprised the following countries: Belgium, Norway, Denmark, Colombia, Peru, and Chile.

Although citizenship is a present issue, it is a challenge insofar as, for its effectiveness, it presupposes an active and responsible action. However, from the analyses studied in the third part of this article, it was possible to verify a certain lack of collective commitment. It is in this sense that the proposal for citizen education in basic education structures proves to be relevant, given that it mainly targets children and adolescents with information about their rights and, above all, about their duties in a given society.

Consequently, this article aims to go through the inferences between the contribution of education aimed at citizenship, in order to promote an active and responsible citizenship, active in democratic participatory processes, not to mention the resolution and/or reduction of social demands.

Active and Responsible Citizenship

Citizenship comprises a range of rights and duties inserted in a society and, therefore, refers, among other issues, to democracy, participation, justice, and culture. Dalmo Dallari, when defining the term, stated that 'it expresses a set of rights that give people the possibility to actively participate in the life and government of their people' and concludes by stating that 'the absence of citizenship implies marginalization and social exclusion'.[1]

In Greece, public space was formed by collective decisions articulated by councils, assemblies and courts, in defence of the expansion of the so-called city-states. However, it urges to emphasise that a citizen was only one who acted in public life, so that those who did not fulfil this role (slaves, etc.) could not be considered as such.

This way, though participation was more active and direct, there was a rupture between classes, given that the demands related to the poorest were hampered by other concerns. With the rise of the Roman Empire and the conflicts existing at the time, the exercise of citizenship collapsed.[2] Pinsky and Bassanezi[3] concluded that:

> In summary: the history of ancient citizenship can only be understood as a long historical process, whose outcome is the Roman Empire. From

1 Dallari (1998) p 14.

2 Pinsky and Bassanezi (2013).

3 Pinsky and Bassanezi (2013).

> belonging to a small agricultural community, citizenship has become, over time, a source of claims and conflicts, as different conceptions of the obligations and rights of citizens within the community clashed … until a higher power established itself over the set of city-states and progressively removed from community citizenship its capacity to be a potential source of claims.[4]

It is, therefore, a historical process of struggle and oppression, with a multiplicity of meanings and factors, depending on the period, generation, mobilisation and limitations, but which generally refers to the public sphere.

According to Pinsky and Bassanezi[5], 'the essence of citizenship, if we could define it, would reside precisely in this public, impersonal character, in this neutral environment, in which social situations, aspirations, desires and conflicting interests confront, within the limits of the community, conflicting aspirations, desires and interests.[6] Then, it summarises that it may even be possible to have a community without citizenship, but it is certainly only possible to observe effective citizenship in a 'concrete community', which could be defined as a privileged universe of collective actions.[7]

To Rousseau,[8] the social contract fulfils this role of participation by bringing together all common concerns, which results in a more 'just' state. For Coutinho, on the other hand, democracy is synonymous with popular sovereignty, implied by 'active participation in the formation of government' and 'in the control of social life'.

Currently, pro-collective action can be exercised either by active citizenship or by passive citizenship. To Benevides,[9] while the first is up to the individual, purposing to create, transform, and control power and/or powers;[10] the second is granted to the State, which according to Fernandes,[11] if exercised by individuals, it causes a distance between the people and those in power, as it reveals a complacent, omissive, and non-claiming action.

The exercise of citizenship ensures social, civil and political rights which, for Marshall, are the three elements that presuppose it. The first, created in the 18th century, were called civil rights, which were composed of individual freedom. The second element, established in the 19th century, was based on participation and the exercise of political power. Finally, social rights correspond to economic well-being, that is, the minimum quality of life.

4 Pinsky and Bassanezi (2013).
5 Pinsky and Bassanezi (2013).
6 Pinsky and Bassanezi (2013).
7 Pinsky and Bassanezi (2013).
8 Rousseau (1992) p 92.
9 Benevides (1994) pp 13–6.
10 Benevides (1991) p 20.
11 Fernandes (2009) p 184.

Debates on the inspection and active action of society have been recurring, due to numerous social demands, for that matter, Vera Telles states that:

> The absence of spaces for recognition and proper civil bonds translates into the difficulties of formulating everyday dramas (individual and collective) in the public language of rights, tending, for that very reason, to be equated within the moral codes of private life. This is where the denial of rights, the non-recognition of others as subjects of legitimate interests and aspirations, affects sociability, culture and identity.[12]

There is, then, a complex scenario around which mechanisms could be used to allow this active and responsible citizen action, to defend their rights and exercise their duties. To resume this role of active citizen, Telles argues that an identity is necessary, the 'feeling of a citizen', in order to exercise their duties, mainly, of diligence with regard to guaranteeing their own rights.

Citizenship, therefore, must be continually rebuilt and reformulated in the modern world with a view to strengthening the understanding of the rights and duties of each individual, which can only be achieved when there is a situation of belonging, respect, and information. This is the only way to think about 'active and responsible citizenship'. Active by acting incisively, committed and responsible, according to the awareness of their rights and responsibilities within a society.

This distance for Vianna and Rezende de Carvalho[13] occurred at the time of the Brazilian military regime, triggering an 'injury to the social fabric', since with the expansion of capitalism, political indifference, individualism and, consequently, 'the passage from the individual to the citizen deepened' promoting negative consequences to civic culture. The responsiveness model, in this sense,

> It cannot be, as its authors warn, a path to the death of the law, but rather to a democratic order that, demonstrating permeability to social demands, old and new, puts principles, laws and public policies under tension, in the sense of a permanent renewal of the right done with the participation of all.[14]

Hence, active and responsible citizenship prioritises practices in favour of the common good, avoiding waste, controlling public accounts, respecting differences, sharing ideas, and seeking more adequate solutions for society. For Jennings et al. it is the ability to actively participate in democratic processes,

12 Telles (1994) p 45.

13 Vianna and Carvalho (2000) p 28.

14 Vianna and Eisenberg (2010) p 9.

in dialogue about just and egalitarian societies, then, active and responsible citizenship prioritises practices in favour of the common good, avoiding waste, controlling public accounts, respecting differences, sharing ideas and seeking more adequate solutions for society. For Jennings et al., it is the ability to actively participate in democratic processes, in dialogue about just and egalitarian societies, as well as in their creation and maintenance.[15] To Valentim,[16] this exercise promotes more conscious behaviours and attitudes, as it fosters the 'spirit of belonging' and so understands that:

> The responsibility conquered by groups and classes that over the years have struggled for their rights to be recognized cannot be limited to the enjoyment of these same rights, but rather to a participation that continues to fight for changes that improve people's quality of life. Even if these changes do not directly affect you, since this is a characteristic of responsible citizenship, not only living for yourself but also for the communities.[17]

Therefore, active and responsible citizenship allows for conscious action, for feeling involved and committed to the future projections of the society in which they live, for this reason, participation, involvement, supervision and commitment, are all amplified, promoting resolution and/or reduction of social demands.

Social Demands and Global Perception: A Study Compared with Brazil

Active and responsible citizenship corroborates, above all, with the effective exercise of the duties of surveillance, inspection, participation, and respect for differences, in short, with the full performance of the citizen in the society to which he is inserted, in order to protect the collectivity by ensuring the preservation of fundamental rights.

From this perspective, a comparative analysis was made between Brazil and both European and Latin American countries, with the purpose of verifying whether the implementation of an education focused on citizenship in schools would enhance democratic participatory processes and the resolution and/or reduction of social demands, in order to effectively exercise active and responsible citizenship.

For that, besides bibliographies, indexes and surveys from the following institutes were used: 'International Association for the Evaluation of Educational Achievement', 'Transparency International', 'Mexico Security,

15 Jennings, Neves, and Gomes (2014) p 12.
16 Valentim (2012) pp 23–5.
17 Valentim (2012) pp 23–5.

Justice and Peace Secretariat', 'Institute for Economics and Peace', 'Social Progress Imperative', 'World Health Organization', 'World Economic Forum', 'Foundation Institute of Economic Research', 'National Council of Justice', 'Institute for Criminal Policy Research', 'Prison Pastoral', and the 'Department of Economic and Social Affairs'.

In the meantime, with a view to allowing a retained and comprehensive analysis of all the above-mentioned indices and surveys, it was essential to select the countries to be compared with Brazil. This choice was based mainly on the diagnosis performed by the 'International Civic and Citizenship Study' (ICCS), supported by the 'International Association for the Evaluation of Educational Achievement' (IEA), since not all countries were analysed by it. This study, conducted in 2016, involved the participation of 24 countries in order to monitor civic engagement in schools by evaluating students aged approximately 14 years old (see Table 3.1).[18]

With regard to social demands, it was also essential to provide the selection of the analytical categories in Table 3.2.

Table 3.1 Countries chosen for analysis purposes

Europe	*Latin America*
Belgium	Chile
Norway	Colombia
Denmark	Peru

Own source.

Table 3.2 Analytical categories selected for analysis purposes

Analytical Categories
1. Corruption
2. Violence
3. Security
4. Homicíde
5. Tolerance
6. Imprisonment
7. Democracy
8. Electronic government

Own source.

18 International Association for the Evaluation of Educational Achievement, 'International Civic and Citizenship Education Study: Framework', https://iccs.iea.nl/home.html, accessed 10 February 2019.

School education can favour a more democratic and engaged public space, with regard to reducing social ills. It is, therefore, in this context of defining citizenship as the realisation of active and responsible participation that the current situation of the countries selected above was analysed. It is worth mentioning, though, that it will not be the object of this article to specify each category analytically, which were examined according to world analyses already carried out.

Having said that, social demands are frequent and require effort regarding the constant participation of individuals. This is because only with an active and responsible action is its resolution and/or reduction feasible.

Debates about corruption prevail in all fields, whether through the discussion of action plans, coping strategies, punishments, rights restrictions, or public policies. The reason is because it prioritises individual over collective wishes and, consequently, restricts and violates guarantees.

With the vision of measuring the perception of corruption in the world, in 1993, the movement called 'Transparency International' was created, which since then has been working to promote a collective conscience in this regard. The index ranks 180 countries and territories using a scale from 0 (highly corrupt) to 100 (greater integrity), considering, among other criteria, the incorporation of integrity mechanisms, effective judgment, bureaucracy, adequate legislation, and protection of witnesses and informants.[19]

In 2018, the study found that more than two-thirds of countries scored below 50, contributing to a global democratic crisis. Hence, it can be said that the higher the score, the greater the protection of rights, so that lower levels portray a deterioration of the rule of law.[20] From this angle, when comparing the scale of corruption between Brazil and European and Latin American countries, we have this scenario in Europe: Belgium with 75 points, Norway with 84 points, Denmark with 88 points. On the other side, in Latin America, we have Chile with 67 points, Colombia with 36 points, Peru with 35 points, and Brazil also with 35 points. [21]

As can be seen, Brazil is below the minimum average established by the index, consolidating its position at 105th in the world rankings. This scenario, according to 'Transparency International', favours, among other aspects, the weakening of the free and independent media, the silencing of civil society, the increase in social discrimination, and interference in the separation of powers. European countries stand out with an average above 70 points, while Latin

19 Transparency International, 'Corruption Perception Index 2018', www.transparency.org/files/content/pages/2018_CPI_Executive_Summary.pdf, accessed 29 January 2019.

20 Transparency International, 'World Map', www.transparency.org/cpi2018#world-map, accessed 29 January 2019.

21 Transparency International, Corruption Perception Index 2018' www.transparency.org/files/content/pages/2018_CPI_Executive_Summary.pdf, accessed 29 January 2019.

American countries have an average score of 35, with the exception of Chile, which exhibits a greater perception of integrity.

With regard to violence, in 2017, in Mexico, the Secretariat for Security, Justice and Peace developed a methodology that brought together the cities with the highest level of violence to call for political action in the listed regions. The defined criteria are basically: i) urban area; ii) cities with populations above 300,000 inhabitants; and iii) relationship with official homicide rates. Among the countries chosen for this article, only two are mentioned, namely: Colombia—represented by three cities—and Brazil, counting 17.[22]

Furthermore, the report 'Global Peace Index' promoted by the 'Institute for Economics and Peace' and published in 2018 was analysed, which assessed the perception of peace in 163 countries through 23 indicators, being considered the main 'measurer' of world peace. Based on comprehensive data analysis, it provides updates on global peace trends, economic values, and criteria definitions to qualify as peaceful societies.

This study also pays particular attention to eight pillars of the so-called 'Positive Peace, namely: i) 'the good functioning of the government'; ii) 'the equitable distribution of resources'; iii) 'the free flow of information'; iv) 'good relations with neighboring countries'; v) 'the high levels of human capital'; vi) 'the acceptance of the rights of other citizens'; vii) 'the low levels of corruption'; and viii) 'the solid business environment'.[23]

By this way, comparing the level of peace between European and Latin American countries, you have: Belgium at 21st position, Norway at 16th, Denmark at 5th, Chile at 28th, Colombia at 145th, Peru at 74th, and Brazil at 106th.[24]

As can be seen, Brazil reached 106th position, in view of the high crime rates, coming closer to Colombia (145th). While European countries and Chile did not even surpass 30th position in presenting acceptable levels of violence.[25]

It also emphasises the work made by the non-profit entity 'Social Progress Imperative'[26] which carried out a survey in 146 countries, allowing comparisons

22 OEA, 'Seguridad, Justicia y Paz: Consejo Ciudadano para la Seguridad Pública y la Justicia Penal AC', https://www.oas.org/ext/es/seguridad/red-prevencion-crimen/Recursos/Biblioteca-Digital/ranking-2017-de-las-50-ciudades-mas-violentas-del-mundo, accessed 30 January 2019, pp 1–4.

23 Institute for Economics and Peace, 'Global Peace Index 2018: Measuring Peace in a Complex World', https://www.economicsandpeace.org/wp-content/uploads/2020/08/Global-Peace-Index-2018-2-1.pdf, accessed 30 January 2019, pp 60–5.

24 Institute for Economics and Peace, 'Global Peace Index 2018: Measuring Peace in a Complex World' https://www.economicsandpeace.org/wp-content/uploads/2020/08/Global-Peace-Index-2018-2-1.pdf, accessed 30 January 2019, pp 60–5.

25 Institute for Economics and Peace, 'Global Peace Index 2018: Measuring Peace in a Complex World', https://www.economicsandpeace.org/wp-content/uploads/2020/08/Global-Peace-Index-2018-2-1.pdf, accessed 30 January 2019, pp 14–7.

26 Social Progress Index, 'Compare Countries 2018', www.socialprogress.org/, accessed 30 January 2019.

to be made between numerous measures. In the case of security, the index considers: i) 'homicide rate'; ii) 'murder and torture'; iii) 'perceived crime'; and iv) 'traffic deaths'. As can be observed, Brazil and Colombia again stand out in relation to the others selected.

Comparing the security level between European and Latin American countries with Brazil we find Belgium at 30th, Norway at 8th, Denmark at 13th, Chile at 45th, Colombia at 116th, Peru at 92nd, and Brazil at 124th.[27]

From this it can be seen that, in a classification from 0 to 100, European countries do not surpass the 30th place. In Latin America, Chile is the country with the best security level.[28] This scenario of insecurity, as presented, can be consolidated by the data made available through the report 'World Health Statistics',[29] formulated by WHO. The document, published in 2018, compiled data from 194 countries from studies by both the WHO and the United Nations. Comparing the number of homicides, the level between Brazil and European and Latin American countries is: Belgium 1000 deaths per 100,000 inhabitants, Norway 600 deaths, Denmark 800 deaths, Chile 4,400 deaths, Colombia 43,100 deaths, Peru 11,600 deaths, and Brazil 31,300 deaths per 100,000 inhabitants.[30]

Through the aforementioned report, it is noted that Brazil and Colombia again have emphasis, corresponding to the 9th and 4th countries with the highest homicide rate in the world, respectively.[31]

Another relevant demand is the case of tolerance and respect between individuals. For this purpose, the report 'Social Progress Imperative'[32] and the Global Gender Differences Index,[33] the latter, promoted by the World Economic Forum, analysed disparities in 144 countries through economic, educational, and political criteria.

In this regard, the report compiles all the data collected in relation to the countries selected by this study. The tolerance level for homosexuality between

27 Social Progress Index, 'Compare Countries 2018', www.socialprogress.org/, accessed 30 January 2019.

28 Social Progress Index, 'Compare Countries 2018', www.socialprogress.org/ accessed 30 January 2019.

29 World Health Organization, 'World Health Statistics 2018: Monitoring health for the SDGs, sustainable development goals' https://apps.who.int/iris/bitstream/handle/10665/272596/9789241565585-eng.pdf?ua=1, accessed 30 January 2019.

30 World Health Organization, 'World Health Statistics 2018: Monitoring health for the SDGs, sustainable development goals' https://apps.who.int/iris/bitstream/handle/10665/272596/9789241565585-eng.pdf?ua=1, accessed 30 January 2019.

31 World Health Organization, 'World Health Statistics 2018: Monitoring health for the SDGs, sustainable development goals' https://apps.who.int/iris/bitstream/handle/10665/272596/9789241565585-eng.pdf?ua=1, accessed 30 January 2019.

32 Social Progress Index, 'Compare Countries 2018', www.socialprogress.org/, accessed 30 January 2019.

33 World Economic Forum, 'Global Gender Gap Index 2017', www3.weforum.org/docs/WEF_GGGR_2017.pdf, accessed 30 January 2019.

Brazil and European and Latin American countries is: Belgium at 7th position, Norway at 2nd, Denmark at 5th, Chile at 26th, Colombia at 34th, Peru at 48th, and Brazil at 22nd.[34]

For minorities, the research identified Belgium at 40th position, Norway at 4th, Denmark at 10th, Chile at 15th, Colombia at 90th, Peru at 108th, and Brazil at 79th. For gender, it is possible to verify: Belgium at 31st position, Norway at 2nd, Denmark at 14th, Chile at 63rd, Colombia at 36th, Peru at 48th, and Brazil at 90th.[35]

In the case of homosexuals, among Latin American countries, Brazil has the best position. With regard to discrimination against minorities, even behind Chile, it ranks 79th. In gender issues, Brazil deserves even more attention, as it stands out at 90th position. Among European countries, Norway and Denmark are more tolerant, however, Belgium shows a higher level of intolerance, even being in a much lower position than Chile.

For this reason, when diagnosing prejudice and discrimination in 501 schools in 27 Brazilian states, with the participation of more than 15,000 students, the 'Research on Prejudice and Discrimination in the School Environment',[36] concluded that the level of prejudice in the Brazilian school environment is above 90% when it comes to 'have some kind of prejudice', 'people with special needs', 'ethnic-racial prejudice', 'gender' and, 'generation'. For 'socioeconomic' and 'sexual orientation' the percentage is above 80%, and for 'territorial prejudice', 70%.[37]

In this sense, the school setting is permeated by countless conditions that give rise to discrimination or bias among students, whether due to ethnic-racial, gender, sexual, or economic orientation.

It is also worth mentioning the demand regarding incarceration. Data provided by CNJ[38] and also ICPR,[39] revealed that Brazil has over 700,000 prisoners and that 71.15% of the prison population has completed primary

34 World Economic Forum, 'Global Gender Gap Index 2017', www3.weforum.org/docs/WEF_GGGR_2017.pdf, accessed 30 January 2019.

35 World Economic Forum, 'Global Gender Gap Index 2017', www3.weforum.org/docs/WEF_GGGR_2017.pdf, accessed 30 January 2019.

36 Fundação Instituto de Pesquisas Econômicas, 'Pesquisa sobre preconceito e discriminação no ambiente escolar', http://portal.mec.gov.br/dmdocuments/diversidade_apresentacao.pdf, accessed 30 January 2019.

37 Fundação Instituto de Pesquisas Econômicas, 'Pesquisa sobre preconceito e discriminação no ambiente escolar', http://portal.mec.gov.br/dmdocuments/diversidade_apresentacao.pdf, accessed 30 January 2019.

38 Conselho Nacional de Justiça, 'Painel banco nacional de monitoramento de prisões – BNMP 2.0' https://paineis.cnj.jus.br/QvAJAXZfc/opendoc.htm?document=qvw_l%2FPainelCNJ.qvw&host=QVS%40neodimio03&anonymous=true&sheet=shBNMPIIMAPA, accessed 30 January 2019.

39 Institute for Criminal Policy Research, World Prison Brief', http://www.prisonstudies.org/highest-to-lowest/prison-population-total?field_region_taxonomy_tid=All, accessed 18 February 2019.

education.[40] Compared to European and Latin American countries, the prominence of numbers in Brazil is visible.

CNJ[41] and ICPR[42] identify, by comparing prison populations between Brazil and European and Latin American countries, the following scenario: Belgium with 10,073 at 98th position, Norway with 3,373 at 134th, Denmark with 3,635 at 130th, Chile with 41,068 at 46th, Colombia with 118,513 at 14th, Peru with 89,494 at 18th, and Brazil with 700,432 at 3rd.

Linked to this, the research entitled 'Anti-prison Struggle in the Contemporary World: A Study on Experiences of Reducing the Prison Population in Other Nations',[43] traces Brazil as the only country, among the nations in the world with most incarcerations (United States, China, Brazil, Russia, India, and Thailand), to show a constant trend of growth in these rates.

In order to verify the propensity with regard to social participation in the countries studied, the research undertaken by UNDESA about e-government was analysed.[44] This is due to the diffusion of technologies and the development of measures that foster political-social-economic discussion bringing individuals together, then intensifying their participation in social demands.

Yet, even achieving a better position in the last report, Brazil must still advance in this area to allow greater interaction between the citizen and the government. For electronic government: Belgium is at 23rd position, Norway at 14th, Denmark in 1st, Chile at 42nd, Colombia at 61st, Peru at 36th, and Brazil at 44th.[45]

In this same perspective, the 'Democracy Index', formulated by 'The Economist Intelligence Unit', verified the level of democracy in 165 countries and territories, based on the following criteria: i) 'electoral process and pluralism'; ii) 'civil liberties'; iii) 'functioning of the government'; iv) 'political participation'; and v) 'political culture'. In view of the analysis gained through

40 Conselho Nacional de Justiça, 'Cadastro Nacional de Presos', https://www.socialprogress.org/static/9b25a2a187a2638e806fd39d0a7e3ab0/2018-social-progress-index-methodology.pdf, accessed 18 February 2019., p 45.

41 Conselho Nacional de Justiça, 'Painel banco nacional de monitoramento de prisões – BNMP 2.0', https://paineis.cnj.jus.br/QvAJAXZfc/opendoc.htm?document=qvw_l%2FPainelCNJ.qvw&host=QVS%40neodimio03&anonymous=true&sheet=shBNMPIIMAPA, Accessed 30 January 2019.

42 Institute for Criminal Policy Research, 'World Prison Brief', www.prisonstudies.org/highest-to-lowest/prison-population-total?field_region_taxonomy_tid=All, accessed 18 February 2019.

43 Instituto Betty e Jacob Lafer, 'LUTA Antiprisional no Mundo Contemporâneo: Um Estudo sobre Experiências de Redução da População Carcerária em Outras Nações' http://carceraria.org.br/wp-content/uploads/2018/09/relatorio_luta_antiprisional.pdf, accessed 18 February 2019, p 11.

44 United Nations Department of Economic and Social Affairs (UNDESA), 'E-government Survey 2018', https://publicadministration.un.org/egovkb/Portals/egovkb/Documents/un/2018-Survey/E-Government%20Survey%202018_FINAL%20for%20web.pdf, accessed 18 February 2018.

45 United Nations Department of Economic and Social Affairs (UNDESA), 'E-government Survey 2018', https://publicadministration.un.org/egovkb/Portals/egovkb/Documents/un/2018-Survey/E-Government%20Survey%202018_FINAL%20for%20web.pdf, accessed 18 February 2018.

the criteria above, each country is categorised into four regimes, namely: i) 'full democracies'; ii) 'failing democracies'; iii) 'hybrid regimes'; and iv) 'authoritarian regimes'.[46]

To this end, they explained that in democracies considered full, all freedoms and rights are respected and, thus, there is a 'flowering' of democracy, fostered by political culture. In failing democracies, although free elections exist, there are significant weaknesses, such as the low level of participation and an underdeveloped political culture. In hybrid regimes, on the other hand, elections present substantial irregularities. Finally, in authoritarian regimes, the state political pluralism is absent or strongly circumscribed and, for this reason, they are considered dictatorships.[47]

It was proven, with this, that Europe has 14 countries in full democracy, without any authoritarian regimes. In Latin America, in addition to the primacy of failed democracies, there is the presence of authoritarianism in two countries.[48]

From the above, in view of the analyses of social demands, it was possible to observe the existing mismatch between European and Latin American countries, but especially in relation to Brazil, which still presents quite significant data.

Responsible Citizenship and Expanding the Democratic Participatory Process: An Analysis on Citizen Training in Brazilian Schools

Active and responsible citizenship comprises, therefore, an action aimed at facing social demands, to exercise social control, to share practices in favour of the common good, to respect differences, in short, to promote conscious actions as well. In this sense, Vera Telles[49] issues citizenship in the following way: 'how is it possible for these men and women to recognize themselves as citizens if they do not find spaces, signs or discourses that name and constitute them as such?'[50] and she concludes:

> Then, we should not be surprised by the increase in criminality and juvenile delinquency, the growth of private justice practices, prejudice and racism, as well as the collusion with political authoritarianism or even police

46 The Economist, 'Democracy Index 2015', www.yabiladi.com/img/content/EIU-Democracy-Index-2015.pdf, accessed 30 January 2019, pp 1–2.

47 The Economist, 'Democracy Index 2015', www.yabiladi.com/img/content/EIU-Democracy-Index-2015.pdf, accessed 30 January 2019, pp 45–6.

48 The Economist, 'Democracy Index 2015', www.yabiladi.com/img/content/EIU-Democracy-Index-2015.pdf, accessed 30 January 2019, p 23.

49 Telles (1994).

50 Telles (1994) p 45.

> violence. Before crediting all this to a supposed political backwardness of majorities or to an equally supposed pathology inherent to poverty, it could be said that they are consequences of non-citizenship.[51]

Through this meaning, it is essential to debate about an education focused on citizenship, with the purpose of analysing whether the perception of fundamental rights and duties would enhance democratic participatory processes and, consequently, the full exercise of active citizenship. Guarinello,[52] when questioning what measures could be used for collective action in a scenario permeated by setbacks, resumes the idea of belonging:

> Every citizen is a member of a community, however it is organized. And this belonging, which is a source of obligations, also allows it to claim rights, seek to change relations within the community, try to redefine its principles, its symbolic identity, redistribute community goods. [53]

For Gadotti,[54] the school that proposes an education for citizenship, 'assumes itself as a center of rights and duties', 'enables the citizenship of those who are in it and those who come to it' and 'is consistent with the formative, liberating discourse', 'lives the tense experience of democracy'. According to Santos,[55] although it does not constitute citizenship, civic education provides the fundamental instruments for its exercise and, for this reason, school education is a prerequisite for the formation of an active and responsible citizen.

Accordingly, education aimed at citizenship provides a culture based on fundamental values to be present in the formation of youngsters, actively and responsibly participating in social issues. It is not just about transmitting general and superficial information to students, but above all, promoting a dialogical and pro-collective reflection on fundamental rights and duties.

Nothing is more suitable for this model of awareness than the school environment, as it creates spaces for constant interactions between young people, whether through questioning, reflection, judgment, norms, in short, it allows for complete training for acting in the society in which you live. Juste[56] states that in school life, the student can, among other opportunities, work as a team, collaborate, show solidarity with colleagues, participate in collective decisions, and debate.

In this sense, the 'International Association for the Evaluation of Educational Achievement' created, in 2009, the 'International Civic and Citizenship Study',

51 Telles (1994) p 45.
52 Guarinello (2013) p 46.
53 Guarinello (2013) p 46.
54 Gadotti (2019).
55 Santos (2001) p 65.
56 Juste (2008) p 250.

with the purpose of improving the analyses in the scope of world education, being currently considered the greatest diagnosis on the subject. The assessment permeates aspects of civic knowledge, understanding, involvement, and behaviour of students regarding citizenship.

> The aim of the International Study for Civic and Citizenship Education is to investigate, in a group of countries, the degree of citizenship developed by young people to assimilate the prerogatives that offer their rights, freedoms and responsibilities and obligations, which implies their role as citizens. To achieve this goal, it promotes an assessment of student performance, in a test of knowledge and understanding of aspects related to civic education, also analyzing data on their beliefs, attitudes, behaviors and perceptions. The study recognizes the need for constant evaluation and is a response to the challenge of educating young people in the current contexts of democracy and civic participation.[57]

Through a civic knowledge scale, the cognitive skills and performance of young people in society are presented, thus, for each item there is a percentage of qualification, so that the established average is 500 points, that is, countries above this score demonstrate better levels of citizenship in the school environment.[58] The approach aims to answer the following questions:

1. How is civic and citizenship education implemented in participating countries?
2. What is the extent and variation of students' civic knowledge within and across participating countries?

57 International Association for the Evaluation of Educational Achievement, 'International Civic and Citizenship Education Study 2017: Informe nacional: Estudio Internacional de Educación Cívica y Ciudadana', https://iccs.iea.nl/fileadmin/user_upload/Editor_Group/Documents/ICCS_2016_National_Report_Colombia.pdf, accessed 29 January 2019, pp 12–15. Authors' translation. Original: 'El objetivo del Estudio Internacional para la Educación Cívica y Ciudadana es investigar, en un conjunto de países, el grado de civismo desarrollado por los jóvenes para asimilar las prerrogativas que ofrecen sus derechos y libertades, y las responsabilidades y obligaciones que implica su rol de ciudadanos. Para la consecución de este objetivo, acude a la evaluación del desempeño de los estudiantes en una prueba de conocimiento y comprensión de aspectos relacionados con la educación cívica y la ciudadanía, de igual forma analiza datos sobre sus creencias, actitudes, comportamientos y percepciones. El estudio reconoce la necesidad de una evaluación constante y es una respuesta al desafío que supone la educación de los jóvenes en los actuales contextos de democracia y participación cívica'.

58 International Association for the Evaluation of Educational Achievement, 'International Civic and Citizenship Education Study 2017: Informe nacional: Estudio Internacional de Educación Cívica y Ciudadana', https://iccs.iea.nl/fileadmin/user_upload/Editor_Group/Documents/ICCS_2016_National_Report_Colombia.pdf, accessed 29 January 2019, pp 12–5.

3. What is the extent of student involvement in different spheres of society and what factors within or between countries relate to them?
4. What beliefs do students from participating countries have regarding important civic issues in modern society and what are the factors that influence their variation?
5. How are schools in participating countries organised in relation to civic and citizenship education and what is their association with student learning outcomes?[59]

In this scenario, four contexts are analysed: i) community in general, including the school and family environment; ii) school environment; iii) family environment; iv) individual context, which includes the student's characteristics, containing the following content structure: society, civic principles, participation, and identity.[60]

From the comparative analysis carried out between the countries selected based on the ICCS, it is noted that Brazil was not even interested in participating, which already demonstrates some attention, since the research intends to identify the flaws and improve teaching methods regarding civic education, with the purpose of encouraging school formation aimed at raising awareness of rights and duties.

This reality can be verified when there is no stimulus to propagate school plans that direct students to understand the reality in which they are inserted. An example of this is consolidated when philosophy is removed from the national curriculum base as a compulsory subject and destined for mere 'studies and practices', as provided for in arts. 36, IV and 35-A, §2 of Law No. 9,394/96, amended by Provisional Measure No. 746/16. Then, although philosophy alone does not indicate an education focused on citizenship, it comes close to stimulating the promotion of the common good and social values.

It is worth highlighting that, as a result, it was found that the majority of high-school students from Latin American countries supported justifications of dictatorial regimes, and two-thirds of these students understand that this situation can be grounded in order, security, and economic benefits. Completely the opposite position of students who showed high levels of civic knowledge.[61]

59 International Association for the Evaluation of Educational Achievement, 'International Civic and Citizenship Education Study: Framework', https://iccs.iea.nl/home.html, accessed 10 February 2019.

60 International Association for the Evaluation of Educational Achievement, 'International Civic and Citizenship Education Study 2017: Informe nacional: Estudio Internacional de Educación Cívica y Ciudadana', https://iccs.iea.nl/fileadmin/user_upload/Editor_Group/Documents/ICCS_2016_National_Report_Colombia.pdf, accessed 29 January 2019, pp 11–5.

61 Wolfram et al. (2019).

Also, in a research[62] performed by the Institute of Economic Research Foundation, with the participation of more than 500 Brazilian schools, it was found that 99.3% of the students have some form of prejudice, whether ethnic-racial, territorial, gender, or sexual orientation.

Then, supporting students only with regard to objective subjects (mathematics, language, biology, chemistry, etc.), does not enable the main purpose for the formation of a citizen. Furthermore, according to 'Transparency International',[63] it can be seen that Brazil has a very low level of democracy.

It is important to mention that Brazil fits into the so-called 'failed democracies', which conveys 'problems with governance', 'underdeveloped political culture', and 'low level of social participation'.[64] In accordance with Comparato,[65] 'in all quarters the deficiency of popular representation has been felt',[66] but warns that countless power centres have undeniable social roles in society, such as the school establishment, which could allow for greater social grouping:

> The effectiveness of group representation, especially in a country like ours, clashes with the low degree of organization of society. Many classes, professions or statuses exhibit the lack of a minimum of agglutination or coalescence capable of generating collective awareness of their own interests.[67]

With regard to security, according to the 'Social Progress Index',[68] the country is the last one among those selected in this study, showing 124th position in the world. From this perspective, it was also possible to verify that the level of incarceration is increasing in the country,[69] occupying 3rd place in the world in relation to the theme, according to data from the CNJ and the ICPR. More than that, the CNJ[70] underscores that the level of prisoners' education basi-

62 Fundação Instituto de Pesquisas Econômicas, 'Pesquisa sobre preconceito e discriminação no ambiente escolar' http://portal.mec.gov.br/dmdocuments/diversidade_apresentacao.pdf, accessed 30 January 2019.

63 Transparency International, 'Corruption Perception Index 2018', www.transparency.org/files/content/pages/2018_CPI_Executive_Summary.pdf, accessed 29 January 2019.

64 The Economist, 'Democracy Index 2015', www.yabiladi.com/img/content/EIU-Democracy-Index-2015.pdf, ccessed 30 January 2019.

65 Comparato (1986) p 430.

66 Comparato (1986) p 420.

67 Comparato (1986) p 421.

68 Social Progress Index, 'Compare Countries 2018', www.socialprogress.org/, accessed 30 January 2019.

69 Instituto Betty e Jacob Lafer, 'LUTA Antiprisional no Mundo Contemporâneo: Um Estudo sobre Experiências de Redução da População Carcerária em Outras Nações' http://carceraria.org.br/wp-content/uploads/2018/09/relatorio_luta_antiprisional.pdf, accessed 18 February 2019, p 11.

70 Conselho Nacional de Justiça, 'Painel banco nacional de monitoramento de prisões – BNMP 2.0', https://paineis.cnj.jus.br/QvAJAXZfc/opendoc.htm?document=qvw_l%2FPainelCNJ.qvw&host=QVS%40neodimio03&anonymous=true&sheet=shBNMPIIMAPA, accessed 30 January 2019.

cally corresponds to the complete elementary school curriculum, representing a total of 71.15%.

In this vein, it is observed that the vast majority of the prison population has completed primary education, which evidently highlights the importance of an education focused on citizenship, especially for young people, training conscientious and responsible individuals to perform their duties and protect their rights within Brazilian society.

It was in this sense that the Bill no 38/15[71] which is currently being processed by the Federal Senate, was proposed by suggesting the inclusion of item V in art. 36 of the Law of Directives and Bases of Education (Law no 9.394/96) in order to introduce 'Citizenship' as a compulsory subject in the curriculum. Oraisón and Pérez underscore that the school is:

> [...] a privileged area of public deliberation, building citizenship and generating social transformations. Hence, the school as a political agent must redefine its function, transcending pedagogy and assistance to community action and assuming the social responsibility of its self-referential context. But, as a place where the State and civil society converge, it becomes a stage for the formation of citizenship, not only for students, but also for teachers and members of the educational community in general.[72]

Given this, it can be concluded that citizenship education provides the exercise of active and responsible citizenship, with the purpose to act with regard to the resolution and/or reduction of social demands, promoting a more harmonious and democratic environment.

Final Considerations

This article aimed to analyse the interferences between citizen education, social demands, and social participation, in the sense it investigated, within the limits initially proposed, whether awareness of fundamental rights and duties would enhance democratic participatory processes and, consequently, full exercise of citizenship, in order to promote active and responsible actions.

71 Senado Federal, 'Projeto de Lei no 38/15', https://www25.senado.leg.br/web/atividade/materias/-/materia/119721, accessed 30 January 2019.

72 Oraisón and Pérez (2006) pp 18–9. Authors' translation. Original: 'ámbito privilegiado de deliberación pública, construcción de ciudadanía y generación de transformaciones sociales. En tal sentido, la escuela como agente político debe redefinir su función, trascendiendo lo pedagógico y asistencial hacia el accionar comunitario y asumiendo la responsabilidad social de su contexto autoreferencial. Pero, en tanto lugar en el que convergen el Estado y la sociedad civil, se convierte en un escenario de formación de ciudadanía, no sólo de los alumnos sino de los docentes y de los miembros de la comunidad educativa en general'.

There are multiple mechanisms for the realisation of active and responsible citizenship, however, the knowledge about their rights and duties, by providing a sense of belonging, stimulates the performance of the individual in society, to combat social ills and contribute to democratic-participatory development.

As it was highlighted throughout this article, it is not enough to offer students information by itself, it is essential to engage the school, teachers, and family in the development of daily actions aimed at citizenship practices.

As it was seen, the Foundation Institute of Economic Research, carried out a survey that included more than 500 schools and identified that 99.3% of students have some prejudice, whether ethnic-racial, territorial, gender, or sexual orientation. Another issue about the school environment, found by the ICCS, was about dictatorial regimes, which for most Latin American students is justifiable, so that two-thirds of these students understand their legitimacy based on order, security, and economic benefits. The research concluded that this result is inverted when analysing students with high levels of civic knowledge. In addition, the CNJ, when analysing the prison population in Brazil, showed that 71.15% of prisoners have completed primary education.

Therefore, the school reveals itself as a unique environment for the citizenship education of young people, by providing spaces and means to promote participation, creativity, relationships, understanding, interaction and, above all, the construction of a collective identity for expanding the democratic participatory process.

Consequently, the pedagogical project must be aimed at civic education, in order to integrate the curricular content, studies and practices that raise awareness, mainly, of children and adolescents about the constitutionally guaranteed values, to promote a civic culture, focused on the common good and collective action.

References

Wolfram et al (2019) 'International Civic and Citizenship Education Study. Percepciones de los jóvenes acerca del gobierno, la convivência pacífica y la diversidad em cinco países de América Latina', International Association for the Evaluation of Educational Achievement.https://iccs.iea.nl/fileadmin/user_upload/Editor_Group/Pictures/Infographics_Latin_American_report_jpgs/ICCS_2016_LA_release_version_Spanish_11Apr_update.pdf, 30 January 2019.

Maria Victória Benevides (1991) *A cidadania ativa: Referendo, plebiscito e iniciativa popular*, Ática.

Maria Victória Benevides (1994) 'Democracia e cidadania' in Renata Villas Boas et al (eds) *Participação Popular nos Governos Locais*, Pólis.

Fábio Konder Comparato (1986) 'Um quadro institucional para o desenvolvimento democrático' in Hélio Jaguaribe et al (eds) *Brasil, sociedade democrática*, 2nd Edition, Editora José Olympio.

Carlos Nelson Coutinho (1999). *Cidadania e modernidade*, Perspectivas.

Dalmo Dallari (1998). *Direitos Humanos e Cidadania*, Moderna.

Antônio Teixeira Fernandes (2009). *Democracia e Cidadania. Revista da Faculdade de Letras da Universidade do Porto*, Volume XIX, Universidade do Porto.

Moacir Gadotti (2019) 'Escola Cidadã: Educação para a cidadania', http://www.acervo.paulofreire.org:8080/jspui/bitstream/7891/1645/3/FPF_PTPF_13_009.pdf.

Nelson Luiz Guarinello (2013) 'Cidades-estado na antiguidade clássica' in Jaime Pinsky e Carla Bassanezi Pinsky (orgs). *História da Cidadania*, 6th Edition, Contexto.

Louise Jennings, Vanessa Neves e Maria Gomes (2014) 'Oportunidades de aprendizagem e cidadania responsável: Práticas democráticas em sala de aula' 50(36) *Revista Educação em Questão*, Natal, set/dez.

Mercedes Oraisón e Ana Pérez (2006) 'Escuela y participación: El difícil camino de la construcción de ciudadanía' 42 *Revista Iberoamericana de Educación.*

Ramón Pérez Juste (2008) 'Educación, ciudadanía y convivencia. Diversidad y sentido social de la educación' 59(2–3) *Bordón Revista de Pedagogía, Madrid.*

Jaime Pinsky e Carla Bassanezi (2013) *História da cidadania*, 6th Edition, Contexto.

Jean Jacques Rousseau (1997) *O Contrato Social*, Nova Cultural.

Gislene Santos (2001). *A Universidade formação cidadania*, Cortez.

Vera Telles (1994) 'Sociedade civil, direitos e espaços públicos' in Renata Villas Boas et al (org) *Participação Popular nos Governos Locais*, Pólis.

Marta Gabriela Ferreira Valentim (2012) *Responsabilidade social e cidadania responsável: Um caso de estudo da missão sorriso*, Instituto Universitário de Lisboa.

Luiz Werneck Vianna e Maria Alice Rezende Carvalho (2000) 'República e civilização brasileira' 5(8) *Revista Estudos de Sociologia.*

Luiz Werneck Vianna e José Eisenberg (2010) 'Apresentação à edição brasileira' in Philippe Nonet and Philip Selznick (eds) *Direito e sociedade: A transição ao sistema jurídico responsivo*, Editora Revan.

Chapter 4

The Value of Twitter in Building a Community of Students

Does This Go Toward or Against the Concept of 'Human' Students?

Katherine Langley

Introduction

The introduction of social media into our daily lives is not a new thing. *The Oxford English Dictionary* defines social media as, 'websites and applications which enable users to create and share content or to participate in social networking'.[1] Indeed, the introduction of more media, referencing software, online library resources, and artificial intelligence have been emerging increasingly over the last several decades in higher education.[2] This chapter considers the value of some of these resources in assisting education, and in the impact that they can have on community building in higher education; with emphasis on the value of social media in higher education following the seismic shifts created by the COVID-19 pandemic.

This chapter further examines whether Twitter or similar can be used a teaching tool,[3] and whether the use of such platforms influences the tradition of classroom and face-to-face teaching for good.[4] In a world where teaching is regularly supplemented by virtual learning environments (VLEs), online library, video tutorials, recorded lectures, and distance learning, does this dehumanise the student experience? Is social media a supplementary tool or does it detract from effective scholarship? The chapter considers two perspectives on the use of Twitter or social media, first, that of the undergraduate law student, and second, the position of the early career academic.

There are some who would suggest that the use of social media makes the world a smaller place, and in educational circles this could be very true.[5] As a tool for early career academics and students, Twitter and similar platforms can be useful, if not crucial mechanisms for networking.[6] This chapter explores

1 www.oed.com/view/Entry/183739?redirectedFrom=social+media#eid272386371.
2 Willems et al. (2019).
3 Rinaldo et al. (2011) pp 193–203.
4 Kassens-Noor (2012) pp 9–21.
5 Green et al. (2002).
6 Ferguson and Wheat (2015) pp 3–13.

DOI: 10.4324/9781003179283-6

whether this online network of peers has a tangible impact on the experience of the undergraduate student, and early career academic (ECA), respectively. Further, with the recent COVID-19 global pandemic, there have been fewer opportunities for academic communities to be physically together and share knowledge in the traditional sense, with many conferences being cancelled.[7] The shifting of some of these events in itself requires some reflection, and undoubtedly has its own pitfalls.[8]

In the contemporary context of providing legal education, many providers are striving for a more global and transformative product.[9] International student numbers in law continue to thrive post-pandemic, and emphasis continues to be placed on skills across the sector.[10] In the year ending March 2022, there were 466,611 sponsored study visas granted (including dependents). This is the highest annual number of study visas granted on record in the UK and represents both a recovery from the lower number of visas granted during the COVID-19 pandemic but also an increase on pre-pandemic levels.

The number of law students and aspiring lawyers has reached an all-time high in the UK according to new data from the Universities and Colleges Admissions Service (UCAS) and London law offices. It shows applications from international students to study law in the country have risen by a staggering 238% over the last ten years.[11] Against the background of higher numbers of students, and a higher number of international students, it is prudent for educators to consider the adaptability and value of their courses. Vogel et al.'s work is useful to show that social media can be valuable to all types of students, lecturers, tutors, and supervisors; it is a mechanism for communication. Whilst there can be no argument that social media plays a valuable part in building study or employment networks,[12] can this be counted as a global or transformative skill in the same way?

Establishing a local peer support network represents an important capability of online neighbourhood social networks (ONSNs). By segmenting the inhabitants of neighbourhoods into separate online communities, such as modules, course, or cohorts, ONSNs offer 'neighbours' a direct channel for requesting and provisioning volunteer support not automatically available on other social media. During the COVID-19 pandemic, a peer support network such as a dedicated Facebook page or WhatsApp group provided vital assistance

7 Goebel et al. (2020) pp 797–816.

8 Paudel (2021) pp 70–85.

9 Morgan and Carey (2009).

10 Twining (1988) pp 4–13 and Guth (2020) pp 161–73. See also; www.universitiesuk.ac.uk/universities-uk-international/explore-uuki/international-student-recruitment/international-student-recruitment-data.

11 https://gsl.news/2022/02/18/intl-student-applications-for-uk-law-degrees-sky-rocket-despite-brexit-and-covid-19/.

12 Yeo (2014) pp 53–62.

to at-risk individuals such as members of a group or the particularly vulnerable, easing the burden of confinement and preventing the violation of stay-at-home orders.[13]

Developing Pedagogy around Legal Teaching

This chapter is predicated on the theory that legal curricula have evolved significantly in the last 50 years.[14] Law as a discipline is seen as a classical subject, traditionally dominated by white male, and upper-class students. Currently, most law schools have moved away from these traditional and constrained roots and towards more skills-embedded curricula for law, accessible to a more diverse student body.[15] Aside from these large-scale shifts in legal education, there continues to be smaller scale changes such as the move to open book assessments, or online assessments,[16] the inclusion of more reflection in legal education, and the inclusion of non-traditional core modules.[17] In preparing for the competitive legal workplace, students need to be adept at online forms, online communication, and conferencing, in addition to online versions of what have always been included in a law degree, legal research, critical thinking, and evaluation skills. One way to move away from these traditional methods of legal education is to bring in more modern technology into the classroom, and it makes sense that this should be the same or similar technology to that which is proliferating legal practice.[18]

Law students now are better placed for a global employment market, and for employment beyond legal practice with a range of practical and transferrable skills.[19] The use of online platforms for teaching throughout the pandemic and beyond equips students with exemplary skills of moderation and attentiveness to participants from differing backgrounds and experience.[20] These types of large Zoom session call for a particular type of empathy and dialogue across cultures and backgrounds; skills which cannot fail to assist those in legal practice. Further than this, long gone are the days of the 'chalk and talk' as the only lecture approach where the students are passive recipients of knowledge.[21] Within this context, there is a place for the introduction of more global and transformative opportunities for teaching law, shifting the power dynamic of

13 Vogel et al. (2021).
14 Chesterman (2008) pp 58–67.
15 Knox and Stone (2019) pp 90–101.
16 Bansal (2021) pp 1–14.
17 Rogers (2013) p 387.
18 Hafner (2009) pp 299–302.
19 Ribstein (2010) p 1649.
20 Ilker Yakin and Hasan Tinmaz (2013).
21 Serbessa (2006) p 129.

the traditional lecture theatre and enabling students to have greater autonomy in their own career journey.

The emergence of social media and online technology are often perceived as fundamentally altering traditional communication and restoring a voice to the public; rehumanising communication which has been limited by mainstream media.[22] Northcote notes that whilst there are clear benefits to online learning environments, there is a 'lack of humanity' in some online courses.[23] In order for there to be a more welcoming environment for students, tutors have to create an environment of belonging and community. One way to do this is to introduce the tutor using a short sound file; this would be easy to facilitate using social media.[24] Using social media as a form of individual contact between students and tutors remains important, especially for students new to higher education.

There are numerous commentators and pedagogy about law and tech or legal education. Klopfer, Osterweil, Groff, and Haas argued that social networks have all the characteristics and potential of achieving good learning, as users are now creating, learning, and communicating in new ways.[25] When considering the use of social media as part of the future of higher education, many academics comment on the need for those online mechanisms to mirror human values such as empathy, respect, collaboration, and trust. Thus, since time, lack of skills, and financial constraints constitute the major barriers to the use of conventional VLEs, the application of social networking sites in education seems to address some of these challenges. Further, social networking sites, specifically Facebook, have the capacity to facilitate online discussions and collaboration among students, and between students and teachers, in addition to providing opportunities for the sharing of ideas, educational content as well as enhancement of communication among stakeholders.[26] This is very important because the current generation of students are digital natives.[27] When considered on pure face value, these social media tools can be useful for both undergraduate students and ECAs. However, as referred to above, legal curricula are transforming into more globally understood qualifications, and therefore, there are more modern and niche opportunities for embedding social media, one example of this is the growth of clinical legal education. Such popularity in clinical opportunities evidences the attraction of practical legal skills, not only to students, but to marketing mechanisms and, of course, to the graduate legal recruiters.[28] There is clearly a remit for the use of a variety of methods,

22 Picard (2015).
23 Northcote (2008).
24 Keough (2005).
25 Klopfer et al. (2009).
26 Klopfer et al. (2009).
27 Buzzetto-More (2012) pp 63–90.
28 Matambanadzo (2006) pp 90–5.

but where is the balance?[29] How seriously would recruiters, and students, take a heavily social media–based degree?

It must also be borne in mind that for many students, including mature students, it is difficult to remember a working life without the use of the Internet; accordingly, it would almost be inconceivable that a degree qualification in law would not be taught with some type of Internet interaction.[30] This notion poses more questions about the commercial nature of higher education qualifications. Even with the most superficial investigation it is clear that the growth of social media is underpinned by advertising, business interests, and political elites.[31] As such, the use of existing social media brings with it and interesting power dynamic driven by corporate interests and the not the aims of course designers or the best interests of their students, or indeed the future of the legal profession.

Background to the Chapter—Early Career Symposium

The catalyst to this chapter is reflections around the Association of Law Teachers (ALT) Early Career Symposium (2019). This chapter specifically reflects on how online and social community building can support or detract from traditional legal education.[32] This symposium was devised by the author and another ECA colleague to bring together early career academics from across the UK. The event was held over two days in Leeds and brought a community of 80 legal academic delegates from the Isle of Wight to Belfast. For the event, the organisers recruited a diverse range of more senior academic speakers to talk about several topics relevant to the early career academic community. These topics included the art of preparing for teaching, supporting students in an academic environment, managing your mental wellbeing, and finding your place as a new teacher.[33]

The symposium was advertised on Twitter, and the organisers took a deliberate decision to release information like a 'festival style line-up'.[34] A short profile of keynote speakers and other session speakers was released via Twitter every few days, and then questions and teasers for the event were also shared in a piecemeal way. The event sold out in just a few days, with extra tickets having to be released to the maximum capacity of the venue. To build upon the momentum of the rapid ticket sales, and in the usual practice of larger academic conferences, the organiser used a hashtag to invite delegates and speakers

29 Kaplan and Haenlein (2016) pp 441–50.
30 Selwyn (2012).
31 Scott (2013).
32 Pozniak and Skrypchenko (2021).
33 As is noted further in this chapter, undergraduate students can be introverts.
34 Manthiou et al. (2014).

to share information about the event, during the event, and to build upon a network of shared experiences after the event.[35] The feedback for the symposium was overwhelmingly positive with plans in place for this to become an annual event. Delegates found a good balance of teaching and research related content and found ample opportunities to meet and speak with people of similar experience levels or practice areas.

Following the symposium, the organisers tried to maintain momentum in the conversation on Twitter and used the hashtag in several other tweets.[36] Perhaps unsurprisingly, without the draw of the event, there was waning interest in sharing some of these tweets and experiences. Another interesting reflection on this event was the use of the OneHE platform, which was used alongside the event as a networking tool. Uptake in this platform as one which was new and unfamiliar was much smaller, and so many students and delegates are already on larger social media platforms such as Facebook and Twitter.[37]

Without question, this symposium provided an ideal meeting point for many academics to grow their networks, and to have conversations related to the event; some of these connections, for the author anyway, are ongoing, and would have been less likely to come to fruition without the catalyst of the event. The symposium evidenced that social media worked well to market an event, to initiate conversations, and to open networks, but this begs the question as to whether social media could be used in relative isolation as a teaching or networking tool?

Social Media as a Teaching Tool or a Support Mechanism?

Planning and organising such an event gave the author the impetus to consider the role of Twitter and other social media as a teaching tool in the more traditional legal curriculum. These reflections have only been magnified by the effects of the COVID-19 pandemic. The advantages of social media in the classroom are easy to identify, it is instant, students are already adept at using it, and so it does not require any further instruction.[38] However, there are also well-rehearsed disadvantages too. Social media is hard to regulate.[39] The instant nature of posts and communications can lead to incorrect or improper content, which in turn makes the aims and objectives of the teacher more complex with regard to specific material. Finally, and perhaps anecdotally, as students often already engage with these platforms, it is easy for them to disengage with the

35 Jackson et al. (2018) pp 188–91.
36 Greenhow et al. (2019).
37 Palmer and Koenig-Lewis (2009).
38 Callagham and Fribbace (2016).
39 Tess (2013).

task at hand and instead catch up with their own 'friends' or newsfeeds rather than be concerned with knowledge acquisition.

There are examples of Facebook groups being used meaningfully within the classroom context,[40] though within the authors' experience, these have been viewed with slight suspicion by other members of a wider module teaching team. The use of a social media group in one seminar set can lead to a discrepant student experience and therefore has been discouraged.[41]

A further complicated application of social media has been the creation of cohort chat groups, particularly using the WhatsApp platform.[42] As another consequence of the pandemic, many of the usual induction and social activities which provide students with the opportunity to form and develop friendship groups have been cancelled.[43] Many students have created larger scale WhatsApp discussion groups with the primary aim of sharing information. However, as these groups and content of other social media platforms fall outside of the university jurisdiction, they are difficult to regulate by academic staff, and any issue within these groups (bullying, harassment, hate crime) are near impossible to address from a compliance and governance standpoint.

Some of the difficulty in using these methods, as with any technology, is the confidence of the tutor to employ something different. The lack of guidance or training on how to adopt social media can influence staff decisions on whether to introduce it in their classes or not.[44] Second, the students often need a lot of guidance as to what is permitted and what is expected within the context of their studies.[45] It is important at this juncture to note that the online shift of many degree programmes meant that many students and ECAs were navigating these platforms or methods with varying degrees of guidance and support.

What could not be foreseen at the time of planning and reflecting on the early career symposium was the mass shift to online teaching due to the COVID-19 global pandemic. In the face of uncertainty about teaching, student numbers, engagement, and process, there was the opportunity for discussion to take place about more radical curriculum design.[46] Under the umbrella term of pandemic teaching—many academics were more open to casual forms of communication including Teams chat, VLE messages, Padlet boards.

During the initial stages of the pandemic, much time, energy, and thought was invested in shifting the large LLB programmes online; this left many ECAs with a lack of clarity as to their position[47]. Many ECAs were in non-permanent

40 Towner and Muñoz (2011).
41 Roblyer et al. (2010) pp 134–40.
42 Quispe et al. (2021).
43 Foster et al. (2020).
44 Cao et al. (2013).
45 Neal (2012).
46 Burgos et al. (2020).
47 Eti Herman et al (2021).

teaching roles and studying as well[48]. Considering this, some academics have worked hard to provide a meaningful and lasting platform to support all academics, but especially ECAs.[49] One example of this type of support has been the Connecting LegalEd Hangout. This forum is a short session hosted via Microsoft Teams and is used in varying ways to support community, discussion, research, and all things legal education. The session, organised by three senior legal academics, has hosted several sessions directed specifically at ECAs, one of which was hosted by the author. These hangout sessions are advertised only via social media channels, and also by way of the ALT newsletter; these sessions continue to run online even post-pandemic. The Connect LegalEd Hangout is an interesting example of ECAs having power and autonomy over their own network and doing so via interactions and through online technology. Whilst some of these sessions did specifically focus on social media, the effect here was community building and networking where conferencing options had been cancelled.[50]

Is This a New Normal for Law Schools?

Having considered all the above, thought must be given to whether the use of social media as a community building mechanism or teaching tool can be something sustainable within a higher legal education context, especially as we navigate the changes in our higher education provision, and in routes to qualification post-pandemic. In the author's own experience in teaching throughout the pandemic, there has been a varied use of social media. Some academics are happy to use these platforms to have direct conversations with their students. Some have used the platforms to highlight other relevant opportunities for students to supplement their degrees, and other academics have been so busy with the online shift and workload that social media will have played little role in day-to-day work functions.[51]

As a reflective opportunity, the pandemic has given an ideal space for many law schools to consider the wider impact of their structure and methods.[52] For example, the return to on campus closed book exams seems unlikely in favour of online and remote options. Further, there are tangible benefits to having some aspects of the academic role continue to take place online. One example of this for undergraduate students is the personal tutoring element. Having an available slot in the week where students can book in or drop in, and without having to make an 'unusual' journey to campus or 'face to face'

48 Canan N Kınıkoğlu and Aysegul Can (2021).
49 Langley et al. (2021).
50 Pegg et al. (2014).
51 Flaherty (2020).
52 Castello (2021).

appointment with their tutor is attractive for many students. For tutors, this means that many personal tutees can be seen and written up more efficiently, if a little less personably then pre-pandemic. Another advantage for the ECAs has been the advent of online conferencing and seminars; for many academics, the introduction of online and hybrid events via social platforms have enabled more accessible and cost-effective networking opportunities. As institutions work towards their post-pandemic offerings, only time will tell whether the use of social media in the classroom or for networking will become the 'new normal' in the law school.[53]

Does This Dehumanise the Student Experience?

Throughout the pandemic, some would argue that the student experience was very much limited by online learning, and there were news articles almost daily about the value for money or lack thereof in an online degree.[54] Converse to this is the huge success and growth of the Open University where online learning has been the norm for much longer.[55] There can be no doubt that having a large community of like-minded or experienced scholars to draw upon can have a benefit for students, however, this has to be something which is accessible.[56] Part of the benefit of the early career symposium was that people had the opportunity to meet 'their network' in a space, one which was designed to support them at their particular stage. This naturally provided a springboard for delegates and speakers to continue some of those conversations online. Undergraduate students without a safe space event would have to feel confident to reach out to new contacts, and whilst Twitter provides a certain level of distance, in the authors view, this type of confidence in undergraduate students is rarer. Ahn notes that engaging in interactions using social networking sites is viewed as a form of literacy practice which contributes to learning.[57] Generation Z prefers to learn through 'chunking' of information rather than listening to a long-drawn-out lecture.[58] Given the short attention spans of Generation Z, chunking would be a welcome advancement to the classroom and some institutions have already moved to a micro-lecture format. Lessons will need to be brief, broken down into sizeable bites that capture their attention with visuals. Spencer highlights the prevalence of introverted personality types in law courses, and this is something which curriculum designers should bear in mind, especially as a result of the nearly two years of home learning,

53 Richardson (2020).
54 Watermeyer et al. (2021) pp 623–41.
55 Sclater (2008) pp 1–13.
56 Curro and Ainswroth (2018) And Kelly K McCormick (2008).
57 Ahn (2011).
58 Minarcin (2020).

and online classrooms.[59] The COVID Generation Z may well prefer more socially distant methods of learning, and this may be part of a 'new normal' for legal education providers.

In the authors view, the pinnacle of student experience is to manage expectations and be clear about the parameters of what you are teaching.[60] This clarity was very much harder to achieve during the pandemic. On reflection, there could be a valuable place for the inclusion of social networks as an embedded part of university courses. The difficulty then is looking at the parameters of these mechanisms. One of the attractions of social media is the short version opinions, there is little real censorship or regulation of these mechanisms. Bringing such a mechanism within the context of a written curricula would mean it would have to comply with university charters and regulations; as a result, this is undoubtedly less attractive for students and course validators alike.[61]

Students like to be able to benefit from the more informal methods of communication, chat functions, and informal message or email functions via VLE platforms. However, this is arguably doing a disservice to students who wish to enter a traditional profession such as law, where traditional communication skills are often a benchmark for success, and for recruiters[62].

Conclusions

Like many aspects of a professional qualification, there needs to be a balance achieved in student experience versus innovation and traditional core modules. Having considered the value of social media networks and the advantages of using these tools for both undergraduates and ECA positions, does it matter if students have a broader or narrower experience? For many academics, and ECA colleagues, social media platforms are already part of our personal lives. However, there needs to be further thought about how to use these networks in a way which is supportive of students' autonomy, and safe for staff as individuals, and of course in a method commensurate with university policies. When put in these terms, social media is immediately less attractive for the red tape which it creates.

Manca and Ranieri emphasise a generally more favourable attitude towards personal sharing and connecting with peers in professional networks rather than integrating these devices into their teaching practices.[63] Ultimately, it seems that for ECA colleagues, Twitter and other social media provide a very

59 Spencer (2022) pp 1–15.
60 Odeku (2021) p 101.
61 Hamadi et al. (2021) pp 55–85.
62 Michael A Peters et al. (2019).
63 Manca and Ranieri (2016).

useful and safe sounding board, and extended network. However, there remain official processes for each institution which create barriers to its wider inclusion in undergraduate programmes.

Social media remains highly contentious as an online learning resource; it is still artificial, impersonal, and a means of exerting control rather than empowering the individual. Further, if we are to learn lessons from the pandemic about the use of online technology and social media, it is that students need a place to belong to, this was traditionally a campus and cohort. If it is to remain online in some way, this sense of a 'place to belong to' needs to be more humanised, more supportive, and a little less formal than previous iterations. That sense of place is created by recognising the identity and value of each party to any communication and to foster positive relationships and develop community throughout a whole course. It is clear that the use of social media affords a greater opportunity for people to share observations, communication, and content.

It may be that social media is the current popular pedagogy, and it may be that the pandemic has exacerbated its usefulness in the classroom. Selwyn et al. discuss the future of education being a seller's market and note that the future is in the balance as regards to the juxtaposition of critically reflective learning and the company interests for new markets.[64] Further, as academics we need to consider that no (wo)man is an island, and it is a combination of factors, opportunities, technologies, experiences, and interactions which produce the best outcome for our individual students. So, the final question remains, can we work with our students to establish the parameters which are needed for a proper use of social medial in the classroom? #tweetlawpossibilities

References

June Ahn (2011) 'The Effect of Social Network Sites on Adolescents' Social and Academic Development: Current Theories and Controversies' 62 *Journal of the American Society for Information Science and Technology* 8.

Daniel Bansal (2021) 'Open Book Examinations: Modifying Pedagogical Practices for Effective Teaching and Learning' 56 *The Law Teacher* 1.

Daniel Burgos et al. (eds) (2020) *Radical Solutions for Education in a Crisis Context: COVID-19 as an Opportunity for Global Learning*, Springer Nature.

Nicole A Buzzetto-More (2012) 'Social Networking in Undergraduate Education' 7 *Interdisciplinary Journal of Information, Knowledge, and Management* 63.

Yingxia Cao et al. (2013) 'Using Social Media Applications for Educational Outcomes in College Teaching: A Structural Equation Analysis' 44 *British Journal of Educational Technology* 4.

George Callagham and Ian Fribbace (2016) 'The Use If Facebook to Build a Community for Distance Learning Students a Case Study from the Open University' 31 *Open Learning* 3.

64 Selwyn et al. (2020).

Rosa Castello (2021) 'The New Skill on the Block: Using Social Media in the Law School Classroom to Facilitate Learning' 45 *Southern Illinois University Law Journal* 3.

Simon Chesterman (2008) 'The Globalisation of Legal Education' *Singapore Journal of Legal Studies* 58.

Gina Curro and Nussen Ainswroth (2018) 'Social Media and Higher Education: Does Digitally Enabled Learning Have a Place in Law Schools?' 18 *Journal of the Scholarship of Teaching and Learning* 3.

Hazel Ferguson and Katherine L Wheat (2015) 'Early Career Academic Mentoring Using Twitter: The Case of# ECRchat' 37 *Journal of Higher Education Policy and Management* 1.

Colleen Flaherty (2020) 'Not "Glorified Skype"' Inside Higher Education.

Monika Foster et al. (2020) 'Exploring Coping Strategies of Transfer Students Joining Universities from Colleges' 11 *Student Success* 2.

Janna Goebel et al. (2020) 'Academic Conferencing in the Age of COVID-19 and Climate Crisis: The Case of the Comparative and International Education Society (CIES)' 66 *International Review of Education* 5.

Madeleine F Green et al. (2002) *The Brave New (and Smaller) World of Higher Education: A Transatlantic View*, American Council on Education.

Christine Greenhow et al. (2019) 'From Tweeting to Meeting: Expansive Professional Learning and the Academic Conference Backchannel' 50 *British Journal of Educational* 4.

Jess Guth (2020) 'The Pasts and Futures of Legal Skills in English Law Schools' in *Key Directions in Legal Education*, Routledge.

Christoph A Hafner (2009) 'Designing, Implementing, and Evaluating an Online Resource for Professional Legal Communication Skills' 16 *International Journal of Speech Language and the Law* 2.

Mostafa Hamadi et al. (2021) 'A Social Media Adoption Framework as Pedagogical Instruments in Higher Education Classrooms' 18 *E-Learning and Digital Media* 1.

Eti Herman et al. (2021) 'The Impact of the Pandemic on Early Career Researchers: What We Already Know from the Internationally Published Literature' 30 *Profesional de la Información* 2.

Jennifer Jackson et al. (2018) '"The Power of Twitter": Using Social Media at a Conference with Nursing Students' 68 *Nurse Education Today* 188.

Andreas M Kaplan and Michael Haenlein (2016) 'Higher Education and the Digital Revolution: About MOOCs, SPOCs, Social Media, and the Cookie Monster' 59 *Business Horizons* 4.

Eva Kassens-Noor (2012) 'Twitter as a Teaching Practice to Enhance Active and Informal Learning in Higher Education: The Case of Sustainable Tweets' 13 *Active Learning in Higher Education* 1.

Mark Keough (2005) 'Relationships Not Technology are the Key to Online Learning' paper presented at the 17th Biennial Conference of the Open and Distance Learning Association.

Canan N Kınıkoğlu and Aysegul Can (2021) 'Negotiating the Different Degrees of Precarity in the UK Academia during the Covid-19 Pandemic' 23 *European Societies* S817.

Eric Klopfer et al. (2009) 'Using Technology of Today in the Classroom of Today: The Instructional Power of Digital Gaming and Social Networking and How Teachers Can Leverage It' *The Education Arcade*, https://education.mit.edu/wp-content/uploads/2018/10/GamesSimsSocNets_EdArcade.pdf.

Jenny Knox and Melanie Stone (2019) 'Embedding Employability Skills for the Legal Professionals of the Future' 53 *The Law Teacher* 1.

Katherine Langley et al. (2021) 'A Conversation with the Connecting Legal Education Community of Practice' 55 *The Law Teacher: The International Journal of Legal Education* 4.

Stefania Manca and Maria Ranieri (2016) '"Yes for Sharing, No for Teaching!": Social Media in Academic Practices' 29 *The Internet and Higher Education* 63.

Aikaterini Manthiou et al. (2014) 'The Experience Economy Approach to Festival Marketing: Vivid Memory and Attendee Loyalty' 28 *Journal of Services Marketing* 22.

Sarudzayi M Matambanadzo (2006) 'Fumbling Toward a Critical Legal Pedagogy and Practice' 4 *Policy Futures in Education* 1.

Kelly K McCormick (2008) 'Building and Modelling How to Build a Community of Learners' 2 *IUMPST: The Journal* 1.

Robert Minarcin (2020) 'Ok Boomer—The Approaching Dizruption of Legal Education by Generation Z' 39 *Quinnipiac Law Review* 1.

Tannis Morgan and Stephen Carey (2009) 'From Open Content to Open Course Models: Increasing Access and Enabling Global Participation in Higher Education' 10 *International Review of Research in Open and Distributed Learning* 5.

Diane R Neal (ed) (2012) *Social Media for Academics: A Practical Guide*, Elsevier.

Maria Northcote (2008) 'Sense of Place in Online Learning Environments' http://www.ascilite.org.au/conferences/melbourne08/procs/northcote.pdf.

Kolawole S Odeku (2021) 'Conducting Law Pedagogy Using Virtual Classroom in the Era of COVID-19 Pandemic: Opportunities and Existing Obstacles' 11 *Journal of Educational and Social Research* 1.

Pitambar Paudel (2021) 'Online Education: Benefits, Challenges and Strategies During and After COVID-19 in Higher Education' 3 *International Journal on Studies in Education* 2.

Michael A Peters et al. (2019) 'The Curious Case of Educationalizing Technological Unemployment: What Can Places of Learning Really Do About the Future of Work?' 51(3) *Educational Philosophy and Theory* 242.

Robert G Picard (2015) 'The Humanisation of Media? Social Media and the Reformation of Communication' 1(1) *Communication Research and Practice* 32.

Jerine Pegg et al. (2014) 'Finding FRiENDS: Creating a Community of Support for Early Career Academics' 24 *Brock Education* 1.

I Ye Pozniak and SS Skrypchenko (2021) 'Advantages and Disadvantages of Social Media' *Science and Innovations in the 21st Century* 59.

Nayely Quispe, Noe Vicente Rosas and Laberiano Andrade-Arenas (2021) 'Impact of The Use of Telegram and WhatsApp at the University in Pandemic Times' in *2021 2nd Sustainable Cities Latin America Conference (SCLA)*, IEEE, pp. 1–6.

Larry E Ribstein (2010) 'Practicing Theory: Legal Education for the Twenty-First Century' 96 *Iowa Law Review* 1649.

Marianna E Richardson (2020) 'Social Media in the Classroom: The New Normal for University Education after COVID' 7 *International Dialogues on Education* 14.

Shannon B Rinaldo et al. (2011) 'Learning by Tweeting: Using Twitter as a Pedagogical Tool' 33 *Journal of Marketing Education* 2.

MD Roblyer et al. (2010) 'Findings on Facebook in Higher Education: A Comparison of College Faculty and Student Uses and Perceptions of Social Networking Sites' 13 *The Internet and Higher Education* 3.

Scott L Rogers (2013) 'The Role of Mindfulness in the Ongoing Evolution of Legal Education' 36 *University of Arkansas at Little Rock Law Review* 387.

Niall Sclater (2008) 'Large-Scale Open Source E-Learning Systems at the Open University UK' 2008(12) *Research Bulletin* 1.

Neil Selwyn (2012) 'Social Media in Higher Education'.

Neil Selwyn et al. (2020) 'What Might the School of 2030 Look Like? An Exercise in Social Science Fiction' 45(1) *Learning, Media and Technology* 90.

DD Serbessa (2006) 'Tension between Traditional and Modern Teaching-Learning Approaches in Ethiopian Primary Schools' 9 *Journal of International Cooperation in Education* 1.

Rachel Spencer (2022) '"Hell is Other People": Rethinking the Socratic Method for Quiet Law Students' 56 *The Law Teacher* 90.

Paul A Tess (2013) 'The Role of Social Media in Higher Education Classes (Real and Virtual) – A Literature Review' 29 *Computers in Human Behaviour* A60.

TL Towner and C Lego Muñoz (2011) 'Facebook and Education: A Classroom Connection?' in Wankel, C (ed) *Educating Educators with Social Media (Cutting-Edge Technologies in Higher Education, Vol. 1)*, Emerald Group Publishing Limited, pp. 33–57.

William Twining (1988) 'Legal Skills and Legal Education' 22 *The Law Teacher* 1.

Pascal Vogel et al. (2021) 'Fostering Social Resilience Via Online Neighbourhood Social Networks during the COVID-19 Pandemic and Beyond: Status Quo, Design Dilemmas and Research Opportunities' 1 *Proceedings of the 54th Hawaii International Conference on System Sciences* 3037.

Richard Watermeyer et al. (2021) 'COVID-19 and Digital Disruption in UK Universities: Afflictions and Affordances of Emergency Online Migration' 81 *Higher Education* 623.

Julie Willems et al. (2019) 'The Increasing Significance of Digital Equity in Higher Education' 35 *Australasian Journal of Educational Technology* 6.

Ilker Yakin and Hasan Tinmaz (2013) 'Using Twitter as an Instructions Tool: A Case Study in Higher Education' 12 *The Turkish Online Journal of Educational Technology* 209.

Michelle ML Yeo (2014) 'Social Media and Social Networking Applications for Teaching and Learning' 2 *European Journal of Science and Mathematics Education* 1.

Chapter 5

The Role of Legal Educators in Disruption of Hierarchies within Education and the Profession

Kryss Macleod

Introduction

In England and Wales, an increasing number of law students are from diverse socio-economic and ethnic minority backgrounds, a level not yet matched in the professions.[1] This contribution enquires into the role of legal educators in advancing diversity within the legal profession, using Bourdieusian concepts to examine how the changes wrought by the propagation of uses of legal technologies can provide the impetus to disrupt and reconsider existing approaches to legal work, education, and employment.

The chapter begins with an outline of diversity in the profession, and then discusses research on the role of symbolic and other capital in social reproduction in the profession, and how unexamined, these developments could serve to exacerbate existing inequality of access in the professions. The next section highlights key changes caused by the increasing awareness, uses, and availability of legal tech, defined here as software using advanced technology in practice of law, suggesting that if framed as an event or *crises*, these could be used to stimulate transformation within legal education and the professions to address the current inequalities.[2] The piece focuses on the possibility of change, and the increased use and availability of legal technology (legal tech), encompassing software for legal practice that utilises advanced technology, as an event that could be used to instigate change. It adopts the classification of legal tech by Gowder of effect on legal practice, and further focuses on the second of Gowder's classes: the 'transformative' types of technology that facilitates legal practice processes in ways that were not previously possible.[3]

Considering the possible reproduction of forms of capital in legal education, the chapter then examines the role of educators in disrupting these hierarchies, through creation of 'heresies' or *symbolic revolutions*,[4] and how this might be

1 Webley (2014).
2 Fowler (2020).
3 Gowder (2018).
4 Bourdieu (2013).

DOI: 10.4324/9781003179283-7

realised in legal education, utilising the legal tech 'event' as a catalyst, to create a more equal and diverse profession.

(In)Access to the profession

The predominantly white and elitist nature of the legal profession is well-documented.[5] Lawyers from racial minorities are predominantly found in areas of the profession considered to be less prestigious,[6] concentrated in private client and criminal work.[7] Further effects of racial stratification can be seen across a range of factors, including disciplinary action[8] and career progression,[9] and firm location, size,[10] and profile.[11] Solicitors from minorities are more likely to be solo practitioners, or practising in firms with fewer than four partners,[12] which may be attributed to the barriers they face to access in larger, more established firms.[13] Class is also a significant issue. The Milburn Report in 2012 highlighted the over-representation of privately educated individuals from financially advantaged backgrounds, contributing to the elite nature of the legal profession.[14] The SRA's most recent biennial survey confirms this issue persists, with disproportionate numbers of lawyers who benefit from private education, and the education and professional advantage of their parents.[15]

These figures paint a picture of a deeply stratified profession. Yet despite numerous initiatives to change this, exclusion continues.[16] The following sections use Bourdieusian concepts to examine the ways in which this happens, and is maintained and perpetuated.

Symbolic Capital and Access to the Profession

Central to Bourdieu's theories is the notion of differentiation, how some groups are able to exert control or privilege over others.[17] Educational credentials

5 E.g., Sommerlad (2007), Sommerlad (2008) The Ouseley Report – Solicitors Regulation Authority (2008), Sommerlad – Legal Services Board (2010), The Law Society (2010), Headworth et al. (2016), Aulack et al. (2017).
6 The Law Society (2010).
7 Solicitors Regulation Authority (2019).
8 Solicitors Regulation Authority (2008), Webley (2013).
9 Tomlinson et al. (2019).
10 Solicitors Regulation Authority (2019).
11 Tomlinson et al. (2019).
12 Solicitors Regulation Authority (2008).
13 Webley (2013).
14 Milburn (2012).
15 Lawyers who attended fee paying schools are over-represented in law by 14%, which rises to 47% in corporate practice; 51% of lawyers have parents with degree-level qualification, as compared to 19% in the general population; 15% had a parent who was employed in a 'traditional' profession, and a further 26% in a modern profession.
16 Webley et al. (2016), Ashley et al. (2015).
17 Bourdieu (1994).

have been found to be a significant form of capital in recruitment processes. Despite larger numbers of students from diverse backgrounds in higher education, advantage is given in the form of institutional capital to those who attend elite and redbrick universities,[18] and to ensure that those admitted to firms 'fit' into the social environment where specific types of cultural and social capital are used as proxies of merit.[19] Attendance at new or post-1992 universities is viewed as an indicator of 'lower' class, and attendance at elite (Oxbridge) universities indicates upper class status.

Leading law firms have also been found to prioritise employment of trainee lawyers with embodied and symbolic capital such as 'accent, speech, mannerisms and dress'.[20] Embodied and institutionalised cultural capital, such as types of hobbies, clubs, societies, experiences, travels, and prestigious internships and city work experience acquired are also all used as evidence of a person's character, drive, and of being able to succeed in city law firm environments.[21]

These 'arbitrarily legitimised'[22] forms of institutional and embodied capital are disproportionately available to those from upper-middle class, private schooling, and elite university backgrounds. This discriminates against those from minority ethnic groups and those from lower socio-economic backgrounds,[23] and are requirements even in the face of an applicant holding appropriate institutional and human capital.[24] Thus, those who have fewer material advantages, and are unable to acquire the legitimised forms of cultural capital are excluded from the profession, 'no matter how great their intellect'.[25]

There also exists a doxa of being 'professional' specific to the city law field.[26] Although there is formal representation from a range of backgrounds, inclusion is still contingent on conforming with 'hegemonic cultural understandings of "being professional"'.[27] Diversity only exists as defined by the very strict boundaries of the elite city law culture, and its particular doxa, which leads to the reproduction of a homologous city culture and social exclusion.[28] This is enforced by recruitment processes, which despite neutral language of skills and qualifications, consistently emphasise and prioritise certain forms of cultural capital. These are 'treated as symbolic evidence' of the ability to succeed in the environment, selecting only those candidates thought to 'fit' or who can be moulded to fit in the city.

18 Wakeling et al. (2015).
19 Ashley et al. (2015).
20 Ashley et al. (2013).
21 Cook et al. (2012).
22 Ashley et al. (2013).
23 Webley et al. (2016).
24 Ashley et al. (2013).
25 Ashley et al. (2013) p 223.
26 Deer (2008).
27 Cook et al. (2012) p 1759.
28 Cook et al. (2012).

Webley et al. argue also that conceptions of 'merit' in hiring processes reproduce the privilege of the dominant group, which might eliminate aspiring 'BAME' lawyers as legitimate professionals in the localised conceptions of habitus, conceived by Bourdieu as the accumulation of structurally situated, socialisation experiences, that determine individuals as social agents.[29] They further propose that those who do succeed may have had to compensate for 'deficits' of embodied cultural capital with higher levels of institutional capital, and that the success of these individuals is used as evidence to legitimise the doxa as an 'objective meritocracy'.[30]

This continues beyond recruitment and into career progression. Tomlinson et al. note that promotion decisions are premised upon certain symbols which act as proxies for quality, performance, and reputation, and are made by 'middle class white men' who favour those in their own model.[31] These symbols include forms of social and cultural capital such as accents, self-presentation, taste, interests, and mutual connections, which, again, have clear gender, racial, and class dimensions.[32]

In city firms, this exclusion is often a conscious commercial strategy, either to avoid risk through homogenisation of culture, or to signal an image of quality and thus value to clients.[33] Where knowledge is least open to objective assessment, the projection of this upper-class image becomes most important.[34]

The Intractability of the Situation

Webley et al. argue that '[r]eal change is unlikely until the current proxies are recognised as subjective constructions of merit, ill-designed to provide a meaningful assessment of legal ability and skill, until they are replaced with a more sophisticated competencies-based method of assessing potential lawyering ability'.[35] They further note that the ongoing focus to increase 'BAME participation in elite schools (positive though that may be), the habitus reproduces to the benefit of those already privileged by the field' leaving unchallenged both definitions of merit, and the assumption that they are objectively defined.[36] Sommerlad notes that despite the adoption of diversity initiatives, merit-based recruitment processes, and the prominence of discourses focusing on the agentic power of individuals 'social differences have been reinforced:

29 Bourdieu et al. (1992).
30 Webley et al. (2016).
31 Tomlinson et al. (2017).
32 Webley et al. (2016).
33 Ashley et al. (2013), Tomlinson et al. (2019).
34 Ashley et al. (2013).
35 Webley et al. (2016).
36 Webley et al. (2016).

the significance of class, ethnicity, and gender in what the profession recognizes as "talent" has not only persisted but actually strengthened'.[37]

Legal Tech and the Legal Profession

Underpinning how 'transformative' legal tech can be understood as a catalyst for change, is Bourdieu's notion of *crises*, as events that impact within and across fields.[38] These *crises* result from the synchronising of fields' temporality, offering the possibility for transformation, particularly due to 'maladjusted habitus'.[39] It is suggested that this point in the digital transformation of legal work is such *crises*, linking fields of legal professionalism, practice, technology, and legal education, and causing the current habitus in professionalism and education to become unstable. This is further exacerbated by the introduction of the SQE, which calls into question both the nature of knowledge in legal education[40] and of professionalisation and attainment of professionalism acquired in legal education and the training contract, and thus, that accumulation of experience that shape and direct social agents.

The incorporation of digital technologies has already impacted a wide range of practice areas, with increasing implications for legal practice.[41] As the use and availability of legal tech increases, so is there an increased demand for digital capabilities and understanding of the uses of technologies to increase efficiency in practice.[42] At the same time, change is also predicated to the shape of the law firms as boundaries of who performs what actions and functions in the legal profession.[43] Moving across fields, the advances in artificial technologies has pushed the tech sector to increase their focus on ethics, and how this relates to diversity in that sector. The tech industry also struggles with diversity,[44] and is relatively new to considering ethics as an integral part of their work.[45] In law, principles of justice, fairness, and ethics, have long since been a core part of study, but now need to be reviewed as we consider the impact of technology on not only legal work, but on justice and the means and mechanism through which it is secured.

Richard Susskind's ongoing critique of the impact of technology on the legal profession proposes the imminent decline of the traditional lawyer due to

37 Sommerlad (2016).
38 Bourdieu (1987) and (1993).
39 Fowler (2020).
40 Madhloom (2023).
41 McGinnis et al. (2019), Caserta et al. (2019), and Thornton (2019).
42 Ribstein (2012).
43 Ribstein (2012).
44 'An exploration of tech founders, employees and leaders' (*Tech Nation*, 2022) https://technation.io/diversity-and-inclusion-in-uk-tech/ accessed 26 August 2022, and Holtzblatt et al. (2016).
45 Metcalf et al. (2019).

the use of technologies to replace parts of the role.[46] He suggests there will be a complete reconfiguration of the role of lawyers, bifurcating the role from tradition work,[47] to a wide range of necessary skills, reducing knowledge to a single component.[48] Although initially radical, this was echoed by The Law Society in 2019, who recognise the significant impact that new technologies will have on the legal profession, requiring new skills and new delivery models.[49]

Adapting to this new environment will be a key concern for legal professionals seeking to remain relevant,[50] and those seeking to gain admission, as the ongoing 'digital revolution' continues to disrupt legal work.[51] Fenwick et al. note that key lawyer characteristics and core skills sets in the current models of legal education are 'incompatible with the demands on lawyers of the twenty-first century',[52] agreeing with Susskind that lawyers are not usually known for characteristics such as agility and innovation.[53] They suggest this is because most law firms still employ an 'old textbook' model, even as alternative modes of working 'call for a revision if not rejection of that model'.[54]

These changes call for new knowledge, skills, capabilities, and models of practice, which will, in varying timeframes across the sector, result in significant changes to the roles and ethical obligations of legal professionals. In legal education, commentators have proposed varying levels of incorporation of digital technologies into curricula,[55] to address skills deficits. What is left undiscussed are possibilities of using these new approaches as a catalyst for change in addressing how we understand justice to be conceived, in the way it is articulated within the law, and in the way it does, or does not, form part of the foundational aspects of functional legal professionalism.

As these interlinked fields are faced with change, it is suggested that legal education uses these *crises* to examine the status quo with a view to transformation that exposes and interrogates hierarchies rather than reproduces them.

46 See Susskind (2008), Susskind (2013), Susskind et al. (2015), and Susskind (2020).
47 Susskind (2013) pp 134–5.
48 Susskind (2013).
49 The Law Society (2019).
50 Corrales et al. (2019).
51 Fenwick et al. (2019).
52 Fenwick et al. (2017) p 353.
53 Susskind (2013) pp 53–4.
54 Susskind (2013) pp 53–4.
55 For example, see Wang (2019), arguing for 'technological competency' and 'basic understanding of general principles of technologies', Fenwick et al. (2017) focusing on the new skills required in legal education to support disruptive technologies, such as blockchain, Ireland et al. (2020), suggesting the inclusion of basic programming concepts and capabilities such as document automation in UG law degrees, Ryan (2020) discussing the benefits of introducing technological skills as part of UG law degrees, and Contreras et al. (2020) arguing that law schools should teach law students to code to make them 'future-proof'.

Inclusion and Exclusion in Changing Legal Services

The danger is that, precisely because of the ways in which control of the field is currently constituted, change will impact on those who are already marginalised. In respect of the ongoing compartmentalisation of legal work, Sommerlad identifies the emergence of a distinct sub-profession whose 'highly insecure working conditions and negligible prospects of a future professional career warrant the description legal precariat'.[56]

It is likely that smaller firms will struggle with adoption, and their ability to survive will be impacted.[57] Smaller, single practitioner, and lower-paid work firms, where there are a concentration of lawyers from racial and ethnic minorities, may be hit the worst, and junior lawyers and support staff will likely be 'the first victims' of evolution.[58] Some larger firms have created technology training contracts.[59] Others, with the specific aim of maximising the business opportunities made available by legal tech, have created the corresponding graduate tracks, as a distinct branch of business operations.[60] Recently, more common are roles for legal technologists, requiring law degrees, but without paths to qualification,[61] which may risk creating other tiers of work in the 'precariat'[62] noted by Sommerlad.

Thornton suggests that despite the extensive restructuring of legal services delivery as a consequence of digital technologies, professional hierarchies are still visible, where human capital still predicates success, and new lawyers must still be professionalised in old structures.[63] The Solicitors Qualifying Examination (SQE) is unlikely to help either, with its focus on traditional knowledge acquisition and a static approach to skills where an increasingly dynamic approach is required, leaving a vacuum for where this should be positioned. If restructuring is accompanied by the further closure of the existing space of legal professionalism, and expands only the range of sub-professionals upon whom the elite sector rely, dominant groups will only consolidate power at the expense of others.

56 Sommerlad (2016).
57 Caserta et al. (2019).
58 Fenwick et al. (2017) p 360.
59 Bona, 'Tech Pioneers: Meet Addleshaw's trainee innovators' (2016) www.thelawyer.com/tech-pioneers-new-unicorns/ accessed 28 July 2021.
60 See for example, the Business and Legal operations graduate track scheme, www.nortonrosefulbright.com/en-gb/careers/graduates/business-and-legal-operations-graduate-scheme.
61 E.g., the Legal Technologist – Document Automation roles at Addleshaw Goddard, and a range advertised by agencies for 'leading global law firms' for legal technologists.
62 Sommerlad (2016).
63 Thornton (2019).

Legal Education and the Reproduction of Hierarchies in a Neoliberal World

This is a paradox of legal education: the study of law as premised upon equality, the rule of law, and individual rights, against the reality that many working class and minority students are excluded from the profession or, if admitted, from certain areas of practice. Bourdieu warns of the 'neutral' characterisation of systems of education, which allow for the reproduction of both educators and those within power elsewhere in the field, and the conditioning of individuals to passively accept their place within society.[64] As educators, when we are silent on hierarchies, we reinforce them.[65] For legal educators, as the professional conditioning of lawyers already risks contributing to the reproduction of the status quo,[66] questioning this neutrality becomes an imperative.

Assessments or employability initiatives that promote acquiring or adopting 'professional behaviours' based on embodied capital favoured by the dominant group could further legitimise the arbitrary requirements favoured by that same group, reinforcing doxa that exclude and maintain the profession's tiered structures.[67] Legal pedagogies that obscure or make irrelevant contextual social or moral factors, such as the method of legal analysis identified as 'Thinking like a Lawyer',[68] create a powerful habitus that erase or ignore social differences and reinforce the idea that legal actors are situated equally.[69]

Many 'new' institutions have shaped their courses to equip students with skills ostensibly required by the profession, and yet graduates are still devalued since they lack the requisite symbolic and cultural capital.[70] If conceived as symbolic capital, any widening of professionalism necessarily impacts its scarcity, and thus its value and status.[71] Closure of the profession is visible even at the regulatory level, as noted in a report for the Law Society: '[i]f anyone who wants to could become a solicitor, the profession would lose much of its prestige'.[72] Sommerlad notes that it is exactly this type of closure that demonstrates the neoliberal contradiction of choice and agency, and the 'reality of a profession that continues to practice closure'.[73] Ignoring this attributes the failure of excluded groups to their individual weaknesses,[74] creating what Fowler

64 Bourdieu et al. (1990).
65 Bourdieu (1977) p 188.
66 Čuroš (2023).
67 Jewel (2008) p 1208.
68 Mertz (2007).
69 Jewel (2008).
70 Sommerlad (2016) p 249.
71 Noordegraaf et al. (2011).
72 Dixon (2011) p 15, cited in Sommerlad (2016).
73 Sommerlad (2016) p 261.
74 Bourdieu et al. (1990) pp 204–5.

terms a 'new legitimatory "sociodicy"'.[75] This reinforces the habitus purporting that admittance is merit based, yet the proxy for merit is specific forms of scarce symbolic capital.

Without addressing the power inherent in the field overall, presenting the acquisition of digital and technological skills and capabilities as a 'solution' to access for individuals may simply further entrench existing barriers, and create a factory supply of law graduates to lower tiered jobs, in a digital and technological strand of excluded, declassed, and precarious work.

The Role of Legal Educators

Bourdieu encourages academics to study and critique the role of institutions in replicating the established order.[76] Thus, the focus is a project of transformation for legal education: but not, as demanded by neoliberal market consumerism, of adopting curricula to develop skills for an individual's readiness for the job market, passively accepting their roles within the existing structures. The transformation is of the way we approach and contribute to the composition of the field of law and legal practice itself. As Brian Simpson notes of the role of law schools in relation to the changing place of law firms in a digitalised world, 'the law school must move beyond mere training of lawyers in the "use" of technology and begin to engage with how that technology may disrupt the justice of the law'.[77]

Conceived in this way, this move does not turn the study of law into a narrow, technocratic exercise, nor does it go against principles underpinning the liberal law degree, which ward against employability as playing any integral part of undergraduate studies in law.[78] The law is a study of actions and outcomes impacted by those with power within that field. As Fowler notes, those actors who possess significant cultural capital in any particular field also possess the ability to restructure that field and to revalue its values.[79] As such, it is contended that it is appropriate for legal educators to work with students and the profession to collectively negotiate and reconstruct the fields that are pivotal to the application of law.

A Framework for the Disruption of Hierarchies within Legal Education and Legal Employment

It is proposed that the distilling of transformative legal technologies in legal education is conceived not as a simple formula for consumption by the market,

75 Fowler (2020).
76 Bourdieu (1977).
77 Simpson (2016).
78 See e.g., Bradney (2003) and Guth et al. (2014).
79 Fowler (2020) p 19.

or a mechanism for ratification of the arbitrary, but to engage collective action, and challenge and reconstruct understandings of law and the legal profession.[80] Ultimately, legal educators can thus act to generate 'heresies' or 'symbolic revolutions'[81] which turn 'cognitive structures upside down and sometimes, to a degree, social structures',[82] in favour of a reconstituted understanding of law and the legal profession, and act as facilitators between students, firms, and regulators to interrogate the social preconditions of the current hierarchies.

Interrogating the Social Preconditions

This requires investigation of the field of professionalisation, and the possibilities for these to expand to support the re-evaluation of who and what it is to be a legal professional critiquing and exploring the new demands of law, with a specific reference to the position of existing sub-fields, which serve to consolidates the power of the dominant group. To prevent further rationalisation of lower-type work and roles of the professional factory to those of the 'wrong' ethnicity, class, and gender,[83] and the further prioritisation of 'archaic signs of privilege' and 'commodification of upper middle-class Englishness', the impact and potential value of legal tech to the legal system and profession should become part of our overall exploration of how law is shaped, created, applied, and practised. Of Webley et al.'s three narratives of attitudes towards 'lawtech' in the profession,[84] their 'status professional' narrative posits 'true legal professionals' encapsulated within a defensive discourse of 'classical' professionalism, and describing the specific range of 'symbolic designations' of legal work, norms, and training.[85] They note that

> in the status professionalism story, the archetype of the True Legal Professional not only endures in a LawTech future but also possibly thrives. Its historical privileges and powers allow it to assimilate within an existing sense of what it means to be a 'lawyer' and further within the existing firm structures, while incorporating or excluding possible non-law LawTech competitors.[86]

This is the essence of reproduction and exclusion by an already dominant class.

In relation to small firms and less lucrative areas, examination is crucial to prevent the obsolescence of new or emerging firms, sole practitioners,

80 Bourassa (2010).
81 Fowler (2020).
82 Bourdieu (2013) p 13.
83 Sommerlad (2016) p 260.
84 Webley et al. (2019).
85 Webley et al. (2019) p 11.
86 Webley et al. (2019).

and existing firms, with concomitant impacts on whole areas of practice. Universities are ideal places to situate cross-disciplinary interrogations to help understanding of critical social relations with technology which will impact the practice and application of law, but also to centre emancipatory technological practices to better enable access to justice.[87]

Instead of reducing the developments in digital to a niche or employability issue, it is key to recognise the significant issues of power and privilege within the profession, and reconstitute what is now required in the field, and how we could reconstitute what is valued within the field.[88]

Generating Heresies

Bourdieu's concepts of heresies, or symbolic revolutions, should cause the rethinking of the existing order and orchestration of change, by dispelling current doxa.[89] This requires examination of the changes to legal practice, and how the populations of workers within the legal industry will be impacted, instead of viewing it as without connection to context. However, to do this, law schools and academics must work with the profession to engage critically with the possibilities of transformative tech in law and the profession. Bourdieu criticised the notion of profession as a bureaucratic concept, because of the assumption in the ordinary use of the term, affording it uncontested and universal recognition which results in distinctive profit and symbolic value.[90] He saw the concept of professionalism as a mechanism of difference, imbued with power to assert dominance, and believed it presented a sociological issue as a consequence: the uncritical ratification of an arbitrary social construction. Advocating an academic position that simply supports or entrenches the 'status professional' model as outlined by Webley et al.[91] ignores the reality of access to the profession for many law students, and ignores our responsibilities to examine positions of power within our own discipline. While, in our heresies, we may not be contesting that professionalism as a concept should exist, we should certainly be attempting to situate how as a field it is impacted by these changes, such as the need for renewed examination of ethics and codes of conduct to equip the law and lawyers for how technology, in particular artificial intelligence, occurring at this time, and how these margins allow innovation and transformation to support those in subordinated groups.

Instead of inculcating 'disabling professions' within our teaching, we could explore a generation of enabling professionals, who actively seek new ways to

87 Emejulu et al. (2019).
88 Sommerlad (2016).
89 Deer (2008).
90 Bourdieu et al. (1992).
91 Webley et al. (2019).

reconfigure legal work to ensure access to the widest range of legal needs. This requires firms to actively do this, and law schools to work to produce students who are able to view both law and the profession as one which is not only able to change, but in need of change, and to deliver curricula that offer the range of cross-disciplinary subjects that support them in engaging holistically with how legal tech is and can be used to change the practice of law. It requires law schools to deliver these curricula in a way that engages all tutors and students, not just those from diverse backgrounds, to examine the study and practice of law in a culturally responsive way, and uses justice and the access to it, to underpin this.

Rethinking the attributes and abilities of lawyers may also act as a catalyst to dispel current doxa about what lawyers sound, look, and act like, and where the 'value' in the services provided lies. This requires not only a new curriculum but a renewed look at how we teach: adopting critical approaches to pedagogy, that challenge or remove hierarchies within the classroom, and actively embody diversity and justice as a key component of education and the practice of law.

It could mean examining the role of digital transformation in providing access to justice, via supporting the small firms and sole practitioners in less lucrative areas of practice that provide these services, or further incorporating a wider recognition and understanding of work of the professionals within these areas, and the career plans of students planning to enter these areas of practice.

Conclusion

That the legal profession has changed and will change further as the use of digital technologies continue and increase is clear. This contribution has proposed using this time of change as an event, to re-evaluate the 'space of competition and struggle'[92] in the fields of legal professionalism and work. This examination, if accompanied by the subsequent creations of heresies, which dispel current doxa, and enable the disruption of existing hierarchies, may enable a path for social transformation toward a long-awaited diversity in both composition and practice in law, where the wide and increasing range of dynamic skills now required by lawyering is predicated on ability, and not the arbitrary made legitimate in a pre-digital age.

References

Louise Ashley et al (2015) *A Qualitative Evaluation of Non-Educational Barriers to the Elite Professions*, Social Mobility and Child Poverty Commission London.

Louise Ashley and Laura Empson (2013) 'Differentiation and Discrimination: Understanding Social Class and Social Exclusion in Leading Law Firms' 66 *Human Relations* 219.

92 Bourdieu et al. (1992) p 234.

Sundeep Aulakh, Andy Charlwood, Daniel Muzio, Jennifer Tomlinson and Danat Valizade (2017) 'Mapping Advantages and Disadvantages: Diversity in the Legal Profession in England and Wales', Solicitors Regulation Authority.

Gregory N Bourassa (2010) *A Review of "Power, Crisis, and Education for Liberation: Rethinking Critical Pedagogy" Noah De Lissovoy*, Taylor & Francis.

Pierre Bourdieu (1977) *Outline of a Theory of Practice*, Cambridge University Press.

Pierre Bourdieu (1987) *Distinction: A Social Critique of the Judgement of Taste*, Harvard University Press.

Pierre Bourdieu (1993) *The Field of Cultural Production*, Polity.

Pierre Bourdieu (1994) 'Structures, Habitus, Power: Basis for a Theory of Symbolic Power' in Nicholas B Dirks, Geoff Eley et al (eds) *Culture/Power/History: A Reader in Contemporary Social Theory*, Princeton University Press.

Pierre Bourdieu (2013) *Manet: Une révolution symbolique*, Seuil, Raisons d'Agir.

Pierre Bourdieu and Loic Wacquant (1992) *An Invitation to Reflexive Sociology*, Polity.

Anthony Bradney (2003) *Conversations, Choices and Chances: The Liberal Law School in the Twenty-First Century*, Bloomsbury Publishing.

Salvatore Caserta and Mikael Rask Madsen (2019) 'The Legal Profession in the Era of Digital Capitalism: Disruption or New Dawn' 8 *Laws* 1.

Alfredo Contreras and Joe McGrath (2020) 'Law, Technology, and Pedagogy: Teaching Coding to Build a "Future-Proof" Lawyer' 21 *Minnesota Journal of Law, Science & Technology* 297.

Andrew CG Cook et al (2012) 'London's Legal Elite: Recruitment through Cultural Capital and the Reproduction of Social Exclusivity in City Professional Service Fields' 44 *Environment and Planning A* 1744.

Marcelo Corrales et al (2019) 'Digital Technologies, "Legal Design" & the Future of the Legal Profession' in Marcelo Corrales, Mark Fenwick et al (eds) *Legal Tech, Smart Contracts and Blockchain, Perspectives in Law, Business and Innovation*, Springer.

Peter Čuroš (2023) 'Educating into Aware Subjects instead of Unaware Objects' in L Siliquini-Cinelli and T Giddens (eds) *Biopolitics and Structure in Legal Education*, Routledge.

Cécile Deer (2008) 'Doxa' in Grenfell, Michael James (ed) *Pierre Bourdieu: Key Concepts*, Acumen Publishers.

David Dixon (2011) *Entry to the Solicitors' Profession 1980–2010*, The Law Society.

Akwugo Emejulu and Callum McGregor (2019) 'Towards a Radical Digital Citizenship in Digital Education' 60 *Critical Studies in Education* 131.

Mark Fenwick et al (2017) 'Legal Education in the Blockchain Revolution' 20 *Vand. J. Ent. & Tech. L.* 351.

Mark Fenwick and Erik PM Vermeulen (2019) 'The Lawyer of the Future as "Transaction Engineer": Digital Technologies and the Disruption of the Legal Profession' in Marcelo Corrales et al (eds) *Legal Tech, Smart Contracts and Blockchain*, Springer.

Bridget Fowler (2020) 'Pierre Bourdieu on Social Transformation, with Particular Reference to Political and Symbolic Revolutions' 49 *Theory and Society* 439.

Paul Gowder (2018) 'Transformative Legal Technology and the Rule of Law' 68 *University of Toronto Law Journal* 82.

Jessica Guth and Chris Ashford (2014) 'The Legal Education and Training Review: Regulating Socio-Legal and Liberal Legal Education?' 48 *The Law Teacher* 5.

Spencer Headworth et al (2016) *Diversity in Practice: Race, Gender, and Class in Legal and Professional Careers*, Cambridge University Press.

Karen Holtzblatt et al (2016) 'Beyond the Pipeline: Addressing Diversity in High Tech' in Jofish Kaye et al (eds) *Proceedings of the 2016 CHI Conference Extended Abstracts on Human Factors in Computing Systems*, Association for Computing Machinery, pp. 1063.

Chris Ireland and Ryan Hockley (2020) 'A Call for Introducing LegalTech in the Classroom' 36 *Computer Law & Security Review* 105399.

Lucille A Jewel (2008) 'Bourdieu and American Legal Education: How Law Schools Reproduce Social Stratification and Class Hierarchy' 56 *Buffalo Law Review* 1155.

The Law Society (2010) *Ethnic Diversity in Law Firms Understanding the Barriers*, The Law Society.

The Law Society (2019) *Lawtech Adoption Research*, The Law Society.

Omar Madhloom (2023) 'Biopolitics and the Solicitors Qualifying Examination' in L Siliquini-Cinelli and T Giddens (eds) *Life and the Structures of the Law School: The Biopolitics of Legal Education*, Routledge.

John O McGinnis and Russell G Pearce (2019) 'The Great Disruption: How Machine Intelligence Will Transform the Role of Lawyers in the Delivery of Legal Services' 82 *Actual Problems of Economics* 1230.

Elizabeth Mertz (2007) *The Language of Law School: Learning to "Think Like a Lawyer"*, Oxford University Press.

Jacob Metcalf and Emanuel Moss (2019) 'Owning Ethics: Corporate Logics, Silicon Valley, and the Institutionalization of Ethics' 2 *Social Research: An International Quarterly* 449.

Alan Milburn (2012) *Fair Access to Professional Careers: A Progress Report by the Independent Reviewer on Social Mobility and Child Poverty*, Cabinet Office.

Mirko Noordegraaf and Willem Schinkel (2011) 'Professionalism as Symbolic Capital: Materials for a Bourdieusian Theory of Professionalism' 10 *Comparative Sociology* 67.

Herman Ouseley (2008) *Independent Review Into Disproportionate Regulatory Outcomes For Black And Minority Ethnic Solicitors*, Solicitors Regulation Authority.

Larry E Ribstein (2012) 'Delawyering the Corporation' *Wisconsin Law Review* 305.

Francine Ryan (2020) 'Rage Against the Machine? Incorporating Legal Tech into Legal Education' 55(3) *The Law Teacher* 1.

Brian Simpson (2016) 'Algorithms or Advocacy: Does the Legal Profession Have a Future in a Digital World?' 25 *Information & Communications Technology Law* 50.

Solicitors Regulation Authority (2019) *How Diverse is the Legal Profession?* Solicitors Regulation Authority

Hilary Sommerlad (2007) 'Researching and Theorizing the Processes of Professional Identity Formation' 34 *Journal of Law and Society* 190.

Hilary Sommerlad (2008) '"What Are You Doing Here? You Should Be Working in a Hair Salon or Something": Outsider Status and Professional Socialization in the Solicitors Profession' 2 *Web Journal of Current Legal Issues* 1.

Hilary Sommerlad et al (2010) *Diversity in the Legal Profession in England and Wales: A Qualitative Study of Barriers and Individual Choices*, Legal Services Board.

Hilary Sommerlad (2016) 'The New "Professionalism" in England and Wales: Talent, Diversity, and a Legal Precariat' in Spencer Headworth, Robert L Nelson et al (eds) *Diversity in Practice: Race, Gender, and Class in Legal and Professional Careers*, Cambridge University Press.

Richard E Susskind (2008) 'The End of Lawyers' 32 *Rethinking the Nature of Legal Services* 50.

Richard E Susskind (2020) 'Hot Topic: Online Justice: The Way of the Future?' 63 *LSJ: Law Society of NSW Journal* 24.

Richard E Susskind (2013) *Tomorrow's Lawyers: An Introduction to Your Future*, Oxford University Press.

Richard E Susskind and Daniel Susskind (2015) *The Future of the Professions: How Technology Will Transform the Work of Human Experts*, Oxford University Press.

Margaret Thornton (2019) 'Towards the Uberisation of Legal Practice Symposium: Automation, Innovation and Disruption in Legal Practice' 1 *Law, Technology and Humans* 46.

Jennifer Tomlinson et al (2017) *Privileges and Penalties in the Legal Profession in England and Wales: Analysis of Solicitors Regulation Authority Records in Relation to Career Progression and Diversity Characteristics*, SASE.

Jennifer Tomlinson et al (2019) 'Privileges and Penalties in the Legal Profession: An Intersectional Analysis of Career Progression' 70 *The British Journal of Sociology* 1043.

Paul Wakeling and Mike Savage (2015) 'Entry to Elite Positions and the Stratification of Higher Education in Britain' 63 *The Sociological Review* 290.

Zhiqiong June Wang (2019) 'Between Constancy and Change: Legal Practice and Legal Education in the Age of Technology' 36 *Law in Context: A Socio-legal Journal* 64.

Lisa Webley (2013) 'United Kingdom: What Robinson v Solicitors Regulation Authority Tells Us about the Contested Terrain of Race and Disciplinary Processes' 16 *Legal Ethics* 236.

Lisa Webley (2014) 'Legal Professional de (Re) Regulation, Equality, and Inclusion, and the Contested Space of Professionalism Within the Legal Market in England and Wales' 83 *Fordham Law Review* 2349.

Lisa Webley et al (2016) 'Access to a Career in the Legal Profession in England and Wales: Race, Class and the Role of Educational Background' in Spencer Headworth, Robert L Nelson et al (eds) *Diversity in Practice: Race, Gender, and Class in Legal and Professional Careers*, Cambridge University Press.

Lisa Webley et al (2019) 'The Profession(s)' Engagements with LawTech: Narratives and Archetypes of Future Law Symposium: Automation, Innovation and Disruption in Legal Practice' 1 *Law, Technology and Humans* 6.

Part II

Internal Resistance

Chapter 6

Law Teacher as Poet

Transcending the Mechanics of Legal Education

Prue Vines

Introduction

This chapter is about developing the area of teaching we are mostly too afraid to pursue because it often feels out of control—judgment. Coming to judgment requires taking into account all the exigencies of the situation and the fact that these are real people with real lives. Doing this well involves including emotions and values in our strict legal reasoning. I define judgment here as more than simply playing the game of whether the doctrine of precedent says 'yes' or 'no'. The reference to the doctrine of precedent will reveal that my background and teaching experience is in common law, and the experience may be different for law students from other disciplines. Including emotions may frighten us because it might ignite our own emotions or those of our students, and we know emotions can be powerful and can wreak havoc. However, our emotions are also a pointer to our moral values,[1] and, as such, have a significant role to play in the education of lawyers. My approach is biopolitical in the naïve sense, in that it takes into account our and others' biological selves as actors and objects of legal thoughts and actions. It might be regarded as an example of naturalistic biopolitics in that it seeks to draw on the biological base of human emotion and apply this to teaching law. Whether it fits into a Foucauldian notion of biopolitics is unclear, and is not the focus of this chapter.[2] The focus is on the student and the teacher as human, with human characteristics.

The analogy of the poet for the law teacher is useful for teaching law as a human/to humans. For me, teaching law very well means facilitating students' learning in a myriad of ways so they can develop their own sense of judgment. Coming to judgment is the thing that distinguishes lawyers from philosophers—lawyers *have* to make determinations that apply to real people in real time, and they cannot duck the need to decide. Judges, of course, must come to judgment, but ultimately all lawyers need to develop this art which

1 Nussbaum (2003).

2 This view of biopolitics draws on the outline by Lieson and Walsh (2012).

DOI: 10.4324/9781003179283-9

begins as mechanical, and then should turn from mechanical to art, and at its best requires insight into human conditions and the possibilities of law.

The Poet as Model

It may be surprising to think that the law teacher might be analogised to the poet, but there are many similarities, and sometimes an unusual analogy is more illuminating than a more common one. This chapter only briefly considers using poetry in law teaching. Rather, it concerns thinking about the poet and the poet's techniques, habits and aspirations as a model which we, as law teachers, might use. It is useful to consider some definitions of poetry[3] to start us off:

'Poetry' has been defined as:

> Literary work in which the expression of feelings and ideas is given intensity by the use of distinctive style and rhythm; poems collectively or as a genre of literature.
>
> ...
>
> **1.1** A quality of beauty and intensity of emotion regarded as characteristic of poems.
>
> *'poetry and fire are nicely balanced in the music'*
>
> **1.2** Something regarded as comparable to poetry in its beauty.
>
> *'the music department is housed in a building which is pure poetry'*[4]

What is it about poetry that makes it useful for us to consider? This definition speaks of intensity of feeling and ideas, distinctive style and rhythm, qualities of beauty, and the use of 'poetry' as a metaphor for 'beauty'.

The poet seeks to go beyond the mechanical and the obvious, to illuminate things that may otherwise be ignored by using intensity and emotion in a distinctive style. Where the definition uses 'beauty' we might see a particular coming to judgment as 'pure poetry'. Poetry might lift or lower the spirit as part of the development of insight, to instil in the listener or reader a sense that there is more than just the words on the page. The techniques the poet uses to achieve these things vary from following strict rules to breaking the rules, using our human-ness including emotional and bodily awareness to force us to see things differently. Law teachers can learn from both the aspirations and the techniques of the poet. This analogy may inspire us to try to achieve transcendence (going beyond the limits, beyond ordinary limitations) in the teaching of law.

3 Disclaimer: Although I did study English literature at university as an undergraduate, this is very much a lay view of poetry and poets. I do not pretend to be a literary scholar of any kind.

4 *Oxford English Dictionary* Online.

Considering the poet as a model can help us recognise the need to move students from the mechanical learning of techniques (the familiar 'learning to think like a lawyer'[5]) to the meta-cognitive coming to judgment which looks like effortless 'art' and becomes the mark of the effective practitioner. That is the mastery that is needed to be a good lawyer.[6] Poets and law students have to hone their craft by paying attention to the mechanical parts of their craft before they can achieve mastery. The poet must attend to grammar, to choice of words, to determining how to create the wished-for rhythm. They must understand simile and metaphor, assonance, alliteration and allusion until it can all be woven together to create the necessary effect. They need to be persuasive. They need to be able to use connotation and separate it from denotation. Some of these things, such as grammar, choice of words, analogy, denotation are also required of the lawyer.

It is entirely appropriate to focus on skills first. Teaching the mechanics of reading a case or statute allows the student to learn the skill, while also allowing the teacher to demonstrate concern and the students to learn to trust the teacher so they can develop. In early law school the goals associated with this skill development need to be incorporated with three broader goals:

- Tolerance of uncertainty
- Independence of learning
- Intrinsic motivation

Tolerance of uncertainty is required in order to have the student develop the necessary ability to ask critical questions and keep asking them. Independence of learning is required to allow the student to continue to learn long after they have left university. Intrinsic motivation, paradoxically, can be developed so that the student learns to be really interested in the relevant matter.[7]

Along with all those we need to teach the importance of practice—for example, that writing, as for the poet, is a matter of writing, re-writing, and re-writing again. The MIRAT[8] or IRAC form is a classic example of how we teach mechanics, and it is a very good system. However, coming to judgment requires more than MIRAT. A good judgment states the reasoning by which it comes to the ratio decided in a way which is persuasive and incorporates attention to past and possible future cases, and attention to the parties whose dispute is being decided within the context within which the

5 The classic aspiration for law students. See, among many books with similar titles: Schauer (2009) S Fruehwald (2013).

6 I take this to be the kind of reflective practitioner that Donald A Schon is referring to in his classic book: Schon (1991) p 43.

7 For example, Song and Grabowski (2006); Ng (2018).

8 Material facts, Issue, Rule, Application to facts, Tentative conclusion (MIRAT); Issue Rule Application Conclusion (IRAC).

law happens. It pays attention to psychology, sociology, and philosophy as well as law because good law incorporates those things. It is lucid and it is powerful. So, in teaching MIRAT we have to keep the students at it until they are writing a judgment or an opinion in which much more is involved than the mechanics.

Poetry exemplifies this process. We see manuscripts where poets have spent months and years to get a word in a line right. When we see it on the printed page, there is just the one, perfect word.[9] We do not see all the words before, just the final result. Students need to see that hard work and practice is what it takes to move from mechanics to art.

How do we move students from mechanics to art? Teach them to pay attention. The law teacher pays attention, but also teaches the student to pay attention. This is a matter of the student bringing their attention to bear on activities in the classroom, and being present to them. Part of getting students to pay attention includes considering the poetic techniques involving rhythm. Rhythm includes words/sounds and *silences*. Since most lawyers can talk 'under wet cement' it is useful to remind us to stop talking and allow space to *think* in the classroom. It is also a useful way of slowing things down. Our students live in a speedy world in which paying attention is constantly asked for but seldom in a sustained way. One of the best gifts we can give our students is the chance to pause for reflection. Ask not for their first answer, but their thoughtful answer. Slow down the pace so they can think rather than just react. Our students at UNSW Law tend to be very quick, and for them it may be even more important to have slow time so that they can pay attention all around a topic, doing their work mindfully so their concentration and focus are enhanced.

The Poet Follows and Breaks the Rules

Another thing law teachers can learn from the poet is the use of following and breaking the rules and the recognition that the rules can change. Rules, particularly in common law systems, are always in tension—that is why we have to decide which level of the hierarchy a court is in, why we have to determine whether the majority in a plural court decided X while the minority decide Y. That is, indeed, why we have to determine whether the facts in the case are similar or different from the facts in the case which set the precedent.

Rules in poetry have also always been in tension—there are periods of total acceptance of some rule and then it is broken. For example, in Anglo-Saxon

9 See an unusual book which published both the final poem and an earlier version of each: Burr and Wallenstein (eds) (2002).

poetry, the rules involved double alliteration in the middle of the sentence. Here is the beginning of *Beowulf*, probably written between 700 and 750 CE:

Béowulf wæs bréme –blaéd wíde sprang–
Scyldes eafera Scedelandum in.
Swá sceal geong guma góde gewyrcean
fromum feohgiftum on fæder bearme[10]

Later forms of poetry changed the rules—each time that would have increased the impact of the poem. When Lord Byron wrote *The Destruction of Sennacherib*, the rhyming words were at the end of the poem and the rhythm was dominant. His use of rhythm moved him away from classical, more sedate poetry in its echoing of the hordes pouring down on Sennacherib:

The Assyrian came down like the wolf on the fold,
And his cohorts were gleaming in purple and gold;
And the sheen of their spears was like stars on the sea,
When the blue wave rolls nightly on deep Galilee …

And Hopkins brought us more surprises in poetic form:

I caught this morning morning's minion, kingdom of daylight's dauphin,
dapple-dawn-drawn Falcon, in his riding
Of the rolling level underneath him steady air, and striding
High there, how he rung upon the rein of a wimpling wing
In his ecstasy! then off, off forth on swing,
As a skate's heel sweeps smooth on a bow-bend: the hurl and gliding
Rebuffed the big wind. My heart in hiding
Stirred for a bird, – the achieve of, the mastery of the thing! …[11]

And e e cummings, 1894–1962, surprised people again with poems like this:

maggie and milly and molly and may
went down to the beach (to play one day)
and maggie discovered a shell that sang
so sweetly she couldn't remember her troubles, and
milly befriended a stranded star

10 Beowulf was famed – his renown spread wide–
Scyld's heir, in Northern lands.
So ought a young man by good deeds deserve,
(and) by fine treasure-gifts, while in his father's keeping
(translated by Benjamin Slade, copyright 2002–2020: https://heorot.dk/beowulf-rede-text.html).

11 Hopkins (1985).

whose rays five languid fingers were;
and molly was chased by a horrible thing
which raced sideways while blowing bubbles: and
may came home with a smooth round stone
as small as a world and as large as alone.
For whatever we lose (like a you or a me)
it's always ourselves we find in the sea[12]

There are two ways of using this particular aspect of the poet's art in law teaching. The first is to assist students in understanding the constant temporal tension in the rules. Our law follows rules until they are changed to new rules. In Australia we could say, for example that there was a long period where the view that Australia was *terra nullius* applied which was only broken in 1992 by the *Mabo* decision.[13]

We can consider the breaking of rules too. We could consider the normal rules of engagement in the classroom. If you break these rules in some way, the benefit of surprise may be yours. There is evidence that the moment of surprise is a critical moment in learning,[14] partly because surprise induces attention. This means creating moments when a student has that moment of sudden insight. For example, in teaching feudal tenures I might jump on a desk and put myself in a position which most students identify as praying. When I tell them this is the position in which the feudal oath was taken they are surprised, and learning follows. You could establish a pattern: for example, raise a case, ask a student for the facts, then ask a student for the issue, then ask a student for the ratio: establish the pattern over a class and then break it. Suddenly ask a question that is completely different, such as 'Why does this case matter?' The surprise makes the students pay attention and then learn. Other ways to surprise include telling students a surprising fact about a case, for example students in torts being told that many people run out of damages (not so surprising) and then are refused access to social security. This surprises most Australians and the students never seem to forget this.

Poetry and Emotion (and the Body)

Poetry has many ways of ensuring that attention is paid, one of which links to our consideration of emotion. It is common for poetry to draw on emotion to create its effect, to make insight occur. Poets move beyond the obvious to develop insight or wisdom. They use emotion to help them do this and they develop our empathic imagination. Legal analysis is only slowly coming to

12 https://poets.org/poem/maggie-and-milly-and-molly-and-may.
13 *Mabo v Queensland (No 2)* (1992) 175 CLR 1.
14 Holland and Gallagher (2006).

understand that reason is not only about logic. Law and emotion now has a burgeoning literature.[15] I would argue that developing the empathic imagination as an intellectual tool is profoundly important for the developing law student.[16]

Empathic imagination, in my view, is the ability to imagine the situation of another person in as rich a way as possible. To develop the skill of being able to see what the position of another person is, and to think through the implications of that position rationally and intellectually is very significant. This is not about feeling sorry for people, but about being able to create data which can be tested by a slightly different process. This harnesses the imagination in ways which will help to understand the mental processes of another person (without making the mistake of assuming that we are them). Teaching students to use empathic imagination, not as sheer emotionalism but as an intellectual tool, actually requires them to ask themselves such questions as, 'if I were a person in that position, would it be reasonable to require me to do "X"?' 'What implications would that have for my ability to consider various courses of action?'[17] For example: consider the argument that the government owes a fiduciary duty to Aboriginal children [in Australia] who were removed from their parents. In *Cubillo v Commonwealth (No 2)* (2001) 112 FCR 455, it was argued that the government owed such a duty to Cubillo and Gunner. However, O'Loughlin J rejected the argument that the duty of a guardian to a child should be seen as fiduciary on the basis that such a duty had traditionally been considered only to exist in relation to economic interests. But what were the interests of these children which had been impacted by the states' behaviour? If we step into the shoes of the children, we find that they have suffered the loss of their connection with their families, and their connection with their land. We further find that they have lost their ability to bring actions for native title land for this reason. If we consider this logically and intellectually, we come to the conclusion that clearly the economic interests of the plaintiffs have been affected. One of the interests of a ward which a guardian should protect is their economic interest. Taking students through this process teaches them the intellectual value of empathic imagination as a reasoning process. It requires real care, though, to think this through in order to avoid a form of appropriation occurring. There is a danger that the stereotypical white, middle class law student may simply project themselves in a limited way into the position of the people concerned and fail to comprehend the whole scope of the issue for that person. This is the reason I emphasise the word 'empathy' with its element of comprehension, as opposed to 'sympathy' which is more about an emotional

15 For example, Bandes (ed.) (2000), Conway and Stannard (2016), Martha Nussbaum (2003). See also Jones (2020).

16 Here I draw on an article on including Indigenous Issues in the Curriculum, Vines (2012).

17 Vines, above n 16, 53.

response. It is also the reason I emphasise that it is an intellectual tool which must be practised.

The case of *Trevorrow*[18] (the only Indigenous person in Australia found by a court to have been stolen and awarded compensation for his removal as a young child from his family and culture) can be used to teach torts students how to assess damages. I ask them to do a deep reading of the facts of the case and then to think about the impact of those facts on somebody's life and how one would claim damages for them. In reading the facts we use techniques that might be used for poetry—different people to read different facts aloud, taking the time to read in a literary and more emotional rather than dry and factual way. As students read the facts, they take the roles of different people such as Trevorrow, his mother, the social worker, and the foster mother. The students have to think deeply and use their emotional signals to consider what it would really be like to have lost the chance to identify with the Aboriginal community when all your other siblings were significant elders. We think it through in relation to the requirements of the civil liability legislation and come to judgment. This is not easy. It requires some emotional strength as well as the ability to empathise, but the point is to see that Trevorrow was real and that his hurt was not 'just another legal issue'. This is another lesson from poetry—using emotion to teach students to develop their empathic imagination as an intellectual tool, to feel the emotion but then to use it to arouse the intellect.

This empathic imagination approach might also move us to teach preventive law more often. The more we look to the emotional impact of the law on our clients, particularly the emotional impact of litigation on clients who are not corporations, the less we will be satisfied with focusing on law's remedial rather than preventive aspects. Most law school curricula might be classed as remedial, focused on the courts after the harm. But it is far better for the client to prevent the problem in the first place. Law schools have been so focused on courts that they miss the obvious fact that a massive amount of lawyer work is transactional and should be preventive—drafting contracts, drafting trusts, drafting wills—all these are aimed at problem-solving and it is only when they fail that the courts come into play. As a teacher of succession my view is that the good succession lawyer keeps her clients out of court. We don't have to change our teaching completely—we just have to look at the cases we teach and ask a preventive rather than a remedial question—how could that contract or will have been drafted so that this problem would not have happened? Draft a contract that will prevent this person having to litigate, etc.

18 *Trevorrow v State of South Australia (No 5)* [2007] SASC 285.

Descartes' legacy of the split between mind and body has fed the notions of objectivity and universality and neutrality, which have their place, but should not be treated as the only approach to law and reason. Rather than reason in the form of emotionless logic being regarded as the epitome, we are beginning to see richer forms of reason enriched by emotion. The familiar traditional view has been:

> [The individual] must restrain his emotions, so that they do not cloud his reason, and he must reduce his particularities – as a judge, for example, assumes an institutional role that distances him from personal experiences that might affect his view of the issue before him – so that he can reach a more neutral or universally valid answer.[19]

Feminist scholarship has been essential in challenging this view of reason as thought-minus-emotion,[20] and as noted above, it is only more recently that emotion has become (slightly) acceptable in the legal academy.[21]

Teaching techniques that recognise the place of emotion in both law and learning are required. The history[22] of these cases shows the slow move away from the view that mental illness or irrationality should not be pandered to, if they exist at all, illustrated in the 1939 case of *Chester v Waverley Council*:[23]

> Death is not an infrequent event, and even violent and distressing deaths are not uncommon. It is, however, not a common experience of mankind that the spectacle, even of the sudden and distressing death of a child, produces any consequence of more than a temporary nature in the case of bystanders or even of close relatives who see the body after death has taken place.

This is what Latham CJ said when denying the existence of a duty of care for psychiatric harm to a mother who, after searching for hours, saw her dead son taken out of a flooded council excavation some 15 metres long, 4 metres wide, and 2 metres deep. Barricades around it were such that people could walk under it and the Council had placed sand next to it which made it very attractive to children.

Poetry often uses emotion to galvanise insight. Compare the statement of Latham CJ above, which is almost completely emotionless, even anti-emotion,

19 Williams (1993) quoted in Jones (2020) p 3.

20 See for example, Antony and Witts (eds) (1993) and Harding and Hintikka (eds) (1983).

21 See above n 16.

22 For accounts of the history of the action for psychiatric injury see Chamallas and Kerber (1990); E Handsley (1996); Vines et al. (2010).

23 *Chester v Waverley Municipal Council* (1939) 62 CLR 1.

with Evatt J's judgment, in which he uses a poem of William Blake's to show that he understands what has happened here:

> During this crucial period the plaintiff's condition of mind and nerve can be completely understood only by parents who have been placed in a similar agony of hope and fear with hope gradually decreasing ....
>
> William Blake's imaginative genius has well portrayed suffering and anxiety of this kind:
>
> Tired and woe-begone
> Hoarse with making moan
> ...
> Rising from unrest
> The trembling woman prest
> With feet of weary woe:
> She could no further go.

Evatt held (dissenting) that there was a duty owed. The poetry makes the emotional point of the impact of the events on the plaintiff to the student, and it shows the judge using his empathic imagination as an intellectual tool to arrive at a decision. His judgment was the inspiration for legislation which changed the law to allow a parent to recover for psychiatric harm in such circumstances.

Related to the increasing acceptance of emotion in law is the recognition of the body and politics of subjectivity as part of teaching. This has, of course, been used by infants' teachers for centuries, but phenomenologists have begun to develop an approach drawing on the body for learning.[24] We have tended to think of legal education as entirely cerebral, and that we can divorce this from our bodies. But law operates on bodies—bodies are fundamentally part of how the legal system works, so they certainly are not irrelevant, but using the body in our teaching might alter what we think it means to teach people to 'think like a lawyer'. The danger is that 'thinking like a lawyer' can be thought of as like a pair of sunglasses which exclude many complexities of law and foster 'a subtle but insidious form of legal formalism'.[25] Using a bodily approach to learning using phenomenology includes focusing on how the body feels when one is emotional, thinking about a topic, or doing some related activity. The focus is on a 'politics of subjectivity' and may include contemplative techniques to focus the mind. Again, we are using intellectual tools to focus on things which are usually not thought of as intellectual pointers—bodily feelings, and emotions.

24 See Patricia Morgan, https://unsw.academia.edu/PatriciaMorgan/CurriculumVitae; Vines and Morgan (2016).

25 Foley and Tang (2016) p 134.

Tim Parks has described how important the teacher-student relationship is to learning. He is right but his mournful view that online education will kill it should be rejected:

> [T]his is the end of a culture in which learning was a collective social experience implying a certain positive hierarchy that invited both teacher and student to grow into the new relationship that every class occasions, the special dynamic that forms with each new group of students.[26]

That 'special dynamic' is an emotional connection which remains vital however the teaching is done. Teaching is an emotional activity—any teacher will tell you they feel exhausted well beyond the physical activity involved. Emotions in teaching include the love of the subject matter, the relationship with the students, the eliciting of surprise to enhance learning. Engagement, that holy grail of education, also involves emotions:

> Consider unpacking engagement – we all talk about the need for engagement, but we usually have quite a simple vision of it – we mean cognitive engagement with the subject matter, but there is also a need for behavioural engagement and for emotional engagement. Indeed, it is likely that emotional engagement is very helpful for the development of the other forms of engagement.[27]

This brings us back to the idea that reason and cognition involve emotion and that emotion may be a pointer to morality or norms. Many of what we think of as negative emotions are useful indicators that something in the system is wrong. Anger at unfairness may be a touchstone for justice; fear is also a pointer. Shame is a powerful emotion which has a significant effect and use. It has not been common for law teachers to draw on these emotions, to point them out as markers, but perhaps we need to more often. We have tended to consider only the positive emotions in the classroom as assisting with learning. For example, liking and loving classmates/teacher/team; identification as a law student seems to be significant in keeping law students studying, but having an intellectual approach to the recognition of emotions, while allowing them to be felt, may create an extra dimension in teaching. As Nussbaum and others have shown,[28] our felt emotions help us to identify our values. The poet does this all the time, evoking emotions to identify what is bad, good, etc. We can draw on this by asking students to notice their emotions as they read a case—if they feel angry as they read it, is this because it is an unjust situation? If they feel

26 Park (2019).
27 Sagayadevan and Jeyaraj (2012).
28 See n 1 above.

satisfied is this because they feel justice has been done? If they feel disgust does this point to something in the judgment that should not have happened? Awe, fear, anxiety, joy, love—all of these may point us to important values in ourselves and in the case which should be addressed. To ignore these emotional responses is to miss something that is vital in the reasoning.

We might, for example, embrace the reality and truth of emotion as it exists in clients' lives in our teaching. The fact that law resisted compensating psychiatric harm for so long suggests that bringing emotions into the discourse challenges it. Considering emotion, for example, can help us challenge the received wisdom that people who are injured are paid sufficient compensation to make up for what has happened to them. A focus on real emotions and real lives may challenge the hegemony of appellate courts in our teaching—yes there is value in paying attention to the appellate courts, but the impact of the courts on the mass of people flowing through the lower courts and tribunals touches the lives and emotions of far more people than traditional law school discourses often consider. Similar considerations apply to the teaching of preventive as well as remedial law.

Conclusions

When I consider the law teacher as poet, I am hoping to create a classroom environment which will allow students to achieve insights that take them further than they otherwise might go, so that they can exercise a rich and compassionate form of judgment. Sometimes this may claim to be wisdom. The *Oxford English Dictionary* defines 'wisdom' as 'the quality of having experience, knowledge, and good judgement; the quality of being wise'. This is not much of a definition, but it draws on experience and knowledge. Experiences are bodily and emotionally felt as well as intellectually experienced, and I seek to incorporate all of these into the teaching of law. If all these things are drawn into a judgment, we might see wisdom in the judgment. That is truly inspirational, and those are the judgments that are still considered decades later. That truly is transcending the mechanical.

The techniques I have discussed, drawn from the poet's arsenal, are all ways of engaging the whole student by drawing on reasons, emotion, and the body as ways to trigger this richer sort of consideration. Our students need to be able to state the law, but they also need to be able to say 'this law is actually threatening our society/vulnerable groups/individuals'; they need to be able to critique the law in order to protect it and to make it the best that it can be, because law is important for a fully functioning civil society.

When our students can use their legal skills as art, and have insight into law, themselves and others, and have developed some wisdom out of their experience and knowledge we have transcended our limits as teachers. When our students are teaching themselves with all the art, insight, and wisdom they can muster, this is teaching success.

References

Primary Sources

Chester v Waverley Municipal Council (1939) 62 CLR 1.
Cubillo v Commonwealth (No 2) (2001) 112 FCR 455.
Mabo v Queensland (No 2) (1992) 175 CLR 1.
Trevorrow v State of South Australia (No 5) (2007) SASC 285.

Secondary Sources

Louise Antony and Charlotte Witts (eds) (1993) *A Mind of One's Own: Feminist Essays on Reason and Objectivity*, Westview Press.

Susan Bandes (ed) (2000) *The Passions of Law*, NYU Press.

R Burr and B Wallenstein (eds) (2002) *Visions and Revisions: The Poet's Process*, Broadview Press.

Heather Conway and John Stannard (2016) *The Emotional Dynamics of Law and Legal Discourse*, Hart Publishing.

M Chamallas and L Kerber (1990) 'Women, Mothers and the Law of Fright: A History' 88 *Michigan Law Review* 814.

T Foley and S Tang (2016) 'Being, Not Just Thinking Like, A Lawyer' in R Field et al (eds) *Promoting Law Student and Lawyer Wellbeing in Australia and Beyond*, Routledge.

Scott Fruehwald (2013) *Think Like a Lawyer: Legal Reasoning for Law Students and Business Professionals*, American Bar Association.

Elizabeth Handsley (1996) 'Mental Injury Occasioned by Harm to Another: A Feminist Critique' 14 *Law and Inequality; A Journal of Theory and Practice* 391.

Sandra Harding and Merrill Hintikka (eds) (1983) *Discovering Reality: Feminist Perspectives on Epistemology, Metaphysics, Methodology and Philosophy of Science*, Reidel Publishing.

Peter C Holland and Michela Gallagher (2006) 'Different Roles for Amygdala Central Nucleus and Substantia Innominata in the Surprise-Induced Enhancement of Learning' 26(14) *Journal of Neuroscience* 3791–3797. https://doi.org/10.1523/JNEUROSCI.0390-06.2006.

Gerard Manley Hopkins (1985) 'The Windhover' in WH Gardner (ed) *Gerard Manley Hopkins: Poems and Prose*, Penguin Classics.

Emma Jones (2020) *Emotions in the Law School*, Routledge.

LT Lieson and MB Walsh (2012) 'The Competing Meanings of Biopolitics in Political Science: Biological and Post-Modern approaches' 31(1–2) *Politics and the Life Sciences* 2–15.

B Ng (2018) 'The Neuroscience of Growth Mindset and Intrinsic Motivation' 8(2) *Brain Science* 20. https://doi.org/10.3390/brainsci8020020.

Martha Nussbaum (2003) *Upheavals of Thought: The intelligence of Emotions*, Cambridge University Press.

Tim Parks (2019) 'The Dying Art of Instruction in the Digital Classroom' *New York Review of Books*, 31 July 2019.

Vathsala Sagayadevan and Senthu Jeyara (2012) 'The Role of Emotional Engagement in Lecturer-Student Interaction and the Impact on Academic Outcomes of Student Achievement and Learning' 3 *Journal of the Scholarship of Teaching and Learning* 1–30.

Frederick Schauer (2009) *Thinking Like a Lawyer*, Harvard University Press.

Donald A Schon (1991) *The Reflective Practitiioner*, Basic Books.
Hae-Deck Song and Barbara L Grabowski (2006) 'Stimulating Intrinsic Motivation for Problem Solving Using Goal-Oriented Contexts and Peer Group Composition' 54 *Educational Technology Research and Development* 445.
Prue Vines and Patricia Morgan (2016) 'Contemplative Practice in the Law School: Breaking Barriers to Learning and Resilience' in R Field et al (eds) *Promoting Law Student and Lawyer Wellbeing in Australia and Beyond*, Routledge.
Prue Vines (2012) 'Putting Indigenous Issues into the Curriculum – Succession and Equity' 4 *Ngiya Talk the Law* 46.
Prue Vines, Mehera San Roque and Emily Rumble (2010) 'Is "Nervous Shock" Still a Feminist Issue? The Duty of Care and Psychiatric Injury in Australia' 18(1) *The Tort Law Review* 9–32.
SH Williams (1993) 'Feminist Legal Epistemology' 8 *Berkeley Women's Law Journal* 63–105.

Chapter 7

TRAMA: Stories of Situated Pedagogy in Legal Education

Julia Ávila Franzoni

Prelude: The National Faculty of Law in Rio de Janeiro is Located at the 'Central do Brasil'

The *Central do Brasil* (Brazil's Central Station) is a historic metropolitan train station that is located at the heart of the city of Rio de Janeiro. From there, multiple train lines depart, connecting the downtown with its North and West Zones, as well as other municipalities situated along the *Baixada Fluminense*.[1] This central node is also integrated with subway and bus stations, making this region the main hub of urban mobility in Rio, where more than 600,000 people, from the most diverse parts of the city, circulate daily. Among them, hundreds of students that attend the National Faculty of Law of the Federal University of Rio de Janeiro (*Faculdade Nacional de Direito da Universidade Federal do Rio de Janeiro, FND-URJ*), whose historic building is located only a couple of blocks away from the Central Station. As Rio de Janeiro was once the seat of the Portuguese Imperial Court and also, at some point, the Capital of the Republic, it is not entirely surprising that the Faculty of Law is situated in the same building that once was the House of the Senate, during both the Imperial period and the early Republic.

Located at the formerly known *Praça da República* (Republic Square), now named *Praça Conde dos Arcos*, there are not many people among the thousands that circulate daily around it that know that the building belongs to the Faculty of Law, especially the urban workers that transit along the area. In a kind of mimesis of legal alienation, the building almost seems to float ethereally in this territory, simultaneously being and not being there, in sight but not really seen, in a way similar to the laws that hardly seem to engage, or relate in actuality, with the real ways in which bodies and relationships are spatially constituted. On its doorstep, homeless people lay on the sidewalk, using the building's bathrooms as their only alternative for hygienic care. In front of the

1 It is important to note that this train station is the inspiration behind an important Brazilian film, *Central Station*, winner of several national and international prizes, which has the same name as the aforementioned station.

DOI: 10.4324/9781003179283-10

university doors, public lectures are held and marches are organised for large street protests that occur along President Vargas Avenue. The relationships that exist between the building, its surroundings, those who regularly frequent it, and its neighbours, tell important stories about the processes and struggles that have taken place for the country's redemocratisation, and narrate some of the important aspects concerning the deterioration of the central region of the city and the precariousness of the lives of its many workers, while also bearing witness to the life experiences of several young people for whom the Faculty of Law represents the hope for a better future, both in order to achieve personal social mobility and as a way to engage in the collective reconstruction of Brazilian democracy.

For the students that live in the metropolitan region of the city or in its neighbourhoods that are located further away from Rio's main areas, the daily journey of crossing the city and reaching the law school may take up to three or even four hours.[2] Buses, subways, and, most commonly, trains are constantly crammed with people, often suffering delays and, in some cases, even being cancelled due to circumstances such as heavy rains or firefights that occur in certain parts of the city due to police operations. The alchemical process that takes place when walking through the classroom doors and sitting on one of its chairs transforms and labels the different persons who frequent the classroom into an individual-student abstraction, which is constantly shaken and challenged by the perspective of these bodies whose trajectories defy and tear this homogenising fiction in favour of a multiplicity that is echoed by their very lives and daily journeys. Coming and going through the Central Station, these law students experience and weave lines, and build plots whose narratives are essential to work upon the very lines and plots that constitute legal education.

The different perspectives of these students narrate some of the structural transformations that Brazilian public universities have been experiencing during the last ten years due to the implementation of national affirmative action measures. The radical change of student's profiles modifies their traditional position before professors—they do not belong to the same race and class status anymore—, which highlights their aim for other transformations in faculties of law, summarised in an intersectionally oriented legal education, and effective student welfare policies. What we want to present and discuss is part of this recent history of change in Brazilian legal education, focusing on the experiences of our last four years of teaching in the National Faculty of Law at the Federal University of Rio de Janeiro.

***

2 In Rio de Janeiro, these areas are generally the poorest and students who spend hours to get to law school and back are often from situations of great social vulnerability.

Thus, this paper aims to present and discuss the theoretical and practical repertories that have been developed with law students through TRAMA[3] (*Teorias e Redes de Ação Materialista*/Theories and Networks of Materialist Action), both in and outside the classroom. TRAMA is a University Research and Extension Program associated with the Research Group 'Labá – Direito, Espaço & Política'.[4] More than that, TRAMA is a collective that is organised by a teacher and students, which has been having an important role in the integration, engagement, and mobilisation of freshman law students, and as a space of articulation, exchanges, and formulations that go beyond the usual agenda and scope of academic investigation and research. The collective and the project have been experimenting with different imaginative perspectives for dealing with the study and practice of law, notably in the jurisprudence course, in which the pre-conceptual blueprint is the juridical situations (daily life, classroom, relationships, and conflicts) and the experiment that has been developed[5] is the theoretical-practical approach that we call situated pedagogy.

Seeking to register and tell our experiences and, from that, speculate about more critical and inclusive pedagogical approaches, this piece works more as an essay than as an article with metrics and closed results. This does not prevent us from pointing out the strategies that have worked best in our experience and from elaborating theoretical contributions to the field of legal education. Despite the idiosyncrasies of the Brazilian political, social, and institutional context, expressed in everyday university life, we do not understand that there is an exclusively Brazilian specificity in the stories we are going to tell. Moreover, we believe the reflections that these experiences bring can connect our perspectives with other critical approaches, reinforcing radical (rooted, situated) strategies for legal education.

This paper is divided into three parts. First, we shall reconstitute how TRAMA was formed and highlight the epistemic nodes and theoretical references that give meaning to our concepts and practices of legal education, articulating the theoretical repertories of the pedagogy of autonomy, the situated knowledge perspective, and the materialist approach (linked to the spatial turn

3 The word *trama* (*substantive*), in Portuguese, has many different meanings: artifice, trick, plot, trap, astuteness/guile, scheme, among others. We mobilised the polysemy of the term to symbolise the strategies of the project and collective through these ambivalences—*tramar* (*action*) could mean, on one hand, to weave and to entwine, but on the other hand, could mean to plot, to plan, and to scheme.

4 The 'Labá – Direito, Espaço & Política" is an interinstitutional research group (Federal University of Rio de Janeiro – UFRJ/Federal University of Paraná – UFPR/Federal University of São Paulo – UNIFESP) that develops actions of research, teaching, and extension that intended to work the relations between the elaboration of the law and the manufacturing of social space. The TRAMA is a Research and Extension Program developed in the National Faculty of Law of the Federal University of Rio de Janeiro (Faculdade Nacional de Direito da Universidade Federal do Rio de Janeiro, FND-UFRJ).

5 This excerpt is inspired by a passage which is contained in de Castro (2014).

inside of legal theory studies) into spaces of juridical and pedagogical creation. Second, we shall expose the experiences that have been responsible for giving form and substance to our perspectives of pedagogical imaginations, recounting about our spaces of encounter, conflict, and networking development—the spatial triad that composes the different strategies that the group employs inside and outside the classroom, combining activities in research, teaching, and extension. Last, we shall sketch a characterisation of what we are calling a situated pedagogy for the field of legal education.

The Epistemic Nodes and the Practices of Transgression-Consumption/Devouring

In June 2019, after finishing another semester in the jurisprudence course that is taught to freshmen students, I was approached by approximately 15 students that expressed their interest in joining, as monitors, the discipline in the following terms. Notably known as an area with limited capacity of attraction that often gains little to no appreciation by the students, in part because it is traditionally taught with a strong focus on analytic legal theory (experienced by the students as tedious and boring) and abstract discussions about the nature of the law, the students' request presented itself as a surprise. What do these students want with jurisprudence?

Subsequently, all the students that showed interest were invited to participate in a collective conversation and, during the discussion that followed, it became clear that the mobilisation around this theme arose from the affinity they felt with the methodology that was adopted throughout the course: an effort to present the most abstract themes embracing a situated perspective approach, exposing and discussing the subject through the debates that took place between the authors, encouraging the students to think and reflect upon the topics of study based on concrete cases that were presented, combining textual as well as post-textual references, and, moreover, encouraging collective works which involved bodily performances and the sharing of personal narratives, in a way that crossed the abstract encirclement of the content studied, and grounded and situated the debate in real, concrete life. After all, those students—who leave Caxias, Campo Grande, or Itaboraí, regions that are located geographically far away from the University, to arrive at Central Station—when discussing the nature of law as rules and/or principles, rather than just learn and understand these classic debates on the subject of jurisprudence, should learn how to operate this difference in practical terms so that the distances between territories and the journeys do not result in even more distinctions among different realities and individuals.

Who would have thought that the jurisprudence course could be attractive? That first collective conversation gave rise to several others and, in August of 2019, we formed TRAMA. At that time, we had ten researchers, most of them having entered the university through affirmative action policies. We dedicated ourselves to developing and deepening the discussions between law and materialism, as well as their repercussions for the reconstruction of dynamics of teaching and learning in legal education. Our very ground has been composed of young men and women, law students who mostly live far from the Central Station area, and the group supports these individuals whose desires intersect different views: they profess Afro-Brazilian and neo-Pentecostal religions, some are active in youth socialist collectives associated with left-wing political parties, they engage in community actions that aim to promote popular education, they participate in artistic movements, and act as political activists engaged in anti-racist and anti-sexist movements. The initial organisation of the group was structured in the form of a seminar and resulted in the creation of a collective, responsible for providing a space of welcome and affection to the students. As the activities developed, the group rearranged itself into a three-fold structure around different workgroups, each with its own front: popular education, research, and communication. Currently, over 30 students are part of the project and its collective, which has been directing its different workgroups towards the topic of legal education through extension action[6] with different collaborators from inside and outside of the university.

In our seminars, the evidence that we shared was that most of the topics and contents taught in the classroom did not correspond or directly relate to the daily lives of the vast majority of the students—everything was framed and presented as if the rules, from a logical standpoint, had a previous abstract existence and only then the actual flesh and bones, people, and everything else in society were posteriorly merely 'fitted' into them. In that sense, most of the subjects and courses the students take are structured as workshops that aim to offer a rationalisation of the legal logic that is employed by the State-Capital which, in Brazil, operates explicitly through a necropolitical[7] structure. Also, the extracurricular internships available do not meet the desire that the students have to learn tools and mechanisms that could enable them to fight in and against the Justice System in favour of social demands, instead operating solely as the locus for implementing the logic of maximum effectiveness in the application of the already established law, presenting this limited approach as the best possible horizon of social justice. If the standards of rights, as well as their theoretical foundations, are somewhere 'out there' (in a normative, logical, and transcendental sense), then they would be unchangeable and there would be nothing we could do about them.[8] When it comes to pedagogical

6 Public higher education in Brazil is traditionally structured into three main pillars: teaching, researching, and extension. 'Extensão universitária', a common term in Brazilian academic vocabulary, means outreach, and extension work through activities organised by the university itself but also initiatives carried out in conjunction with other institutions and social movements, aimed at a public beyond the university community.

7 Mbembe (2019).

8 Davies (2002).

practice, the repercussion of this kind of discourse manifests itself in the mobilisation of theoretical repertoires that reiterate an organisation of fixed roles between teachers and students, in which prevails a structure for transferring knowledge that reinforces a logic that Paulo Freire called 'the banking model of education'.[9]

These critical reflections about praxis, as they are developed by TRAMA, embrace and incorporate the affective components that permeate the experiences of its group members as a way of recognising the important role that the idea of 'just rage' and legitimate indignation have in the process of education, as taught by Paulo Freire. This anger that motivates the protest against social injustices, against lovelessness, against exploitation and violence, can play a highly transformative role.[10] These perceptions are responsible for fuelling feelings of indignation that have contributed, in a collective sense, to the recognition of the difficulties that hinder our effort, favouring feelings of reciprocity and fellowship, transforming the group into an important space of mutual support and fostering among its members. The collective awareness of the anger and the reasons behind it could increase our abilities to adjust some practices following the ideals of solidarity and the desire for social and political transformation.

TRAMA is situated in a vast tradition of critical legal theory, following the footsteps of authors that have consistently denounced the field of legal education and its strategies that reproduce hierarchies and shorten the horizons of justice and social emancipation.[11] We have been mobilising some of the references in the critical legal studies movement, in its different generations, to work critically on the theme of legal education, drawing inspiration from the works of authors such as Duncan Kennedy, Roberto Mangabeira Unger, Patricia Williams, Angela Harris, and Derrick Bell.[12] These critical repertoires have been reworked through their association with important Latin-American and Brazilian theoretical references that are linked with Paulo Freire's concept of Pedagogy of Autonomy and to the Law Found on The Street movement.

In our practice, this tradition is reinterpreted and reconstructed through anthropophagic practices of spatialisation and corporification:[13] it's about devouring the garments that cover and mask the real, concrete, and material dimensions of the legal discourse, absorbing part of its elements in order to resituate and reconstruct them from the perspective of the desiring bodies engaged with the emancipatory transformation of lived experience. The objective, then, is to increase the chances of success of these critical practices through

9 Freire (1998).
10 Freire (1998), p 41.
11 de Sousa (2021).
12 As just one example among many, see Kennedy (1982).
13 In regards to the relations between anthropophagy, space production, and jurisprudence, see Franzoni (2019).

an alliance with other theoretical imaginations and practical perspectives in legal education.

We have three epistemic nodes in TRAMA, the vertices from where our pedagogical imaginations and practices originate and converge: *situated knowledge*,[14] the *pedagogy of autonomy*,[15] and *legal-spatial materialism*.[16] These three lines of approach intertwine into a meshwork of concepts and practices that have been responsible for outlining the main pedagogical propositions to our course regarding the subject of jurisprudence and directed our activities of research and extension. The goal is to collectively build tools and spaces in order to prevent the students from finding themselves submerged into the conservative and elitist structure that is typical in the field of law. By taking into account the conceptual dimensions and practical efforts employed in our endeavour, we have been able to aggregate these epistemic nodes into processes that are simultaneously acts of transgression and incorporation/devouring,[17] using them as a strategy for mapping and for naming our educational theory and practice.

The transgression aspect of the experiment weaves the lines of the jurisprudence course with these pedagogical procedures, combining the Situated Knowledge approach with the Pedagogy of Autonomy, using them as epistemic, ethical, and political tools. Transgression, or to transgress, means here, first, a) the critical and reflexive dimension that goes beyond the implicit knowledge contained in the consolidated common sense, which is then employed for understanding some of the hidden assumptions that lie behind the theories that are studied, but also to provide the engagement with these theories in their explicit aspects, taking into account the political and non-neutral character of these ideas and conceptions of rights; b) second, that the exposition of the main authors, themes, and subjects of the course is done in a way to avoid a static and linear construction of ideas, doing so through a spatial and temporally oriented contextualisation, as well as through the analysis of the debates that are responsible for the development of the concepts and theories debated in class; and, finally, c) concerns the self-reflecting pedagogical posture of relating the ideas that are discussed with the perceptions and experiences of the students, building a partial path of translation and production composed of a specific approach concerning theory and practice—aware of the perspectives of race, sexuality, and class.

The 'devouring' aspect of the experiment, on the other hand, integrates and complements the first aspect, allowing the weaving of the reflexive and

14 Haraway (1988) pp 575–99.

15 In addition to the works of Paulo Freire, we have also mobilised the theoretical framework provided by bell hooks, such as hooks (1994).

16 In this sense, we refer to the theoretical movement known as critical legal geography, which combined the repertoires of critical theory with studies on the production of space, in accordance with what has been developed by Philipopoulos-Mihalopoulos (2015).

17 Here we refer to the idea of devouring oneself and others in an anthropophagic sense.

self-reflective transgressions into the strategies that are linked to the spatial turn in legal theory and its repercussion for pedagogical practice. To devour, in the anthropophagic sense intended here, means, a) to present and debate the different garments that disguise, in a discursive and practical manner, the law in illusions and simulacrums of reality, especially when it comes to those more abstract and universalist theoretical approaches; b) to absorb them in a process that simultaneously incorporates, overcomes, and reconstructs them, so that the study and analysis of the law are spatialised in a joint production situated along the very things and bodies that it actually affects; and, finally, c) to proceed in a way that multiplies the different meanings contained in the educational practice to expand the repertoire of legal education to include references and learning devices other than the traditional textual ones, adding elements such as songs, TV shows, and movies, and procedures other than the mere practice of reading and writing, which include, but are not limited to, theatrical and dancing performances.

Our experimentation with these repertories to build a situated pedagogy for teaching and learning in legal education is, therefore, both conceptual and empirical. We have been mobilising *conceptual experiments*, which themselves focus on problematising the traditional approaches concerning legal education and in proposing new ways to structure the content and making technical-aesthetic experiments, based on specific educational practices that contest and stretch the outlines of the typical banking model of education, and aim to re-elaborate the dynamics in and outside of the classroom through critical and dialogical practices.[18] We combine the possibilities that are brought about by academic freedom with the antagonistic pressures that currently exist in the extremely conservative political and social context of Brazil, in a process of constant and uninterrupted renewal of the university. Thus, our efforts seek to reconfigure and reposition the educational process in a way that escapes the conceptual binds and ties that are often responsible for limiting and depoliticising this line of study, proposing an alternative that is situated beyond the limits of the typical banking model of education that is prevalent in contemporary university education.

Legal-Pedagogical Spaces: Conflicts, Encounters, and Networking

Traditional law schools in Brazil, such as the Faculty of Law of Rio de Janeiro, tell a tale of the reproduction of prestigious social spheres that are aimed at/destined for an economic and cultural elite, in the space of academic research. These are institutions that have developed, ever since Portuguese colonisation, to educate those in power, to train the 'heirs', 'noblemen', and 'aristocrats' of a country with a vast colonial heritage, which is also prominent in legal culture.

18 Freire (1998).

Thus, legal education,[19] in a hegemonic way, is oriented towards the training of young people 'destined' to occupy prestigious and high command positions, be it in the public or private sector. The gradual change of this situation is due, above all, to the social struggles in the last ten years that have managed to institutionalise affirmative action and curriculum reform policies that gradually changed the students' profile and, partly, the contents that are taught. Nevertheless, the distance that exists between the faculty and the students is still a striking one, especially in regard to racial and class representation.

The dominant approach concerning the jurisprudence course in Brazil revolves around questions such as the debate about the scientific character of law, discussions about the nature and validity of the law, the relation between normativity and legitimacy in the face of post-conventional morality, etc. In the main universities,[20] the course is presented with an emphasis on analytical concepts and an almost exclusively Anglo-Saxon repertoire of themes and authors, with little to no incorporation of Brazilian and Latin-American legal and political debates. The main objective is usually to introduce students to the modern legal rationality, training them to 'fit' the theoretical and practical conflicts that exist in concrete legal practice, into those pre-established normative frameworks.

In dealing with such themes, contemporary legal theory is limited to the logic of consensus and normalisation, unable to grasp the logic of conflict that exists in everyday society. These theoretical approaches via analytical theory fulfil the important task of offering the technical-conceptual repertoires that imprison the normativity of law to a liberal concept of rationality. By doing so, they fail to go beyond the objective of a mere adequate implementation of the already established law. When approached from the perspective of so-called contemporary anti-positivist theories, this discussion sometimes postulates the articulation of theoretical discussions with moral and political dilemmas, without questioning the traps and pitfalls of their universalistic projects, which in

19 To those unfamiliar with legal education in Brazil, it is important to note that, in the country, law schools tend to be organised in a five-year course that is divided into theoretical disciplines (located, mostly, in the first years of the course, in which the jurisprudence class itself is situated) and dogmatic and practical ones. These courses are aimed at a 'generic' professional education inside the field of law.

20 To cite some examples of this, let us take a look at the set of subjects that compose jurisprudence courses (also often called e.g. Introduction to Law or General Theory of Law) available on the websites of some of Brazil's most prestigious universities, USP, UFMG, and UFRJ, in this order: (i) 01. The Universality of the Legal Phenomenon, 02. Law as an Object of Knowledge, 03. The Dogmatic Science of Law and Its Theoretical Status, 04. Analytical Dogmatic or Legal Science as a Legal Norm Theory; (ii) I—Legal Norm Theory, II—Legal Order Theory, III—Legal Technique; (iii) Law and Knowledge. The Concept of Law: plurality of points of view. Dogmatic and Zetetic. The Problem of the Public Law/Private Law Dichotomy. Law and other normative orders. Legal Norm Theory. Logical Structure of Legal Norms. The Legal Relation. Intertemporal Law. Forms of Legal Production.

most cases do not go beyond the established truths of an elitist, white, and patriarchal humanism. There is an insistence on focusing on a formal apprehension of the so-called 'civilizational advantages' of modern law—which presents itself as a remedy against arbitrariness—, but which in reality tends to be an approach that is not spatially situated. The result is alienation and depoliticisation.

This rough sketch of the field of jurisprudence highlights the predominant elements of the traditional approaches but fails to present their important fissures, disputes, insufficiencies, and discontinuities. It is important to note that legal education concerning the topic of jurisprudence operates, above all, as an initiation rite to the secrets that control the conceptualisation of law in liberal rationality: *the good handling of theory and technique will transform the student into an artisan of the rule of law, simultaneously an accomplice and co-responsible for its implementation and maintenance. In this caricature, the hierarchical transference of knowledge is the preponderant educational procedure, with an almost exclusive focus on unilateral practices and expositive lectures. The law professor is that imponent figure that speaks gallantly about the ontological, epistemic, and political reasons concerning the topic of jurisprudence.*

It is not surprising, then, that the jurisprudence course is not usually able to entice the interest of students. Traditional methods and approaches, frequently considered as boring and tedious, rather than drawing the students to the topics discussed in the classroom, promote detachment and disinterest. To rebel against this traditionalism is much more an ethical and political choice, that repositions the conceptual and practical starting points, than a mere adoption of an 'anti-method' focused on demonstrating that everything is necessarily a social construction. To deify or demonise technique and science is a dangerously wrong way of thinking, as Paulo Freire reminds us. Thus, the partial rejection of formalism matters, above all, because this formalism is responsible for deactivating, in the teaching-learning process, the spark of creativity and enthusiasm that stimulates the kind of thought and action necessary for the construction of a different world and a better future.[21]

Transgression, in a pedagogical sense, means taking seriously the libidinal commitment to agree upon/incorporate truths and techniques—exercises in legal fiction—in order to build other and better truths and techniques. This effort requires the consumption of knowledge and its traditional repertoires, not to deny them *in totum*, but to absorb its matters in a way radically situated within the horizon of issues that exist in our daily lives, evidenced by the experiences shared by the students. For analytical purposes, we have organised the different procedures and resources into three contiguous and overlapping

21 In this sense, we highlight the important work of Professor Philippe Oliveira de Almeida: see de Almeida (2018).

pedagogical spaces or 'contest zones':[22] (i) spaces of conflict; (ii) spaces of meeting; and, (iii) networking spaces.[23]

Spaces of conflict. The spatial dimension of conflict intends to focus on the importance of difference and contradiction in the teaching-learning process. What has been possible to do—and weave—evidences our strategies (conceptual and practical) for the spatialisation of the main themes of the course, doing so through a work that combines the presentation of the epistemological basis that underlies these hegemonic theories of law, engaging with the debates held between the authors, and, finally, with the critical inflection of the reflections developed through the analysis of actual cases.

Based on the set of subjects that parametrises the jurisprudence course in the National Faculty of Law of Rio de Janeiro, the course has been divided into four main themes: Law and Science, Legal Form, The Production of the Law, and The Sources of Law. In that sense, the course offers the epistemological basis needed for the situated comprehension of the authors and their discourses, covering these topics through debate with contemporary theorists and lines of thought. We begin with discussions about what is a theory, what are the roles that the abstract mediations, language, and discourses have in our comprehension of reality and the legal phenomenon. In addition to this, there is the choice to present the topic related to the scientificity of law and the legal form through the debate between theoretical schools that are affiliated with German idealism and historical materialism. And then we introduce the theme of the sources and production of law through the development of the linguistic turn in philosophy and its repercussion for the field of analytical and moral theories.

This epistemic strategy is also a pedagogical one. By relating the field of jurisprudence to broader debates that were responsible for shaping the modern paradigm and its hegemonic discursive practices, students have the opportunity to situate the course's themes into conceptual, historical maps, becoming more attentive to the responsibilities that come from adopting a certain paradigm of understanding and being able to perceive the discontinuities and conflicts, both theoretical and practical, that exist in legal rationality. By emphasising the contradictory nature of the field of legal theories and the themes discussed in it, we have opted to deepen our study concerning the epistemic nature of law and the limits of normativity through the debates that took place between the authors. For example, the debate between Hans Kelsen and Evgeni Pachukanis concerning the scientific nature of law and the foundations of its normativity; the discussion between Herbert Hart and Ronald Dworkin about the nature of law, the role of theory, and the limits of jurisdictional activity; and, finally, the debates that are developed by contemporary critical theories that politicise the

22 Haraway (2016).

23 This spatial triad is in dialogue with the ruminations about space that are developed by the geographer Doreen Massey in the book *For Space*: Massey (2005).

limits of normativity and legal discourse when it comes to the reflection (and effect) upon social change and transformation.

These debates operate as a gateway that makes it possible to relate the themes discussed with the Brazilian and Latin-American movements, in a state of constant, difficult, and inglorious, anti-colonialist struggle. In that sense, this strategy involves the constant application of educational practices that situate the course's themes—the debates between the authors and their conceptual repertoire—in the universe of radical political and legal conflicts. As an example of such an approach, we have been working on the following cases: a decision by the Brazilian Supreme Court that has declared constitutional a state law that exempted the rituals of religions of African Ancestry/Afro-Brazilian religions from the hypotheses of animal abuse; the creation, also by the Brazilian Supreme Court, of a criminal offence concerning the practice of homophobia, justifying this decision by considering it to be a crime analogous to racism; the decision of a state court that validated the limits of a legal agreement made between the victims of a large environmental crime and the mining companies that were responsible for it, imposing obstacles to the legal representation of those affected by this disaster and also limiting the scope of monetary compensation; and the debates held between scientists, in the hearings of the Supreme Court, concerning the different and conflicting views about the decriminalisation of abortion.

The aim of this project is not so much to apply these theoretical reflections to real experiences, but rather to experiment with these theoretical-practical reflections using conceptual parameters as guidelines to interpret cases, gaining greater awareness and a better understanding of the complexities involving the practice of law. These procedures are experiments evaluated collectively: the students are randomly selected to answer a specific question about the case in discussion and the rest of the class is entitled to provide up to three voluntary contributions, with the final grade being assigned to the class as a whole. This experience, which aims to move away from a logic of competitiveness and individualism, has proved itself a great opportunity to watch students develop collaborative study practices, promoting affective bonds between the students.

Meeting spaces. The spatial dimension of encounter highlights the importance of having a multiplicity of perspectives, simultaneously, in order to forge better educational dynamics. As the main pedagogical practice, we seek to embody reflective strategies into ethical postures and conducts that increase the engagement of the different individuals involved in the teaching-learning process. We have been plotting/weaving and mobilising some procedures such as the correlation between the student's geographic trajectories with the course's trajectories; the engagement with a wide range of teaching repertories; and the use of the body and its different senses in the construction of the student's knowledge and awareness.

On the first days of the class, a mosaic is collectively built with the class with the different routes that the students take from their homes until they reach the Central Station, highlighting the means of transport and the distance that each one has to travel. This ludic and playful dynamic presents itself as a means to cut through the shyness and initial discomfort of the students, who will perceive themselves more or less with other colleagues, creating a space that allows for jokes, ironies, and non-belligerent conflicts. Furthermore, this pedagogical strategy also wants to 'devour' the institutional labels of traditional legal education that are responsible for transforming the different individuals, as they pass through the classroom door, into a fictional, homogenous, and pasteurised group of students. The transgressive practice, which destabilises this homogenous fiction, can activate a circuit of affection and reflection that will contribute to the presentation of the methods that will be utilised throughout the course, inviting the students to move from the established common sense into an embodied discussion of the different theories.

This theoretical-practical path, which follows the lines of the propositions of situated knowledge that were developed by Donna Haraway, recounts stories that intertwine different authors, theories and experiences, building networks of partial connections, seeking to translate and impart knowledge between the very diverse composition of students in our classroom. Furthermore, different people also experience the concepts described in legal categories (marriage, citizenship, crime, human rights) in markedly different ways, often treated through generic and objectifying approaches in the field of legal doctrine. The established practice concerning legal education tends to mask and hide unquestioned social privileges related to the different ways in which people integrate themselves into social relationships, considering the intersection of different elements such as race, gender, class, and sexuality. Educational practices should enable individuals to question the existence of a supposedly logical, normative, transcendent, and previous plan which would contain theories and/or social norms, in a manner abstracted from social relations. In doing so, these practices multiply the perspectives with which the students experience theories and norms.

These pedagogical choices are crucial in raising students' awareness, making it possible for them to understand how certain foundational assumptions of these theories can tell us a lot about ourselves, our culture, and why we think the way we do about law.[24] Moreover, the exchange of multiple experiences between the different students from different regions, religions, traditions, and social conditions, enables an ethical and political reorientation among students, in a way that can reconfigure the distribution of power in our society.[25] As an example, on different occasions, the development and application of these

24 Davies (2002).

25 A similar experience is reported by bell hooks in the aforementioned work and has served us as a source of inspiration and motivation.

pedagogical practices provided the basis for subversive and provocative discussions about topics such as meritocracy, structural racism, and economic inequality.

The reports provided by the different students concerning their experiences on the cases studied and the debates that were carried out allowed us to gain awareness about several social dynamics that are usually made invisible, as well as an understanding of their connection with the production of law in a way that simultaneously combines compassion and criticism.[26] Students with physical disabilities refused to be limited to that social stereotype of victims, instead choosing to question the practical and symbolic limits of their capabilities; students, when confronted with complex situations, problematised 'identity' as the sole foundation grounding oppression; the dilemmas about economic equality and freedom of religion drew attention to the structural dimension, material and immaterial, of racism in Brazilian society and specifically in legal education. As bell hooks, Angela Harris, and Paulo Freire all ponder, the exercise of affective capacity and otherness (to put yourself as another, visualising and experiencing things from this perspective) presents itself as a fundamental practice for the ethical development of the teaching-learning dynamic.

This powerful association between reflection and emotion is developed through the mobilisation of the different pedagogical strategies that aim to reorient the use of the student's senses in the teaching-learning process. In addition to the usual textual and bibliographic materials, other sources are employed as pedagogical references available in non-traditional formats, such as podcasts, videos, and a collaborative musical playlist entitled O Direito & o direito (The Law and the law), which serve as the basis for the final evaluation of the course. In this last evaluation, the students must present, as a group, a collective performance and/or develop a project related to the topics and themes that were studied in the classroom. The objective, then, is to displace the teaching-learning dynamic from the practice of mere memorisation, repetition, and reproduction, articulating other senses and stimulating the student's creativity as well as the use of other mechanisms of perception and learning. Although it may initially be perceived as a reason for anxiety among students, since it deals with a different pedagogical approach from what they are used to, this mode of evaluation shows itself to be a great way to promote cohesion among students, proportioning insightful and memorable moments involving creative practices such as singing, artistic performances, board games, video arts, all contributing to awaken the passion necessary for a purposeful and effective learning process.

At the centre of this expansion of pedagogical strategies, resources, and platforms, TRAMA developed, during this period of remote and online teaching that was brought upon us by the COVID-19 pandemic, three actions that

26 Harris (2012) pp 326–52.

sought to ensure the continuous activities of the group. The objective was to broaden and deepen the reflections on the political, legal, and social repercussions of the COVID-19 pandemic. With this in mind, we held a series of open seminars entitled *Tramando Com* (Weaving With) and published on the group's social media a special series dedicated to the critical analysis of the health crisis. Furthermore, understanding the importance of listening, learning, and discussing these topics from the perspective of the students themselves, we organised the *NósEntreTramas*, an open seminar based on texts and films. In these self-organised meetings, we proposed an exchanging of functions between professors and students in a way that challenges traditional roles, and, by doing so, were able to improve the seminars dynamics: there was a significant increase in the student's engagement in debates, students that rarely stepped up, and the whole group committing collectively to the quality of the seminars.

Network spaces. The spatial dimension of networking highlights the importance of the process of sharing in teaching-learning dynamics. The inseparability that exists between academic research, teaching, and programmes of academic extension is an inescapable reality in Brazil and a principle that organises our pedagogical proposal. It is through the lines that we weave with our partners that we materialise this project (those with whom we do what we do) and redirect the meanings of our practices (what and why we do what we do). Furthermore, through TRAMA we have articulated a research network in partnership with two other research groups, forming the *Estudos Jurídicos Críticos* (Critical Legal Studies) collective project whose main objective is to produce, disseminate, popularise, and update studies that link critical thinking to the field of law.[27] And, finally, the TRAMA collective also develops its own extension programme through a partnership with the social platform that is responsible for building the International People's Tribunal of the Justice System.[28]

The different projects of academic research that are developed through Labá help us in the definition of which topics and pedagogical strategies will be used in our courses. Our work in the field of people's lawyering allows us to build projects in conjunction with social movements that are involved in real and concrete struggles for social rights. Let us present two examples that show this: through the *ContraCorrentes* project and a partnership with the *Movimento dos Atingidos Por Barragens* (Movement of Persons Affected by Dams) and acting in defence of the rights of those that were affected by environmental crimes, we presented, in our classroom, a discussion about the sources of law and the complexity of defining the formal and material contents in legal reparation through

27 The ECJ collective is a partnership between Labá – Direito, Espaço & Política and the groups CERCO (coordinated by Professor Philippe Almeida, FND-UFRJ) and Pura Teoria do Direito (PTD) (coordinated by Professor André Coelho, FND-UFRJ).

28 *V.* https://tribunalpopulardajustica.org.br/

monetary compensation; through the *Cartografias Jurídicas* (Legal Cartographies) project, in articulation with the *Campanha Nacional de Despejo Zero* (National Campaign of Zero Eviction), and in defence of the right of adequate housing, we established a debate concerning the validity and legitimacy of law, as well as the regressive practices of the Judiciary in eviction actions.

The experiences in the field of people's lawyering also had repercussions on the development of TRAMA's actions alongside the *Tribunal Popular Internacional do Sistema de Justiça* (International People's Tribunal of the Justice System). The People's Tribunal is a platform gathering different entities from both civil society and the universities engaged in building collective processes of mobilisation, investigation, and reporting of rights violations perpetrated by the Brazilian Justice System itself. Our collective is one of the groups that integrate this coalition and, as such, has been developing actions that aim to expand the spaces of education and debate concerning topics such as access to justice and the struggle for the recognition and protection of rights, as a way to develop and strengthen academic research and legal action but also to assist politically in drawing communication strategies to make these struggles more visible.

By promoting the student's engagement with politically active segments of civil society, TRAMA also contributes to the politicisation of traditional legal education. The student's repertoire of action is broadened and there is a process of development of political subjectivities capable of producing collective responses to confront the situation of constant rights violations. The conditions under which our projects have been developed also reflect the social-political situation in which the educational system is under attack: dwindling financial resources and the lack of research grants force us to rely mostly on the voluntary, activist work by faculty and students.

Coda: Situated Pedagogy for Legal Education

Currently, Brazil experiences what has been conventionally called the *Crise da Nova República* (New Republic Crises),[29] being governed by a conservative coalition led by the far-right, a declared enemy of democracy and human rights. The central role of the Justice System and its legal institutions in enabling the severe political blows that we have suffered makes the ethical and transgressive politicisation of legal education a fundamental strategy for carrying out an analysis of our contemporary situation. In face of this challenging scenario, aggravated by precariousness and the COVID-19 pandemic, the act of betting

29 The *New Republic* is the name given to the political and institutional process in the country that began with the redemocratisation process in 1988, which ended the dictatorial government.

on a situated pedagogy is a way to expose and discuss the 'glass ceiling' of legal institutions, while also discussing ways to rebuild its 'workshop floor'.[30]

The TRAMA's approaches, which intend to connect and unfold the university community's social context and the concrete situation of the faculties of law, are the actual basis of understanding the effectiveness of our situated pedagogy method. Every procedure in our legal education strategy is an attempt to create powerful pedagogical mechanisms that relate the political crisis to the epistemic crisis—on how the crisis of political hegemony and its relationship with the justice system produces and is produced by legal education, to address these multiple crises from the perspective of the bodies that experience them, seeking strategies to ensure the well-being of students during the course, and to guarantee the theoretical advantage of intersectional approaches, which allow us to combine the critique of law with the concrete life of students.

Understanding the situated pedagogy in legal education as a combination of spaces of conflict, meeting spaces, and network spaces is an attempt to create a 'contestation zone' as a pedagogical praxis. When we defy the traditional positions of all the subjects located in legal education—the student, the professor, the authors, the things (materials, references), the method, the partners (social movements, civil society organisations)—we can also challenge the main register of what it is to teach law. As a zone—space—of contestation—conflict, meeting, and networking—the educational practice is necessarily collective, wittingly open to their surroundings and more engaged with social justice platforms. This strategy of legal education allows students to develop criticisms on the bases provided by the theories studied, mapping the relations between the predominant hegemonic discursive logic and its correlated, concrete, power dynamics.

Moreover, the strategies that attach criticism and emotion allow the subjects to examine their universe of references (neighbourhood, family, clothing, food), transforming the education process into an experience of enthusiasm and pleasure, as defended by bell hooks. A critique of hegemonic ideologies, or legal atmospheres,[31] needs to mobilise alternative affects (senses and feelings) in order to reorient our commitments to the world. We can say with Paulo Freire, bell hooks, Angela Harris, and Philippe Almeida that all education is a sentimental education, and, therefore, a proposal for critical legal education needs to be situated and based on the deepest hopes of students.

TRAMA's effort is a journey that evokes the importance of laying down a path in walking and struggling against alienation in everyday life. This strategy of situated pedagogy invites us to think that the future is not given, our fates are not yet defined, and we can—and must—take control of them. A multiplying,

30 I owe the formulation of this insightful/astute expression to my colleague and friend Philippe Almeida.

31 As named by Andreas Philipopoulos-Mihalopoulos (2015).

daily practice in the teaching-learning dynamics is part of that. Without giving in to an illusory romanticism, but adopting an embodied view, this materialist-spatial dimension evokes the necessity to think and act in a way that embraces the situated perspectives on law (the bodies involved, the individual's position in society, the concrete conflicts), in a way of teaching and learning about its transformation. In a kind of tropicalist-romanticism, the situated pedagogy approach unites us through anthropophagy, which absorbs, transgresses, and 'devours' in the very same act—'*Down with the vegetable elites. In communication with the soil*'.[32]

References

Philippe Oliveira de Almeida (2018) 'A Faculdade de Direito como uma oficina de utopias: Um relato de experiência' 72 *Rev. Fac. Direito UFMG, Belo Horizonte* 481–511, jan./jun. https://doi.org/10.12818/P.0304-2340.2018v72p481

Oswald de Andrade (1999) 'The Cannibalist Manifesto' *Third Text* 92–5, https://doi.org/10.1080/09528829908576784.

Eduardo Batalha Viveiros de Castro (2014). *Cannibal Metaphysics*, Univocal Publishing.

Margaret Davies (2002). *Asking the Law Question*. The Dissolution of Legal Theory. 2nd Edition, Lawbook Co.

Julia Franzoni (2019) 'Geografia jurídica tropicalista: A crítica do materialismo jurídico-espacial' 10 *Revista Direito e Práxis* 2923–67. https://doi.org/10.1590/2179-8966/2019/45692.

Paulo Freire (1998). *Pedagogy of Freedom: Ethics, Democracy and Civic Courage*, Rowman & Littlefield Publishers.

Donna Haraway (1988) '*Situated Knowledges*: The Science Question in Feminism and the Privilege of Partial Perspective' 14 *Feminist Studies* 575–99.

Donna Haraway (2016). *Staying with the Trouble: Making Kin in the Chthulucene*, Duke University Press.

Angela Harris (2012) 'Compassion and Critique' 1(3) *Columbia Journal of Race and Law* 326–52.

bell hooks (1994). *Teaching to Transgress: Education as the Practice of Freedom*, Routledge.

José Geraldo de Sousa Junior (ed) (2021). *O Direito Achado na Rua: Introdução crítica ao direito como liberdade*, OAB Editora; Editora Universidade de Brasília.

Duncan Kennedy (1982) 'Legal Education and the Reproduction of Hierarchy' 32(4) *Journal of Legal Education* 591–615.

Doreen Massey (2005) *For Space*, SAGE.

Achille Mbembe (2019) *Necropolitics*, Duke University Press.

Andreas Philipopoulos-Mihalopoulos (2015). *Spatial Justice: Body, Lawscape, Atmosphere: Space, Materiality, and the Normative*, Routledge.

32 de Andrade (1999).

Chapter 8

The Comedy of *Corpus Iuris*

Peter Goodrich

It will seem odd, but that of course is the point, to begin by attending *au jus* or to the sauce of law.[1] Such peculiarity is, however, a necessary corrective to the spuriously theological gravity of legality which is lodged paradoxically, as we know, in the limbo of abstraction, in the purgatory of dogma and the incorporeal obnubilations of doctrine. Start then with what Jabet memorably depicts as Lord Brougham's obstinate nose, the unique parchment proboscis of the famed judge, reformer, and jurist:

> It is a most eccentric Nose; it comes within no possible category; it is like no other man's nose; it has good points and bad points, and no point at all. When you think it is going right on for a Roman, it suddenly becomes a Greek; when you have written it down Cogitative, it becomes as sharp as a knife. At first view it seems Celestial; but Celestial it is not; its celestiality is not heavenward, but right out into illimitable space, pointing—we know not where.[2]

It is, in the old language of juristic comedy, the legal *facetiae*, a wax nose (*naris cereum*), a protuberance that will bend with the winds of whichever cause has attracted its affections, whether it be by payment, interest, or other affiliation. Although unclassifiable in any nasological concordance, it is not an exception to the system because, to continue *au point*, the nose nonetheless corresponds to the character.

Admitting that by virtue of situation it must indeed be a nose, the question to be raised, fond to Lawrence Sterne, to Jabet and to pataphysicians, is that of the role of this pre-eminent body part in the practice, which is to say the performance of law. It twitches, it smells and through insufflation by means

1 For the sake of detail, the pun—*au jus*—is from Darling (1879) Preface, but the source of the sauce is Horace (*est operae pretium duplicis pernoscere juris naturam*—loosely translating as: a double scrutiny pays off for a compound sauce).

2 This finely satirical expostulation is to be found in Jabet (1852) p 105. The original source, a nose by any other name will proboscate as well, is Warwick (1848) p 152.

DOI: 10.4324/9781003179283-11

of the dual avenues of the nostrils, senses, by metaphor and matterphor, the aura, character, motive, and affective trajectory of the case and thereby the meaning of the rule. The flared point is that the puisne pugnozzle or suffragan snoutfig of the lawyer will do justice only if it can combine wit and judgement, humour and seriousness, and thus align the body with its reasons, so as to admit the sensory quality of all determinations. The question, now posed, for legal education, for the induction and training of 'youth eager for law', is thus that of inducting noses, of preparing the senses and training the body for the work of the juridical. It is a holistic and material project that has lengthy forebears within the epistemic and jurisliterary tradition of law although I will start in the 18th century, with Vico and the new science or more specifically his lectures on legal education. It is in the discussion of pedagogy that we find a reference to universities of the body and by implication at least to an appreciation of the corporeality of learning and law which recognises that the senses and the sensory are an integral part of any effective and affective apprehension of legality.

It is in discussing legal education, the formation of the jurist and office of the lawyer that Vico expounds a dualistic theory of juridical becoming which distinguishes abstraction and incorporation, vacuity, and materiality. The bulk of those that train as lawyers is far from enthusiastic. For Vico, and it not so different today, it was parental pressure, desire for status (vainglory) or wealth, and we should add an idealistic aspiration to improve the world, that were the propulsive factors in entering law school.[3] Each purpose is external to law or at least to questions of legal structure and philological proficiency, code and cases, that constitute the curriculum. At such a young age, in other words, with motives as extraneous or chimerical as those that propel the neophyte, the apprehension of law is inevitably marginal, wholly abstract and at most partial. It is an oneiric experience, an unremembered and hazy non-encounter, often a somewhat traumatic collision with an algebra of rules. For Vico this meant that the juridical remained predominantly external and extraneous, an abstract mirage, a sign of status, a set of tokens for manipulation rather than an authentic form of life or embodied office.[4]

It was thus for Vico only those who returned to legal studies on their own account, who learned law a second time without extraneous pressures or venal distractions, that would come to understand the legal in its mobile and performative, interior and living senses of an embodied mode of knowing and practice in the world. It is after all Vico who also remarks in the new science that it is only '[m]en of limited ideas take law for what the words expressly

3 Vico (1993) Oration VI, p 126: 'Hence it happens that as long as the respect due to their fathers binds them, they continue to pursue those studies unwillingly and with disdain and do not cultivate them either seriously or with enthusiasm'. For a more modern study of parents as the force behind choosing to study law, see Cownie (2004).

4 An argument that in many respects mirrors that of the Latin language, operative more as a sign than in comprehension and use during this era. See Wacquet (2013).

say'.[5] His point is poetic and probabilistic: encounter creates law which is the manifestation of normative judgement in particularistic contexts and directed at uniquely evolving events. It cannot be certain in any mathematical sense but has rather to be a sensory apprehension of the living image and immediacy. Lord Brougham's nose is part and passion of legal judgement providing, as it must, a comedic human and corporeal element to decision, a reminder of the comical in the casuistical. The university of the body, which theatrical jurisprudence has recently also revivified, inveighs a sense of the importance of affect to knowing as an activity, a routine and performance that acts out an interior understanding. It is the sensibility of the knower that affect theory endeavours to manifest and it is this aspect of the university of the body that will be parsed and pursued, beginning with that extreme that takes the form of the dialectic, already referenced, of gravity and levity, solemnity, and laughter.

Emerging out of a monastic context the early modern tradition was founded upon the twin axes of decorum and reverence. The hierarchical order of law required even the judge to pronounce their determinations 'with downcast eyes', to respect hierarchy, follow the path and stay in the shadow of sovereign and divinity. The order of laws ran from divine to natural to royal and then to common in a trajectory that required an embodiment of deference and deferral to the *hieros* of higher causes. For reformers and recusants alike, government was a matter of gravity and thus solemnity of occasion dictated a constant obeisance to the superior authority of the various emblems, figures, and dictions of the living voices of law. The norm required a mood, an affect of melancholic composure and sombre seriousness of address and discourse. The catholic Edward Stillingfleete in the aptly named *Irenicum* was most direct and dispositive on the necessity of solemnity and the dismissal of 'any Ceremonies, Actions, or Gestures, which tend to the discomposing of men's Spirits, are upon that account to be exploded out of any religious Societies'.[6] The threatening lightness of act or address that was to be conflagrated out of social propriety was to be so jettisoned because it 'either rarifies mens spirits too much into a superficial lightnesse and vanitie of spirit; or else sinks them too much below the command of reason into the power of unruly passions'.[7] Reason, it turns out, like law, is conceived to be free of passion. It is a point that is stressed emotively in terms of the expulsion and outlawing of certain vain and unnecessary affects and most particularly enthusiasm which finds expression in excitement, dance, and laughter.

Where Stillingfleete demands decency and decorum, the Cambridge divine and reformer, Dr Henry More, is more direct in attacking or 'unridling this

5 Vico (1984) p 93. (cix).
6 Stillingfleete (1662) p 93.
7 Stillingfleete (1662) p 94.

Riddle of *Enthusiasm*'.[8] In a polemic of paradoxical verve More castigates enthusiasm as the irreligious, delirious, and narcotic pursuit of idols, variously depicted as wild philosophies, misconceived inspirations, witchcraft, paganism, and sorcery. Enthusiasm is, in sum, unchristian and the cure for this distemper and disease is trinitarian: submission to the will of God through the triad of temperance, humility, and reason.[9] For all its sectarian flaws and monotheistic blindness, More's work does have the insight of a work that addresses the power of affects and the force of imagination as emanating from and impacting through the body. Wild judgements, ecstasy and joy, laughter, fervour, and zeal are physical expressions of delirium or possession by other gods. The attack on 'enthusiasme' is 'resolved into *Complexion* or the present Temper or Distemper of the body arising from natural causes that necessarily act thereupon'.[10] It is a 'tenour of the Body' and in a longer passage, More says more: 'Enthusiasts for the most part are intoxicated with vapours from the lowest region of their Body … inspired through the power of certain exhalations breathed from those caverns they have their recesse in'.[11] Respiration, vapours, the entry and exodus of the spirit, humours that accost the blood, 'Paroxysms', and the 'Apoplectical' are all engagements of the corporeal and encounters of the body with air and substance. So too are dreams manifested in the sleeping body, imaginations in darkness.

It is the shadowy, tenebrous and nebulous, obscure and umbrageous character of the affects that are excluded by the Christian dogma, by what is expressly termed the judicious expression of emotions, the *oikonomia* of affect, that merits more extensive analysis. The university of the body is seemingly cribbed, cabined, and confined by a unitary and highly restrictive concept of obedience to a bodily norm of affective restraint and of holding back so as to allow the superiors of spirit and law to lead the way. Weeping and laughter are alike deemed extremes of bodily rapture that betray a wild zeal and delirious fervour, not spirit, More at one point says, but flatulence.[12] The polemical antinomy between true faith and false gods, between the judicious and the inebriate imaginations of enthusiasm carry with them an affective tensor and opposition. The joy and triumph of the spirit are juxtaposed to 'misconceived inspiration', to 'narcotical extasie', to disease, distemper, and imposture of imagination, all of which suffer not light but lightness of affect and action. Heretical faith manifests in images, dreams, and visions, and is depicted variously as inebriation, '*fantastrie*' or the 'strong spirit of *Phantastrie*'.[13]

8 More (1656) A7 (To the Reader).

9 More (1656) p 51. Vico (2015) makes a similar point about fantasy and laughter out of a mix of polemical ire directed at a critic, and in defence of the Roman Catholic faith.

10 More (1656) p 7.

11 More (1656) p 39.

12 More (1656) p 17.

13 More (1656) pp 7, 23.

The attack upon bodily knowledges leads to a denunciation, technically an antirrhetic pitched against the emotions as irrational and misleading. The examples could be lengthily expanded but the point, which Nietzsche of course also makes at length, is that passion as corporeal knowledge, heated 'architectonical' feelings, love of the world and manifestations of the flesh are to be denounced as threatening to the proper sobriety and solemnity of faith, sovereignty and law. The enthusiast is too emotive, too eloquent, and expansive in their view and at one juncture is dismissed as a Poet 'an Enthusiast in jest', whose rhapsodies are but fits and figments but not truth.[14] Theological dogma aside, it is the affective aura of the judicious and of legality, of sovereign and law, that becomes the emotional induction and inculcated deportment or bodily posture of the proper person of the student. Lightness and jest, levity and comedy are forced under the cloak of syllogism and sombre abstraction, rule and putative reasons, the body tense, sedentary, and docile. For the sages of common law, the corporeal was to be transcended, the flesh both waste and wasted and, as the immortal Reverend Cooper observes: 'it is a common saying in the universities, that, in order to succeed in [the study of law], a man must have an *iron head*, and *leaden posterior*'.[15] It would seem thus that for the young jurist, and across the spectrum of connotations of body parts, learning law entails a gluteal training in passivity, a sedimentation in the sedentary, and a substantial degree of becoming an ass.[16]

The derrière is the other face, but one which, even in the case of Venus Callipyge, lacks a nose. Neither nostrils nor tip for the formation of judgement and expression of wit. The sedentary does not dance and sedimentation suggests a quietus of the corporeal and for lawyers the sleeping wisdom of the text, the humourless dust of bookish learning and filing clerks:

> And at numerous points, the intolerably limited nature of linguistic communication is made apparent, for instance in discussing the inability of words to convey the horror of falling down an elevator shaft, or the meaning of 'ha ha ha' in a text (which, of course, denotes laughter and not someone actually saying 'ha' three times).[17]

The lawyer cannot be an enthusiastic ass, neither demonstratively passionate nor vividly witty. The theologico-juridical dictates, to veer into my topic, gain expression in the common law doctrine of impossibility and here specifically the *casus fortuitus* of comedy. In 1936 the Café de Paris in London, and already we can see that we are headed for trouble, employed a trio of comedians, a

14 More (1656) p 20.
15 Cooper (1869) p 22.
16 A similar point is made in terms of 'petrified pedagogy', by Giddens (2021).
17 Giddens (2021) p 38.

troupe of light entertainers as the expression goes, to perform at the Café for four weeks, in January 1936.[18] The contract had a termination clause allowing severance if the comedians should breach the Lord Chamberlain's regulations, cause a complaint to be lodged to the Lord Chamberlain or fail to perform for three days. On 20 January 1936, the King, George V, who was ill, was reported to have taken a serious turn for the worse and close to midnight on the 20th his physician, somewhat controversially, ended his life. When the comedians arrived at the Café on the evening of the 20th, before the King died, they were told the Café was closed and were turned away. They were barred from performing for the rest of the week. The comedians sued for a week's wages, £300.

The defence pleaded was that of impossibility. Having failed to play for three days, the contract on its face allowed termination. In relaying the facts, the Court notes that the performances 'were of a humorous character'. It also notes that there was no 'public mourning clause' in the agreement and so the question of whether the refusal to let the comedians perform was justified fell to be decided by default or in more contemporary argot, by implication. Could the judge, MacNaghten J, read into the contract an implied term, relieving the owner of the Café from their contractual obligation to permit the performers doing what he had contracted them to do, during a period of mourning, and so justify termination. One avenue of doctrinal argument pursued in the case was that the contract, properly interpreted, could be said to include, by imputation, a clause which stipulated 'tiger days excepted' or in this instance, and more specifically, 'king's death precluding'?[19] In the instant case, in light but not lightness of the circumstances, the death, impending or actual, of the sovereign, the agreement allowed for the determination that just such a clause had to be added to the agreement, quasi-contractually or by fiction of law. It transpires that in common law, as a matter of doctrine, comedy was impossible both before the monarch's death, when the King's condition 'was very serious', and on the day that followed his demise. In the words of the Judge, 'it was not reasonably possible for the defendants to allow the performance to be given'. Humour, lightness, celebration, the vivacity of laughter, and event of comedy were thus expressly held to be impossible on two nights of the week of the King's demise, but not subsequently. Payment for the rest of the week was so ordered.

It is an intriguing example of *casus fortuitus*, or of the maxim *lex non cogit ad impossibilia*. It is a prohibition of enthusiasm, a ban on levity, an explicit expulsion of the humorous and, by extension, of that embodiment of the comedic, the distortion of the face, pectoral collapse, and juddering of the diaphragm

18 *Minnevitch v Café de Paris (Londres)* (1936) 1 All. ER 884.

19 'Tiger days excepted' is from Lord Reid's judgement in *Davis v Fareham Urban District Council* [1956] AC 696, 720, citing Lord Sands in *James Scott & Sons v Del Sel* [1922] SC 592, 597.

that breaking into laughter occasions.[20] To weep is permitted, although in modest moderation, but laughter is a one-way street. The 'tiger days excepted' clause is an instance of implausibility according to Lord Sands in *Scott v Del Sel*. In this hypothetical, a tiger has escaped from a menagerie and killed the 'milkgirl' who therefore fails to deliver the milk. An implied condition that the 'milkgirl' not be devoured by escaped felines is in Lord Sands' opinion too implausible to be imputed by pious fiction of law. The milk, though spilled, must nonetheless be delivered or the breaching party milked or mulcted in damages. The contract would not be frustrated or that at least is one reading of the case which involved a stipulation in the agreement that all questions of contract go to arbitration. Performing their comedic routine for the requisite period in the agreed location would seem by similar logic not to be precluded by the contract and implying a condition that the King be alive, or a clause excepting public mourning seems equally implausible. If such is the case, the pious fiction of frustration of contract by virtue of an exculpatory implied term is inapplicable because implausible and there remains only the direct assertion that it is impossible to engage in jape, jest, jocundity or joke when the King is either imminently dying or dead. As a matter of contract this seems bizarre. It is not the performers who have croaked, and they are physically fully able to take to the stage. The owner of the Café can certainly pay them. As for the viewers, one can admit easily enough that laughter can be involuntary, but no-one is forcing the melancholic to attend the show. The impossibility is theologico-juridical, a symbolic state of exception but one that is arguably predicated upon a dogmatic error. As Kantorowicz pointed out, the King's body natural may have departed but their mystic body continues, the royal 'I and I' subsists.[21] Symbolically, which is also to say dogmatically, the King is not dead but lives on in its mystic estate while the body of the Christian monarch is, in doctrine at least, in a better place. Certainly, in any updated version of the theory of the two bodies, it is the populace that continues, that embodies the 'royal remains', a communal sovereignty and can do so with a more contemporary sensibility of levity and a profane apprehension of the ambiguity or plurality of cracking up.[22] Relief, release, and respect come in many forms, including laughter and play.

The emergent question is that of whether the emotions should continue their institutional ambulation under the deferential yoke of sovereignty and the solemn sign of Saturn. Deportment, disposition, timbre and tone, mood and its manifestations are all impacted by the dismissal of the comic as incidental and at times subversive of the propriety of mourning. The juristic instance of

20 The description of the physicality of laughter dates back to the much-commented Joubert (1980). For a recent study, see Parvalescu (2010).

21 Kantorowicz (1956).

22 Santner (2011).

the impossibility of laughter on the day the monarch died is but an instance, writ large and indicative of the imposition of decorum and a centrifugal legal control of affect and its manifestations. Laws governing contempt of court and public order, dress codes, tacit conventions of office and role, appearance and effacement, as well as the system of examinations, both scriptural and practical, inculcate in the student a sense of the charisma of authority as also a tendency to believe in the truth or veridiction of legal hierarchy. Social media, mobile optimised communication, omnivoyant lenses, omnipresent cameras, streaming and posting, challenge those assumptions and intimate the acceleration of change in the videosphere. Such transitions, however, take the predominant form of deluge rather than conscious performance upon the public stage. In a sense, which could variously be termed that of surrogate experience or passive roles of spectatorship, voyeuristic or vicarious experience, it is what Dr Henry More would term a melancholic mania or narcotic enthusiasm which can again distance knowledge from the body that knows, that apprehends in haptic and material modalities.[23]

It is precisely enthusiasm, the affect and intuition that manifest in the corporeal apprehension of the rulebook, the materiality of transmission and relay of the aura and sense of legality, that require pedagogic perusal and didactic discussion. The question is a complicated one as it involves not only the comedy of the body but also the acceleration and speed of enthusiasm, the *perpetuum mobile* of corporeal sensibilities, the atmospherics of transmission. The force of motive, motion and emotion, love and hate in the Socratic classroom, the lecture theatre, the tutorial or seminar room, office and faculty lounge are heuristic intimacies, aspects of epistemics but also of the ontography of law, of the body coming to know. A series of interventions in legal theory mark the emergence of a sensory apprehension of law and can provide a context for comprehension of the comedic in the corporeal and for what Vico, adverted earlier, describes as coming to know the juridical for a second time and owning it. Jurisography and concepts of the lawscape, with its atmospheres, rhythms, sounds and diverse peripeteia, that place the subject in their wild alluvial and built environment.[24] Feminist jurisprudence and judgements place sex, gender, and desire—for control, determination, certainty—into the practice of decision.[25] Trans* practices expand the biblical binaries into choice of sex and fluidity of the body as further facets of fleshy sense and knowing.[26] Critical race

23 The concept of surrogacy is from Lefebvre (2014); while the classic source on spectacle and spectatorship remains Debord (1994). On melancholic inebriation, see More (1656) p 20.

24 Jurisography, deriving from chorography or the study of people and places, was coined in Genovese and McVeigh (2015). On the more general theme of cartographic jurisprudence, see Suresh (2022) p 323.

25 There are now numerous feminist judgements projects and publications. For an engaging introduction to the themes and purposes, see Hunter (2015).

26 For recent elaborations on trans* and the juridical, see Goodrich and Trüstedt (2022).

theory exposes questions of colour, the graphics of skin, and the perceptual history that underpins genocide.[27] Earth jurisprudence, and wild judgements extend the network that the web of law should comprehend, while matterphorics locates the new materialism in sub-atomic physics and the collision of cells that make up both *corpus* and *iuris* as mutable and mutating entities.[28] Here, as Schopenhauer frames it, 'the world itself is the court of justice' and we but apparitions that stand before its portals.[29]

The university of the body also includes, as apparition suggests, the optical endeavours of visual legal studies, the ocular turn, and the materiality of appearances, of manifestation in the sensorium of seeing. What manifests is real, it matters forth and is the immediate sensory aspect of our encounters which lead to the concept of imaginal law as that fragmented and mobile surfeit of images and of interactions, virtual and real, avatar and person that accost the screens as well as the catallactic lenses, the retina that views everyday life. In Agamben's terms, to relate to and move from the body that knows is to profane the sacral and mythical, to play with the pomposity of the theologico-juridical and its heavy signifiers.[30] Profanation frees for human use or concretises in the corporeal and, one could observe in passing, would allow for comedy to be performed even and especially when the monarch dies. Humour, jesting, play all represent a grounding as a coming to earth, with *homo ludens*, the figure of the wise fool gesturing to the poesis of the profane, the carnival of death, the element of being made up that lies at the heart of all knowledge of rite and law. Where the power of the sacred act, liturgical or legal,

> lies in the conjunction of the myth that tells the story and the rite that reproduces and stages it. Play breaks up that unity: as *ludus*, or physical play, it drops the myth and preserves the rite; as *jocus*, or wordplay, it effaces the rite and allows the myth to survive.[31]

In each instance the play, the joke, is that of refiguring the compound sauce, the *au jus* of common law, in the terms that Horace uses, or that of making it one's own, and so allowing entry into the university of the body, in Vico's account precisely of this double play of learning law a second time.

To play, with myth, rites, language, images, and laws, is to recognise a double scene. The law is staged and so too the first category of legal invention, the juristic person, is equally a plot within the drama of compounded fabrications. Play and punning share the same aleatory relationship of contraries in that both

27 For an introduction, see Williams (1988).

28 On matterphorics, see the special issue 24 *Theory and Event* (2021) 1–430; as also the forthcoming Gandorfer (2023).

29 Schopenhauer (2017) vol. I. p 415, discussed in Masciandro (2014) p 44.

30 Agamben (2007) p 73.

31 Agamben (2007) pp 75–6.

shatter the restraint of the norm, in one case by breaking the rules that govern conventional acts and in the other by turning the meaning of a word to a different sense. In both cases, subjectivity challenges objectivity, wit inserts itself into judgement, and for Freud this means that consciousness here looks on the unconscious and subverts the repression barrier. The ethos of the comic, Freud's joke work, plays upon the unconscious energy, and psychical economy of condensation and displacement that find expression in comedy and so give humour its cognitive effect. The joke, in Weitzman's pellucid analysis of irony, 'is an expression of the repression of the comic, in which repression does not lead to the comic's disappearance but, much like the dream, to its reappearance in altered form'.[32] The humouring of the norm, one might here hypothesise, is precisely the creative collision of form with meaning, and in juridical contexts of repression with release. Jurisprudence becomes theatrical when there is a self-conscious appearance within the rite, when the doubling is recognised and acted upon, body meets abstraction, and the unconscious manifests in all of the symptoms—gestures, tones, flushes, images, expressions, and slips—that Freud has noted. It is appearance that matters, that provides access, and so it is surfaces that require close scrutiny, time, transformation, and on occasion playful attention to the game being played.

The performative dimension of legal studies has come increasingly to the fore and nowhere more so than in the development of theatrical jurisprudence which insists upon attending to the encounter and event, the scene and staging of appearances in any legal interaction. How does the body look, read, gesticulate, proclaim, respond? What is the humour, mood, tone, colour, and timbre of performance? What impression is made and what mark and memory, indelible or ephemeral, is left behind? What Leiboff appositely terms the 'exercise' in theatricality is directed to grounding the student in the present: 'the move from thought and reason to the body, the actual body (not an imagined philosophical body) … disrupts and challenges, because it forces an awareness of different realities and a recognition of the impression that they make.[33] To focus on impressions is to enter the world on the strength of experience, the sensory apprehension of being and acting in immediacy. This lies at the root of the '*gaya scienza*', mirthful science, and wields a powerful critical tool, because embodied and attentive to affect as well as reason, sense as well as the nomic data that constitute the basis of abstraction upon the deletion of alternative realities. Attention is paid to the minor and marginal, to continuities that law prefers to disregard in ignoring the immediate meaning and import of *corpus iuris* by burying its body in texts, the tomb of tomes. In a few valedictory pages on humour at the end of his monumental history of revolution, Rosenstock-Huessy depicts lack of humour, 'cool, disinterested, neutral and dispassionate'

32 Weitzman (2015) p 9.
33 Leiboff (2021) p 99.

science as a fatal mode of repression of the senses, leaving the scientist reliant upon 'vestiges and impressions made by life on others'.[34] The separation of mind and body in dualism sounds a death knell for science: 'The truth is that the great Cartesius, when he obliterated the impressions of the child René, maimed himself for any social perception, outside of natural science'.[35] Consciousness of the world and of the sensorium of its apprehension has to play a part, and be accepted in the devising of our accounts of law and of the impressions that precedent provides to guide the contemporary judge.

It remains to specify that humour must be understood in its classical and broadest sense as disposition and inclination based upon experience and so acknowledge the temperatures and moistness of body and context, not just laughter but anger, fear, love, and hate. The comedy of *corpus iuris* embraces the material dimension of legality and uses humour to regulate and ridicule, warn, and inspire. Returning to the judicial proboscis, Lord Brougham's nose, and the legal snoutfig of judgement, there is much to be learned from that incident and symptom of worldliness that takes the marginal form of the ludic in the legal, the cathartic energy that is released in the twists and turns of the factual, in puns, plays, alliterative and other rhyming manipulations and rhythms of words. The absurdity of rituals, the illogicality of legal liturgy, the human comedy, the flashes of pain, laughter, embarrassment, anger, and fear, form a starting point, a series of (un)fortunate events, a wealth of impressions that ground the subject in the art of law. Humour and the humorous are signs that require attention to the body and its physiological expressions, from blush to guffaw, houl to trears, tingle to insensible anticipation. There is the foundation of thought, in the corpus that thinks, that is law, and needs to be noticed because such affects and expressions portend a different reality, the interruption of expectations, the dissolution of a complacency, that appears most often in suits, in robes, in everyday dress at the office, the courthouse, the police station, the prison.

References

Cases (reported)

Davis v Fareham Urban District Council (1956) AC 696.
Minnevitch v Café de Paris (Londres) (1936) 1 All. ER 884.
Scott & Sons v Del Sel (1922) SC 592.

Secondary Sources

Giorgio Agamben (2007) *Profanations*, Zone Books.

34 Rosenstock-Huessy (1969) p 755.
35 Rosenstock-Huessy (1969) p 756.

Rev. Wm Cooper (1869) *A History of the Rod: Flagellants and Flagellation*, Reeves.
Fiona Cownie (2004) *Legal Academics: Cultures and Identities*, Hart.
Charles Darling (1879) *Scintillae Juris*, Davis.
Guy Debord (1994) *Society of the Spectacle*, Zone Books.
Daniela Gandorfer (2023) *Matterphorics: On the Laws of Theory*, Duke University Press.
Ann Genovese and Shaun McVeigh (2015) 'Nineteen Eighty Three: A Jurisographic Report on *Commonwealth v Tasmania*' 24 *Griffith Law Review* 68.
Thomas Giddens (2021) 'A Series of Unfortunate Events *or* the Common Law' (2021) 33 *Law and Literature* 23.
P Goodrich and K Trüstedt (eds) (2022) *Laws of Transgression: The Return of Judge Schreber*, University of Toronto Press.
Rosemary Hunter (2015) 'More than Just a Different Face? Judicial Diversity and Decision-Making' 68 *Current Legal Problems* 119.
George Jabet (1852) *Notes on Noses*, Bentley.
Joubert (1980) *Treatise on Laughter* [1560], University of Alabama Press.
Ernst Kantorowicz (1956) *The King's Two Bodies*, Princeton University Press.
Henri Lefebvre (2014) *Critique of Everyday Life*, Verso.
Marett Leiboff (2021) 'Theatricality' in Goodrich et al (eds) *Research Handbook on Law and Literature*, Elgar.
Nicola Masciandro (2014) *Sufficient Unto the Day:* Sermones Contra Solicitudinem, Schism Press.
Henry More (1656) [Philophilus Parrestiastes], *Enthusiasmus Triumphatus, Or, A Discourse of the Nature, Causes, Kinds and Cure of Enthusiasme*, Flesher.
Anne Parvalescu (2010) *Laughter: Notes on a Passion*, Massachusetts Institute of Technology Press.
Eugene Rosenstock-Huessy (1969) *Out of Revolution*, Berg.
Eric Santner (2011) *The Royal Remains: The Peoples Two Bodies and the Endgames of Sovereignty*, University of Chicago Press.
Edward Stillingfleete (1662) *Irenicum. A Weapon-Salve for the Churches Wounds* [1653], Mortlock.
Sabarish Suresh (2021) 'Cartographic Jurisprudence: Mapping, Territorializing, and the Creation of National Law' in Goodrich et al (eds) *Research Handbook on Law and Literature*, Elgar.
Arthur Schopenhauer (2017) *The World as Will and Representation*, Cambridge University Press.
Giambattista Vico (1984) *The New Science*, Cornell University Press.
Giambattista Vico (1993) *On Humanist Education* [1699–1707], Cornell University Press.
Giambattista Vico (2015) *Vici vindiciae* [1729], Pinton.
Françoise Wacquet (2001) *Latin, or, The Empire of a Sign*, Verso.
Eden Warwick (1848) *Nasology: Or, Hints Towards a Classification of Noses*, Bentley.
Erica Weitzman (2015) *Irony's Antics: Walser, Kafka, Roth, and the German Comic Tradition*, Northwestern University Press.
Patricia Williams (1988) 'On Being the Object of Property' 14 *Signs* 5.

Chapter 9

Teaching Cultural Legal Studies

Timothy D Peters and Karen Crawley

Introduction

This chapter reflects upon our experiences teaching Cultural Legal Studies as an elective subject in the context of a legal education that generally inculcates hierarchy, orients students towards formalistic reasoning that privileges one answer rather than many, and indoctrinates students into the ways of reading texts that are linear and rational.[1] In Cultural Legal Studies, students encounter diverse representational forms—films, comics, images and other cultural artefacts—and analyse them according to the tools of interpretation derived from the humanities. In doing so, they see how legal narratives of rights, responsibility, and subjectivity are bound up in stories of justice, revenge, and culpability. They witness how cultural forms both embody and challenge the tenets of liberal legalism, 'making strange' law's narratives of neutrality, certainty, and reliability.[2] The process of developing their own readings of cultural legal texts empowers students to reflect upon their own complicity in, and responsibility for, the legal forms through which they engage and exert agency.

Unlike traditional law and literature courses, Cultural Legal Studies as we have taught it has been built around the particular encounter (filmic, televisual, ludic, graphic) with a jurisprudence of popular culture.[3] This is not limited to literature or films dealing explicitly with law and justice. Rather it is a practice of reading texts jurisprudentially and is grounded in a jurisprudential tradition—a way of teaching theory. Cultural Legal Studies is thus a course in legal theory. But it is law as stories, reflecting upon the way that, in law school, we both inhabit and inculcate legal imaginaries which are intelligible to us through images, symbols, and narratives. By starting with the imaginary, Cultural Legal Studies provides ways to visualise the biopolitical frames that govern our teaching of sovereignty, justice, rights, authority, violence, and

1 Manderson (2008).
2 Peters (2022a).
3 MacNeil (2007).

DOI: 10.4324/9781003179283-12

the modern legal subject.[4] Such an approach foregrounds the ways in which legality is constituted through the cultural narratives in which we imagine our lives. This enables students to analyse their investments in, and imaginative attachments to, particular kinds of thinking about law, legality, and justice. It also provides them with training that is particularly apposite for legal education—learning how to speak and write the language of the law.[5] In its blend of cinematic texts and legal theory, and its emphasis on the creative act of making arguments, teaching Cultural Legal Studies becomes a way of pursuing legal pluralism that empowers students to think about their own positionality, power, and privilege as normative agents.[6]

This chapter is split into four sections. The first provides the contextual background and focus of our reflection in three regards: the neoliberalisation of university legal education and the emergence of the 'student consumer'; the emphasis on the threshold concept of 'thinking like a lawyer'; and a critique of an overly narrow perspective on what legal education is. The second section provides a brief outline of the field of Cultural Legal Studies. This provides the basis for the third section, which focuses on our approach and experience in teaching Cultural Legal Studies and how it provides opportunities to challenge aspects of the neoliberalisation of legal education as the production of biopolitical subjects. We then conclude by considering what a cultural legal approach to teaching law more broadly might encompass.

Neoliberal Legal Education, the Student-Consumer, and 'Thinking Like a Lawyer'

Literature on the neoliberalisation of the university has emphasised the shift from a social liberalism which sees higher education as a 'public good' that is 'freely available to all from the public purse', to a market-based approach where education is a 'private good for which users pay'.[7] Students are now 'customers' who purchase educational 'products', universities have shifted from public institutions to business entities and the aim of education is no longer about the furthering of knowledge and citizenship, but improving one's competitiveness in a job-market for which the graduate is supposed to emerge 'work-ready'.[8] In Australia, this emerged from the neoliberal reforms of higher education in the late 1980s and early 1990s and has been exacerbated by additional funding

4 Cultural Legal Studies is distinct from 'law and culture' or the 'cultural study of law', as it focuses on the modes of understanding legality and their cultural constitution, emphasising the nature of representation. See Crawley (2016).

5 Boyd White (2011) p 38.

6 Macdonald (2007).

7 Thornton (2005) p 268.

8 Thornton (2005) p 268; Giddens (2021) pp 39–40. On the connections between biopolitics and the neoliberalisation of education, see Simons (2006).

reforms in recent years, as well as the restructures in delivery models being experienced as a response to, and concurrent with, the COVID-19 pandemic. As Margaret Thornton and others have outlined, such reforms produced both a 'massification' of higher education with the increased reliance on fees as opposed to public funding *also* driving the demand to increase student numbers.[9] The emphasis on being consumers purchasing a 'product' situates students not as those coming to be introduced into a tradition of learning and knowledge, but as already existing capitalist-subjects who are to increase their capacity to exchange their labour for value in the market.[10]

For legal education, a result of neoliberalisation has been a shift 'to a greater focus on traditional market-based legal knowledge that is applied and functional'[11]—that is, an emphasis on a degree as a product which will produce particular and immediately exploitable benefits to the receiver. This has manifested in increased attention on professional content requirements, skills, and areas of law directly relevant for (in particular, commercial) practice as well as a streamlining of programmes. Areas such as critical socio-legal scholarship, theory, and critique are viewed as dispensable because they do not possess an 'obvious use value'.[12] Core and elective courses in those areas are reduced or sidelined both from an institutional and curriculum design perspective *and* because students are often looking for courses that they think will be seen as 'directly relevant' to getting a job—reflecting not only an increased vocationalism, but the already embedded biopolitical entrepreneurial subjectivity making an 'investment' upon which there should be a direct 'return'.[13] As Thornton has argued, the 'teaching of technocratic law' not only induces 'conformity in a way that comports with the market message, it ensures that there is no space for the questioning voice, the theorisation of law's role in the market or the consideration of alternative knowledges'.[14] This is particularly problematic in the context of law's fundamental role in securing the dominance of particular power structures in settler states such as Australia.

This is exacerbated by approaches to legal education that emphasise key threshold concepts such as legal reasoning and learning to 'think like a lawyer' in an uncritical fashion. Such threshold concepts—those key entry points into a discipline that have the potential for transformation of the student's world view—can have a potentially 'colonising' effect.[15] This is because, whilst 'thinking like a lawyer' is both one of the challenging aspects of legal education where students get 'stuck', it is also an approach that transforms their way of

9 Thornton (2005) p 268. See also Thornton (2012).
10 See, in general, Simons (2006); Giddens (2021).
11 Thornton (2017) pp 110–11.
12 Thornton (2005) p 269.
13 Thornton (2017) pp 110–11; Simons (2006).
14 Thornton (2005) p 270.
15 Ricketts (2004) p 5; Meyer and Land (2003) p 10.

viewing the law and the world, encompassing certain assumptions: a particular ordering of the universe, individual volition, the commodification of land, and the legitimacy of centralised authority.[16] These assumptions are what Aidan Ricketts refers to as the 'price of entry to the knowledge (and power) of the discipline'.[17] They reflect, as Peter Goodrich has noted, the way legal education is 'the institutionalisation of the future custodians of the law', and offers a training in a discourse of power, of mastery, of a knowledge, that takes for granted, but goes beyond, the more general biopolitical production of legal subjects.[18] Despite ongoing debates about whether 'thinking like a lawyer' is 'a' (or 'the') key threshold concept in the discipline of law,[19] it is regularly taught as part of law curricula and seen as one of the identifiable and valuable outcomes of legal education. This is both because of its emphasis on a type of critical reasoning and analysis that can be effectively deployed in legal practice and its privileging of a particular mode of seeing the world that provides a sophisticated mechanism for engaging in market relations epitomising the biopolitical entrepreneurial self, able to make rational and 'neutral' decisions without emotion.

Whilst there is a plethora of critiques of 'thinking like a lawyer', William Twining has pointed out that it gets at least one thing right: legal education should involve a central concern with *thinking*.[20] This pithy response forms part of a broader critique of the traditional emphasis of thinking about legal education, which tends to focus on the formal aspects of professional formation provided by universities. To make clear this critique, he presents three ideal types that focus on 'learning about law'.[21] The first is the 'primary school model', which focuses on 'initial professional formation'—that is, the formal educational requirements for admission to the profession.[22] The second is the 'reflective practitioner model', which encompasses the way in which professionals learn from experience primarily in informal ways and in a variety of contexts that cannot necessarily be taught. Third is the 'Lawrence Friedman model', which is more radical and of greater interest to us here. This approach sees 'Western societies as one vast school of law involve[ing] all human beings (and other legal persons) learning about law from cradle to grave'.[23] This approach, which encompasses both formal legal education and informal learning, as well as the complex relations *between* them, 'invites one to try to imagine

16 Ricketts (2004) p 8.
17 Ricketts (2004) p 8.
18 Goodrich (1987) p 200.
19 See, for example, Weresh (2014).
20 Twining (2018) p 243.
21 Twining (2018) pp 251–2.
22 Twining (2018) p 251.
23 Twining (2018) p 251; Friedman (1989).

a total picture of learning about law in a given society'.[24] Such recognises that law is not simply a set of knowledge or skills that can be objectively learnt and assessed, but encompasses an entire way of viewing and interacting with the world.

It is from this third perspective that we consider the significance of Cultural Legal Studies within the law curriculum. This is not only because Friedman's work on law and popular culture that Twining cites is considered to be one of the precursors of Cultural Legal Studies, but also because it takes as one of its fundamental starting points the fact that law is something *broader* than legal institutions, cases, and legislation. Rather, it understands law as emerging as a way of perceiving and engaging with the world—a *nomos*, to use the term famously deployed by Robert Cover.[25]

On the Emergence of Cultural Legal Studies

Cultural Legal Studies, whilst extending out of the fields of Law and Literature, Critical Legal Studies, Law and Film, and Law and Popular Culture, takes as its grounding claim the cultural constitution of law.[26] Its focus is not simply on literature as providing a mirror to the law, or on popular (mis)understandings of judges, lawyers, and court procedure drawn from film and television. Rather, it emphasises the way that our very experience of the law, our construction as legal subjects and the instantiation of sovereignty and authority arise from images, narratives, and representations—both cultural and legal. This goes to the way law is 'a practice of subject formation',[27] and as legal subjects, our attachment to the institutions of law is about more than logic or fear of reprisal—it is the attachment of belief, the acting-out of purpose, the absorption of a narrative. In Robert Gordon's words, law's power

> consists less in the force that it can bring to bear against violators of its rules than in its capacity to persuade people that the world described in its images and categories is the only attainable world in which a sane person would want to live.[28]

The law must continually reform and resubstantiate its authority in the social psyche, and it achieves this by embedding itself within and colonising our cultural representations.[29] For Cultural Legal Studies, what is required is an

24 Twining (2018) p 251.
25 Cover (1983).
26 For key texts on Cultural Legal Studies, see Sharp and Leiboff (2016); Peters and Crawley (2018); Giddens (2018a); Tranter (2018); Peters (2022b). See also Crawley (2016); Duncanson (2016).
27 Pether (2009) p 318.
28 Gordon (1984) p 109.
29 Rush and Kenyon (2004) p 2.

account of what makes law, as a mode of representation, attach to and affect our bodies and life-worlds in this way: of how law 'inscribes itself on everyday life'.[30] It encourages a recognition of the way in which law is not simply represented or imbued *in* cultural texts and artefacts (novels, films, television, video games, comics, art, graffiti), but rather the way in which these texts provide *entries into* law, understood not simply as a specific institution but as a way of viewing and engaging the world.[31] That is, law is not only reflected in and constitutive of culture, but culture infuses, reflects, and determines law.[32]

It is for this reason that Cultural Legal Studies takes representations seriously. It seeks to recuperate the study of law as an *ars rhetorica*, by focusing on questions of form, genre, rhetoric, argumentative strategy, textual interpretation, and reading. This is informed more broadly by Law and Humanities, which views law primarily not as a set of rules or as reducible to politics or power, but as a shared language for making claims about justice and injustice.[33] The primary methodological focus of Cultural Legal Studies, however, is on the nature of representations, whether that it is through an insistence upon *reading* the cultural text or artefact jurisprudentially in the work of William P MacNeil, critical reflection on the experience of *encountering* the 'crime-image' in the work of Alison Young, or an analysis of literature, art, video games, and other images as *sites* and *sources* of inculcation into law—as constitutive of our *nomos*—in the work of Desmond Manderson.[34] In doing so, it analyses the way in which cultural texts—as textual, visual, and affective—allow for access to different registers for understanding legal subjectivity and legal agency in relation to terms like genre, positioning, affect, complicity, ambivalence, and investment. However, Cultural Legal Studies not only has an expansive concept of law but it encompasses what has been called a 'democratisation' of legal theory, which 'recognises productive negotiations of legal ideas happening outside the parameters of legal procedure and academia'.[35] As Kirsty Duncanson has highlighted 'law is produced' and 'given meaning and made material by all those who are subject to it. Each person is a site of legal authority'.[36] And the analysis deployed by Cultural Legal Studies is a means of engaging and reflecting on the way in which cultural representations not only reflect but constitute this form of legal meaning and legal subjectivity.

Given Cultural Legal Studies' emergence in the context of the neoliberalisation of the university, one could question its position in the context of

30 Goodrich (1991) p 235.
31 Manderson (2003).
32 See our discussion in Crawley and Peters (2018). See also Leiboff and Sharp (2016); Giddens (2018b); Peters (2022a).
33 Constable (2014).
34 MacNeil (2007); Young (2009); Manderson (2003).
35 Duncanson (2016) p 208; MacNeil (2007) pp 1–2, 156–7.
36 Duncanson (2016) p 209.

the law curriculum. Is it simply a bastion of the old, holding on to the social liberalism and humanist turn of Law and Literature against the more technocratic shifts of recent decades? Or, given its significant focus on the study of popular culture which, itself, is intertwined with globalised neoliberal ideas, is it complicit with the neoliberal turn? Against these two positions, we argue that Cultural Legal Studies, rather than simply being a nostalgia for critique or a reflection of a globalised legal culture, provides a way to reclaim and envision a sense of Twining's *third* notion of legal education, by embedding a particular understanding and way of seeing law and legality, not simply or only as imbued in legislation, cases and legal treatises, but as a much broader aspect of the cultures in which we live and breathe. One of the reasons it does this is that, in the context of the decreased focus on theory, reflection, and critique (or the instrumentalisation of these in the view of producing particular disciplined bodies and biopolitical legal subjects), it *starts* where students are at, asking them to reflect on their own engagements with the texts and artefacts of popular culture, which provide their own sense of legality.[37] It does this not simply to disabuse them of their generic understandings of law, to replace it with the colonising framework of 'thinking like a lawyer', but rather to engage in a critical consideration of the cultural promulgation of our very notions of law and legality.

Teaching Cultural Legal Studies

Cultural Legal Studies—as each of us has developed and been a part of both at Griffith University and the University of the Sunshine Coast—is a legal theory course that satisfies the requirement of a minimum Jurisprudence elective in the law curriculum.[38] It is not about representations of law and justice in film, literature, comics, or video games, but it is about *reading film (and other texts or cultural artefacts) as legal theory*. Students are introduced to leading texts of jurisprudence (HLA Hart on rules, Giorgio Agamben on the state of exception, Kimberlé Crenshaw on intersectionality) and key legal themes (legal personality, judgement, sovereignty, rights) alongside and through being paired with literary, cinematic, ludic, or visual texts (*The Hunger Games*, *Captain*

37 Teaching Cultural Legal Studies thus provides a point of resistance to what Thomas Giddens describes as the 'indicative appearance of bookish study and scholarly endeavour' that has displaced the need to *actually engage in* the work of study that is the core of not only education but the common law. See Giddens (2021) p 43.

38 At Griffith University, Peters developed and taught *6039LAW: Cultural Legal Studies: Critical Approaches to Law and Popular Culture* in 2015 and 2016 (with Crawley providing one of the guest lectures in 2016). Crawley then took-over, redeveloped, and taught the course in 2017 and 2018 (with Peters providing one of the guest lectures). At the University of the Sunshine Coast, Peters assisted Dr Ashley Pearson and Dr Dale Mitchell develop and teach *LAW412 Cultural Legal Studies* in 2021 (with Crawley also providing a guest lecture).

America: Civil War, The Handmaid's Tale, Persona 4)—and each is taught by a scholar mounting and defending a jurisprudential reading of that text that throws into a new light the animating questions of legal theory: what is law? what is its relationship to authority, violence, justice? Our teaching of these courses has thus been shaped by the work of MacNeil, whose programmatic (and eminently teachable and replicable) approach to 'reading jurisprudentially' forms one methodology explored in the course.[39] 'Reading jurisprudentially' involves identifying a similarity, motif, or design common across the legal and the cultural text (for example, the figure of monstrosity in both Mary Shelley's *Frankenstein* and Mary Wollstonecraft's *A Vindication of the Rights of Women*,[40] the shadow-boxing conflict between John Austin and HLA Hart as figured in the 'rules' of *Fight Club*[41]) and then analysing each text by reference to the other (for example, the cynical character of Sydney Carton in Dickens' *A Tale of Two Cities* explicates critical legal studies contempt for the façade of fairness and neutrality that the law adopts in the pursuit of justice[42]). This method of close reading maintains that the texts of popular culture do not simply convey legal themes like fairness, neutrality, and justice by analogy; rather, the *act* of 'reading jurisprudentially'[43] generates new 'intertexts' that reveal and critique the legality that we are already complicit in. The course gives students the opportunity to craft and then reflect upon these intertexts in making their own jurisprudential readings, thus foregrounding their creativity and agency in crafting popular legal culture.

In this fashion, our teaching of Cultural Legal Studies is explicitly *not* about the production of a biopolitical legal subject—as a disciplined body *produced* to engage in a technocratic application of the law—but rather as a training in the praxis of scholarship and of theorising itself. This is encompassed in Cultural Legal Studies' broad approach to issues of law and justice, its expansive approach to legal theory and its emphasis on the nature of theorising as 'the process of displacing experience into a conceptual framework so that you can have some distance from it to be able to perceive yourself in it and act'.[44] The practice of engaging explicitly in theorising about law, rather than learning 'about' something called legal theory, allows for greater self-awareness as well as greater connectivity with the structures that govern our lives. It is in this sense that Cultural Legal Studies potentially provides a means of allowing students, graduates, scholars, and practitioners a mechanism of recognising and

39 MacNeil's scholarship and teaching have been a constitutive influence on the authors and he also pioneered the early iterations of the *Cultural Legal Studies* electives that we teach.

40 Shelley (2004); Wollstonecraft (2004); MacNeil (2012) chapter 4.

41 Fincher (1999); MacNeil (2007) chapter 3.

42 MacNeil (2012) p 14, chapter 7; Dickens (1982).

43 MacNeil (2012) p 12.

44 MacKenzie Wark, 'A Rave Just for Friends' (2021) https://kunstkritikk.com/a-rave-just-for-friends/

taking responsibility for our own production of law as culture and culture as law. The course's privileging of filmic and other popular visual texts provides for accessible sites of analysis because they are inviting and offer students a form of engagement that differs from the remainder of the law degree which largely remains bound to the written word.

In addition to separately scheduled screenings (where required), classes normally encompass two components: first, the presentation of a cultural legal reading of a particular text or texts; second a student-led discussion of the reading and texts. The texts analysed invite particular ways of reading or seeing, modes of identification, and attachment that underwrite our commitments to the normative worlds that govern us. Analysing the film *World War Z* (2013), for example, we (scholars, teachers, and students together) are able to interrogate the law in the symbolic register, and the limits of the liberal state's discourse of tolerance, offering a way of reflecting on how the international order of legal legitimacy—based around sovereign power—is designed around the biopolitical exclusion of the refugee as other.[45] Alternatively, examining the literary and filmic versions of *The Handmaid's Tale* (1985 and 2017–) in their historical and cultural contexts reveals: a framework for theorising the history of feminist-inspired law reform in Western liberal democracies; the enabling fictions that sustain liberalism's notions of formal equality; and the gendered and racialised nature of nation-state violence expressed through law.[46] By reading *The Handmaid's Tale* alongside the violence against Aboriginal women and children facilitated by the *Aboriginals Protection and Restriction of Opium Act Qld* (1897), students consider how law in the settler colony seeks to erase, legitimate, and justify its violent dispossession.[47] These texts highlight the fragility of the nation state's own performative violence with regards to its violent exclusions, and the performativity and contingency of its own symbolic forms of authority. From a more global perspective, by taking up the rhetoric of the corporation as Frankenstein's monster, and reading it through the B-grade film *I, Frankenstein* and its accompanying comic, we can provide students with a critical way to interrogate both the artificial nature of legal personality and the legal construction of corporate bodies.[48] By pairing the particularly *embodied* depiction of 'Adam' (the monster in the film) and his quest for a soul, with the desires of the demon-villain Naberius to find immortality for his *disembodied* hordes, we are able to unpack the disembodied nature of legal rights discourse and the corporate 'body' as its epitome. At the same time, the film's privileging of love as the formation of a soul provides a means for thinking and reflecting

45 MacNeil (2017); Crofts and Vogl (2019).
46 Crawley (2018).
47 Foley (2020).
48 Peters (2017).

upon the possibilities of our responsibility for more reciprocal modes of corporate being together.

Given the presentation by the educator of *particular* jurisprudential readings of cultural texts, *Cultural Legal Studies* would appear to encompass a teacher-centred mode of education—what has sometimes been referred to as the 'sage on the stage'. However, this is intentionally pluralised in two fashions that go beyond the tendency of student-centred learning to reproduce a form of the neoliberal student-consumer.[49] First, students are invited to engage in a critical discussion and analysis not just of the cultural texts and legal theories in question, but of the particular *reading* being presented. That is, students are positioned not simply as recipients of legal knowledge, but rather as co-creators of it. This is supported by a formative assessment structure that focuses on student facilitation of class discussion and/or a short written piece critically reflecting on the particular reading and perspective presented. Second, in the models that each of us have adopted, the 'sage on the stage' itself is pluralised with multiple guest lecturers each presenting their *own* readings and, again, asking students to critically engage with them. In this sense, what is presented is *not* a unitary voice defining specific legal knowledge, but multiple 'ways in' to a diverse field in which students are asked to develop their own ability to critically reflect on the visions of law and legality that they come across in cultural texts and artefacts. The courses are thus set-up not around knowledge of Cultural Legal Studies but rather the collaborative practice of engaging in cultural legal analysis and critique.

The course's foregrounding of creativity, agency, and responsibility for the production of legal culture is grounded in the summative assessment tasks, which consists of a substantial research essay supported by the class presentation of a research plan. In these tasks the student is invited to craft their *own* cultural reading of a text or artefact of their choice. This provides significant autonomy and agency to the student, which is then supported by the scholarly community between the students and teachers that is developed throughout the course. This scholarly community finds one of its clearest locus-points in the symposium-style presentation of research plans to the class, which provides the opportunity for comments and suggestions from both the teaching team *and* from their peers. The result, we argue, is that teaching Cultural Legal Studies provides a way to think about law that can be carried with the student throughout their life and career. It does this by enabling a sense of 'seeing law' everywhere *not* in terms of the framework of 'thinking like a lawyer'—viewing the world through a particular colonised lens that turns all sites or interactions into potential legal actions—but in terms of critically engaging with the concepts and assumptions of law, justice, and legality that imbue all components of life.

49 Desierto and Maio (2020).

Benefits of Teaching Cultural Legal Studies

We have identified four key benefits to this approach to teaching Cultural Legal Studies. First, it fits with Twining's third ideal-type of legal education. It provides students with a way of reflecting on the different sources and contexts in which they 'learn about law', because it encourages them to identify 'law' not simply with courts, legislation, lawyers, judges, and police, but with a much broader understanding of the frameworks of legality—the *nomos* (and *nomoi*) that underlies, and culturally situates, our legal institutions and systems.[50] In this way, overly reductive and settler-colonial accounts of what 'law' is are fundamentally challenged.[51] Through this legal pluralist approach students become aware of the way in which law functions through, and is constituted by, the diverse aspects of culture—something which will serve them well throughout their career (in whichever field that ends up being) *and* in life.

Second, teaching Cultural Legal Studies provides a space for aspects of the context, theory, and critique that Thornton identifies with the liberal law degree, resisting the neoliberalisation of the university. This is not simply a nostalgia for a past golden era of legal education. Rather, by asking students to engage with cultural texts it recognises and operates *within* the current conditions of globalisation, neoliberalism (and its crises).[52] The result is that students are given the chance to critically reflect on the ideas of law and legality that they have absorbed *from* a globalised popular culture, whilst furthering their own thinking and understanding of law. The fact that this is done in the context of classrooms that emphasise the plurality of voices enables students to not only gain their *own* voice, but to critically reflect on the ideas that go to form that voice. Students are therefore able to recognise the way in which they are co-constitutive of the notions of law that dominate today.

The third benefit extends from the above point about bringing students to a recognition of their co-constituting of law to its impact on us as scholars. That is, as cultural legal scholars, *teaching* Cultural Legal Studies provides a mechanism for understanding our role as *not* simply inculcation into a tradition, but rather a developing sense of responsibility *for* that tradition, including its problems. In this way, the project of teaching Cultural Legal Studies aligns with those movements of legal theory, particularly Australian legal theory, that

50 Cover (1983).

51 This is not simply an academic claim. Numerous students have provided feedback after completing our courses that they completely altered their conception of law—that it has gone from a narrow view to a large and expansive one.

52 At the same time, it is important to recognise the risks of this approach in that it may remain caught within what Mark Fisher termed 'Capitalist Realism': Fisher (2006); Fisher and Gilbert (2013). Our argument is that, by engaging in modes of reflective critical analysis *of* those texts and the way they are constitutive of our legal imaginary, that *Cultural Legal Studies* also provides ways of opening up the cracks of Capitalist Realism and the possibilities of imagining alternatives.

emphasise taking responsibility for law.[53] This is of particular significance in the context of Australia as a settler-colonial state and the always-already existing plurality of laws and legal narratives that are operative here.[54]

Fourth, and finally, Cultural Legal Studies encompasses the teaching of transferable skills in the model of the liberal arts degree. Cultural Legal Studies is fundamentally about modes of creative thinking and critical analysis—skills that are seen as key components of threshold learning outcomes in law programmes.[55] The process of conducting a critical reading requires paying attention to detail, a rejection of the desire for the 'right answers', and the recognition of the plurality *within* cultural texts. In this sense, the courses extend and privilege the textual, rhetorical, and interpretative nature of the study and practice of law. Rather than focusing on *content*, its emphasis on an *approach* and method builds skills that can be deployed in a variety of contexts. In this sense, it continues the tradition of humanities-based education which imbues highly transferable skills that are much less likely to date or expire than those that are often the focus of 'job-ready' initiatives. It also contributes to addressing the expectation of the profession that legal education should produce good critical legal readers, who can comprehend, analyse, interpret, and evaluate texts.[56]

Conclusion: The Potential for a 'Cultural Legal' Law Curriculum

If our outline of the significant 'benefits' above are accurate, then the stakes are high in teaching Cultural Legal Studies and the transformative potential it provides. Part of this arises out of the unique position of Cultural Legal Studies as a boutique upper-year elective, which provides for a clearly defined 'space' for such engagement. At the same time, as we have noted, this teaching of Cultural Legal Studies also fits with Twining's emphasis on an expansive understanding of the nature of learning about law, recognising the way in which society itself is 'one vast school of law involve[ing] all human beings (and other legal persons)' [57]—and one could extend beyond this to capture the non-human or inhuman as well.[58] Given that is the case, we conclude here by reflecting on the way in which a cultural legal approach can (and should) be incorporated into other aspects of law programmes. It should be emphasised that this is *not* simply the inclusion of film clips, literature, comics, and art as 'examples' of

53 Black (2011); Dorsett and McVeigh (2012); Barr (2016); Balint et al (2020).
54 See Balint et al (2020).
55 See TLO 3: Thinking Skills: Kift et al. (2010) pp 10, 18–19.
56 Steel et al. (2017).
57 Twining (2018), p 251; Friedman (1989).
58 See, for example, Matthews (2021).

doctrine or legal issues in core courses.[59] Whilst all scholars should aim to be engaging in their teaching, the risk of this approach is that it plays exactly to the 'student-consumer' in an age of ever-increasing proliferation of images and a general lack of sustained attention and analysis. Rather, what is required is a teaching of the tools of analysis of both legal and cultural texts as *part* of the core curriculum.

Given our argument that Cultural Legal Studies seeks to recuperate the study of law as *ars rhetorica*, a key emphasis should be on the way in which the modes of legal reading, writing, communication, and interpretation are taught within the law curriculum. This, in part, responds to the concerns of judges and the profession more broadly about the need for enhanced statutory interpretation skills and for graduates to be critical readers of texts.[60] The learning of how to craft and interpret legal texts is understood as the generation of legal meaning—going beyond simply an analysis of the written text, to encompassing a rhetorical analysis of cinematic and other visual texts—considering questions of form, genre, argumentative strategy, textual, visual, and aural mechanisms of persuasion.[61] This situates the traditions of reading, writing, and speaking the law in the larger project of Cultural Legal Studies—which is to recognise not only the culturally constituted nature of the law, but our own participation *in* that cultural construction. Such will produce both sophisticated readers and writers, but also reflective individuals and practitioners.[62]

A cultural legal approach is also relevant to emphasising the social and cultural context of law. In Australia, the Law Admission Consultative Committee recently engaged in a project of redrafting the Prescribed Areas of Knowledge that included for *all* areas of law, the importance of including theoretical and conceptual bases' as well as teaching their historical and social context.[63] Whilst we would support such an approach, a risk is that the inclusion of such material remains 'introductory' before getting down to the 'real work' of doctrinal analysis. An embedded cultural legal approach would, rather, highlight and ask students to reflect upon the way in which they embody, for example, the vision of themselves as a contracting subject, a rational individual capable of criminal intent and responsibility, the bearer of sovereignty or the owners

59 For a comprehensive collection of approaches to using popular culture to teach law, see: Corcos (2019).

60 Steel et al. (2017).

61 This approach thereby encompasses the need for a critical *visual* literacy in legal education: Giddens (2021) p 38; see also Richard Sherwin's arguments for the teaching of visual eloquence in law school: Sherwin (2011).

62 See Sharp (2019).

63 In September 2020, however, LACC resolved to 'defer indefinitely' the adoption and introduction of these new prescribed areas of knowledge. Documents in relation to the review and the redrafted Prescribed Areas of Knowledge are available from the Legal Services Council, 'Law Admissions Consultative Committee (LACC)', https://legalservicescouncil.org.au/about-us/law-admissions-consultative-committee.html (last accessed 1 February 2023).

of property, and what that means. This is where drawing upon cultural texts and artefacts can be useful—not so much as simply examples of doctrinal points, but as ways for students to recognise and understand their own cultural developments of their own positions. This needs to be considered on a subject-by-subject basis.

The significance of teaching Cultural Legal Studies is that it builds skills in 'seeing' law more broadly, recognising that we learn about the law from multiple sources, but also builds the possibility for reflection and critique by *starting* with the legal imaginary presented in cultural texts. That is, it has the benefit of 'starting' where students already are, whilst *also* building capacity for the critical reflection that is potentially diminished in other parts of the neoliberal law curriculum. The result is a challenge to the biopolitical production of legal subjects and the basis for a critical interrogation of—and responsibility for—the law. If we were to hand the traditions of law onto legal custodians in this manner it would make for a very different future vision of the law and its possibilities of justice.

Acknowledgements

We would like to thank: the participants in the 2021 Australian Law Academics Association conference, where an early version of this paper was presented; the editors and reviewer for their helpful comments; the students of each of our courses who have embarked on the journey of Cultural Legal Studies with us; and our range of guest lecturers and co-teachers: Kieran Tranter, Edwin Bikundo, Thomas Giddens, Cassandra Sharp, Ashley Pearson, and Dale Mitchell. We dedicate this chapter to Professor William P MacNeil and thank him for his ongoing and unceasing mentorship and support.

References

Jennifer Balint et al (2020) *Keeping Hold of Justice: Encounters Between Law and Colonialism*, University of Michigan Press.

Olivia Barr (2016) *A Jurisprudence of Movement: Common Law, Walking, Unsettling Place*, Routledge.

Christine Black (2011) *The Land is the Source of the Law: A Dialogic Encounter with Indigenous Jurisprudence*, Routledge-Cavendish.

Marianne Constable (2014) *Our Word is Our Bond: How Legal Speech Acts*, Stanford University Press.

Christine A Corcos (ed) (2019) *The Media Method: Teaching the Law with Popular Culture*, Carolina Academic Press.

Robert Cover (1983) 'The Supreme Court, 1982 Term—Foreword: Nomos and Narrative' 97 *Harvard Law Review* 4–68.

Karen Crawley (2016) 'The Critical Force of Irony: Reframing Photographs in Cultural Legal Studies' in Cassandra Sharp and Marett Leiboff (eds) *Cultural Legal Studies: Law's Popular Cultures and the Metamorphosis of Law*, Routledge 183–206.

Karen Crawley (2018) 'Reproducing Whiteness: Feminist Genres, Legal Subjectivity and the Postracial Dystopia of The Handmaid's Tale (2017)' 29 *Law and Critique* 333–58.

Karen Crawley and Timothy D Peters (2018) 'Introduction: "Representational Legality"' in Timothy D Peters and Karen Crawley (eds) *Envisioning Legality: Law, Culture and Representation*, Routledge 1–17.

Penny Crofts and Anthea Vogl (2019) 'Dehumanized and Demonized Refugees, Zombies and World War Z' 31 *Law and the Humanities* 29–51.

Anibeth Desierto and Carmela de Maio (2020) 'The Impact of Neoliberalism On Academics and Students in Higher Education: A Call to Adopt Alternative Philosophies' 14 *Journal of Academic Language & Learning* 148–59.

Charles Dickens (1982) 'A Tale of Two Cities' in Charles Dickens (ed) *Four Complete Novels*, Gramercy Books 589–848.

Shaunnaugh Dorsett and Shaun McVeigh (2012) *Jurisdiction*, Routledge.

Kirsty Duncanson (2016) 'Bodies, Cinema, Sovereignty: Using Visual Culture Methodologies to Think About Other Ways That Law Might Work' in Cassandra Sharp and Marett Leiboff (eds) *Cultural Legal Studies: Law's Popular Cultures and the Metamorphosis of Law*, Routledge 207–27.

David Fincher (1999) *Fight Club*, Fox.

Mark Fisher (2006) *Capitalist Realism: Is There No Alternative?* Zero Books.

Mark Fisher and Jeremy Gilbert (2013) 'Capitalist Realism and Neoliberal Hegemony: A Dialogue' 80/81 *New Formations* 89–101.

Fiona Foley (2020) *Biting the Clouds*, University of Queensland Press.

Lawrence M Friedman (1989) 'Law, Lawyers, and Popular Culture' 98 *The Yale Law Journal* 1579–1606.

Thomas Giddens (2018a) *On Comics and Legal Aesthetics: Multimodality and the Haunted Mask of Knowing*, Routledge.

Thomas Giddens (2018b) 'On Comics and Other Ways of Knowing' in Thomas Giddens (ed) *One Comics and Legal Aesthetics: Multimodality and the Haunted Mask of Knowing*, Routledge 1–27.

Thomas Giddens (2021) 'A Series of Unfortunate Events or the Common Law' 33 *Law & Literature* 23–48.

Peter Goodrich (1987) 'Psychoanalysis in Legal Education: Notes on the Violence of the Sign' in Roberta Kevelson (ed) *Law and Semiotics*, Springer 193.

Peter Goodrich (1991) 'Specula Laws: Image, Aesthetic and Common Law' 2 *Law and Critique* 233–54.

Robert W Gordon (1984) 'Critical Legal Histories' 36 *Stanford Law Review* 57–125.

Sally Kift et al (2010) *Bachelor of Laws: Learning and Teaching Academic Standards Statement December 2010*, Australian Learning & Teaching Council.

Marett Leiboff and Cassandra Sharp (2016) 'Cultural Legal Studies and Law's Popular Cultures' in Cassandra Sharp and Marett Leiboff (eds) *Cultural Legal Studies*, Routledge 3–28.

Roderick A Macdonald (2007) 'Post-Charter Legal Education: Does Anyone Teach Law Anymore?' 28 *Policy Options* 75–83.

William MacNeil (2012) *Novel Judgements: Legal Theory as Fiction*, Routledge.

William P MacNeil (2007) *Lex Populi: The Jurisprudence of Popular Culture*, Stanford University Press.

William P MacNeil (2017) 'The Litigating Dead: Zombie Jurisprudence in Contemporary Popular Culture' 14 *NoFo* 108.

Desmond Manderson (2003) 'From Hunger to Love: Myths of the Source, Interpretation, and Constitution of Law in Children's Literature' 15 *Law & Literature* 87–141.
Desmond Manderson (2008) 'Desert Island Discs (Ten Reveries on Pedagogy in Law and the Humanities)' 2 *Law and Humanities* 255–70.
Daniel Matthews (2021) *Earthbound: The Aesthetics of Sovereignty in the Anthropocene*, Edinburgh University Press.
JHF Meyer and R Land (2003) 'Threshold Concepts and Troublesome Knowledge - Linkages to Ways of Thinking and Practising' in C Rust (ed) *Improving Student Learning - Ten Years On*, Oxford Centre for Staff and Learning Development 412–24.
Timothy D Peters (2017) 'I, Corpenstein: Mythic, Metaphorical and Visual Renderings of the Corporate Form in Comics and Film' 30 *International Journal for the Semiotics of Law* 427–54.
Timothy D Peters (2022a) 'Prologue: Reading the Law "Made Strange"' in Timothy D Peters (ed) *A Theological Jurisprudence of Speculative Cinema: Superheroes, Science Fictions and Fantasies of Modern Law*, Edinburgh University Press.
Timothy D Peters (2022b) *A Theological Jurisprudence of Speculative Cinema: Superheroes, Science Fictions and Fantasies of Modern Law*, Edinburgh University Press.
Timothy D Peters and Karen Crawley (eds) (2018) *Envisioning Legality: Law, Culture and Representation*, Routledge.
Penny Pether (2009) 'Language' in Austin Sarat, Matthew Anderson and Catherine O Frank (eds) *Law and the Humanities: An introduction*, Cambridge University Press 315.
Aidan Ricketts (2004) 'Threshold Concepts in Legal Education' 26 *Journal of Educational Studies* 2–12.
Peter Rush and Andrew Kenyon (2004) 'Alter Egos: The Mise-en-Scène of Law and Aesthetics' in Peter Rush and Andrew Kenyon (eds) *Aesthetics of Law and Culture: Texts, Images and Screens*, JAI Press 1–30.
Cassandra Sharp (2019) 'Why Law Students Should Watch More TV… Reflections on the Deliberate Use of Popular Stories in Training Future Lawyers' in Christine A Corcos (ed) *The Media Method: Teaching the Law with Popular Culture*, Carolina Academic Press 95–113.
Cassandra Sharp and Marett Leiboff (eds) (2016) *Cultural Legal Studies: Law's Popular Cultures and the Metamorphosis of Law*, Routledge.
Mary Shelley (2004) *Frankenstein, or, the Modern Prometheus*, Penguin Classics.
Richard Sherwin (2011) *Visualising Law in the Age of the Digital Baroque: Arabesques and Entanglements*, Routledge.
Maarten Simons (2006) 'Learning as Investment: Notes on Governmentality and Biopolitics' 38 *Educational Philosophy and Theory* 523–40.
Alex Steel et al (2017) 'Critical Legal Reading: The Elements, Strategies, and Dispositions Needed to Master this Essential Skill' 26 *Legal Education Review* 187–213.
Margaret Thornton (2005) 'Gothic Horror in the Legal Academy' 14 *Social & Legal Studies* 267.
Margaret Thornton (2012) *Privatising the Public University: The Case of Law*, Routledge.
Margaret Thornton (2017) 'How the Higher Education "Industry" Shapes the Discipline of Law: The Case of Australia' 5 *Griffith Journal of Law and Human Dignity* 101.
Kieran Tranter (2018) *Living in Technical Legality: Science Fiction and Law as Technology*, Edinburgh University Press.
William Twining (2018) 'Rethinking Legal Education' 52 *The Law Teacher* 241–60.

James Boyd White (2011) 'The Cultural Background of *The Legal Imagination*' in Austin Sarat, Cathrine O Frank and Matthew Anderson (eds) *Teaching Law and Literature*, Modern Language Association 29–39.

Melissa H Weresh (2014) 'Stargate: Malleability as a Threshold Concept in Legal Education' 63 *Journal of Legal Education* 689–728.

Mary Wollstonecraft (2004) *A Vindication of the Rights of Women*, Penguin Books.

Alison Young (2009) *The Scene of Violence: Cinema, Crime, Affect*, Routledge.

Chapter 10

Conversation as Pedagogy

The Use of Popular Stories in the Identity Projects of Law Students

Cassandra Sharp

Introduction

Entry into law school is a direct invitation to traverse discursive landscapes, and to begin a transformative journey—one of self-discovery, professional development, and identity creation. Negotiating and interpreting a variety of discourses, identities, and experiences to decipher the legal world into which they will be graduating, law students become imbricated in the struggle over various meanings within the legal culture. Drawing upon a wide range of resources (both legal and non-legal) to construct meaning about what it means to be a lawyer, the law student embodies a site of interweaving ideas, attitudes, beliefs, and perceptions, and as such, they collectively form an important microcosm within which to facilitate biopolitical awareness and engagement.

The chapter presents a triangular connection between stories, student identity, and biopolitical engagement. Today's generation of law students operate in a predominantly narrative culture, in which they are 'story-addicts' hungry for context.[1] Rather than undergoing passive socialisation, the students' transformation in law school is an active interrogatory to the various discursive practices and processes with which students interact. Law school therefore arguably serves as the foreground for students' active construction of legal identity—a process that can provoke self-awareness and biopolitical engagement. In this chapter I suggest that stories have significant power in legal education for helping students to do just that—to develop critical awareness, be self-reflective and construct identity. I argue that not only do first year law students deploy stories to understand the world of law, but that they also use stories as a form of self-reflection, and as a way of challenging their own (and others') perspectives on the social world. Legal educators have a privilege and responsibility to harness and explore these perspectives with the students as they actively deploy stories towards their developing identity construction.[2]

1 Meyer and Cusick (2004) p 897.

2 This is of course not to argue that encouraging such abilities is currently not a priority in many courses, but simply that sometimes it can be relegated to a secondary objective, or a happy by-product of the primary curriculum. The argument as developed later in the chapter is that there

DOI: 10.4324/9781003179283-13

My aim in this chapter is to commend a legal pedagogy that appreciates the unique position of law students by harnessing their capacity for biopolitically reflective and critical analysis. As such, the chapter first urges for the recognition that developing biopolitical awareness as an indispensable aspect of a student's identity construction within law school. Having demonstrated that law schools are in a unique place to catalyse biopolitical awareness, the chapter next considers stories and conversation as a critical aspect to the student experience of transformation. In the final section, the article seeks to commend possibilities for capitalising on the process of student identity towards biopolitical engagement.

The Role of Law School in Encouraging Biopolitical Awareness

The specific local culture we inhabit will inform and challenge our interaction with other parts of the wider culture. The complexity of a law school education is no exception, as it invites the construction of legal identity by reflecting a pattern of integrated practices and shared meaning-making processes through common speech, symbols, and practices. As its own discursive community, the law school is a locus for the struggle over meaning where students are reflexively involved with a continuous biographical project of identity—attempting to answer critical questions of how to act, what to do, and who to be.[3] This is important for developing and nurturing critical reflection and biopolitical awareness in students, a pursuit that is increasingly being encouraged within contemporary educational discourse.[4]

Interestingly, while many studies in the discipline of law are no stranger to biopolitical considerations, legal education still seems to place little explicit emphasis on biopolitical engagement or awareness as a key learning objective in the mainstream doctrinal curriculum. Unsurprisingly, the hegemony of the 'black letter' tradition, and the 'analytic focus of legal education'[5] which depend on an identified and applied body of self-referential rules, has long resisted a contextual or critical approach to the law.[6] Yet, the rising prominence of cultural legal studies, with its directed attention on the cultural forces implicated in meaning-making about law, has increasingly challenged traditional accounts of law to better understand the various ways in which law

are possibilities for dealing with students' development in a much more explicit and active manner within the curriculum and/or degree structure.

3 Barker (2000) p 167.

4 Particularly within the social sciences disciplines, the literature reflects a substantial scholarly basis for the importance of acknowledging biopolitics in education. See for example: Bazzul (2017); and Bourassa (2011).

5 Pommersheim (1988) p 485.

6 Greenfield, Osborn, and Robson (2001) pp 2–3.

can be perceived, critiqued, and understood.[7] Teaching students to develop biopolitical awareness as part of identity construction could therefore comprise a more central concern of educational objectives. It is argued that there is much scope for legal education to open the door to pedagogical practice that sees students empowered to (rather than inhibited from) exploring and constructing biopolitical awareness and identity construction.

Explicitly embracing the law student's transformative process of 'becoming'[8] thus requires a recognition that legal education is implicated in the construction of biopolitical subjectivities. It also means acknowledging the historical influences of biopower in the constitutive practices of law, including those of legal education. 'Biopower', as conceived by Foucault to be a distinctive form of political rationality, refers to the application and impact of political power on human beings as a species, rather than a focus on the individual.[9] The concept of biopolitics advanced in this chapter invokes this Foucauldian analysis of neoliberal governmentality—namely, that the governance of human life should be understood as institutionally legitimised and regulated through the political technology of biopower.[10] At its core, biopolitics is about 'securing normality and the order of the polis'[11] through technologies of control, surveillance, and governance. As such, 'the law' as both institution and practice has a distinct role in normalising (and legitimising) power and truth relations. With its traditions of objectivity and autonomy, the law can be seen as a mechanism for maintaining the hegemonic cultural values and interests within society or, at the very least, as an accessible arena in which to observe how these interests are maintained, challenged, and altered. Through the operation of biopolitical discourse in social practice, legal education is equally implicated in this exercise. It is argued that law school constructs, defines, and circulates the objects of knowledge about law by regulating which meanings can or cannot be deployed. Both the learning and practice of law is demarcated early in legal education as occupying a special place of responsibility in society, and the institution of law school often ensures that '[e]ntrance into this interpretive community is premised on the mastery' of a certain type of legal language.[12] By disciplining ways of 'speaking' and behaviour through forms of 'knowledge'

7 See for example, Sharp and Leiboff M (eds) (2016) and Peters and Crawley (eds) (2018).

8 Identity is best described as an emotionally charged description rather than a timeless entity. This is the basis of a cultural studies anti-essentialist position, which stresses that identity is a 'process of becoming', built from points of similarity *and* difference: 'cultural identity is not seen as a reflection of a fixed, natural, state of being but as a process of *becoming*': Barker (2000) p 66.

9 'Biological existence was reflected in political existence': Michel Foucault (1980) p 143.

10 As Ewald articulates: 'The welfare state accomplishes the dream of biopower—[it] is a state whose primary aim is no longer to protect the freedom of each individual—but rather to assume responsibility for the very manner in which the individual manages his life' Ewald (1986) pp 8–9.

11 Carter (2017).

12 Pommersheim (1988) pp 478–80 citing Fish (1980).

associated with a specified activity or institution,[13] biopolitical discourse is so easily perpetuated and reinforced within the law.[14] This is equally so for educative practices which participate in the production of knowledge, and seeks to legitimise the links between the construction and reproduction of 'truths' with the maintenance of power. Since law schools often frame and employ this legal knowledge for the purposes of producing graduates who can 'think like a lawyer',[15] a legal education then, is itself, an exercise of biopower that '(re)produces and regulates the economic subject'.[16] As Wittman has deftly observed, a critical component to the success of biopolitics is that a variety of institutions 'operate together as a system of coercion rather than force' such that 'people can become so entrenched in institutional logics that those logics and the institutions that support them become invisible'.[17] I want to argue that law school, and its pedagogy, can (and *should*) operate to make visible these institutional logics, and to interrupt the process of biopower, as part of a law student's transformative process of 'becoming'. That is, the teaching environment in law school should be viewed as an important place where power, and the meanings that uphold power, can be discussed, challenged, or resisted. A place where educative practices demand diversity in theoretical interactions with the political, social, and cultural contexts of law; and where possibilities and opportunities are created for unpredictable and diverse outcomes.

In this way, law school can (and should) be viewed as a site where competing discourses are juxtaposed or played against one another, and as one of the key locations in which student legal identity can be negotiated, developed, and constructed to include biopolitical engagement and awareness. Helping students to develop biopolitical awareness as part of their identity construction is a positive step towards encouraging self-evaluation and the challenging of world-view orthodoxies. As Goldsmith argues:

> Humane understanding and sociological insight into legal problems do not naturally surface from the close study of conventional legal materials; they need to be supplemented by explorations of materials from other disciplines in the humanities and social sciences which nevertheless contextualise and generally deepen students' understanding of legal issues and phenomena.[18]

13 Hall (ed.) (1997) pp 5–6.

14 In particular it is the means by which we are able to act, speak, and make sense of things. Danaher, Schirato, and Webb (2000) p 31.

15 'The traditional process of making students "think like a lawyer" has disconnected them from real world thinking': John Jay Osborn Jr (1990) p 54.

16 Lyn Carter, Matthew Weinstein, and Larry Bencze (2017) 'Biopolitics and Science Education' 12 *Cultural Studies of Science Education* 761–7, p 764.

17 Wittman (2016).

18 Goldsmith (1995) p 300.

The ongoing process of identity development is taking place whether students are aware of it or not; they cannot help but participate in the continuing transformation. As such, I argue that law teachers should be encouraged to deliberately address questions that require reflection, critique, and a developing awareness of self. The remaining sections of this chapter promote the value of stories (re)told through conversations during law school as a significant method for accessing and challenging student identity construction.

The Power of Stories in Student Identity Development

To be educated is to invite the continuous 'self-learning that involves the mind, spirit and body of the whole person'.[19] Education is inexorably 'interwoven with living and with the possibility of retelling our life stories',[20] and contributes to the construction of self-narratives with which we identify.[21] This operative concept of self-identity is understood as a reflexive and discursive construction of self[22] that concerns a culturally contingent production that is specific to particular times and places.[23] One's identity is a continual rehearsal of narration and practice of re-narration.[24] The enduring narration of self is 'always held in context, shaped by contextual factors' that frame and mediate it.[25] It is within the ongoing transformative stage of studying law that students can experience this surge of understanding about their self-identity. Following Anthony Giddens,[26] a connection between identity construction and transformation can be explored within the context of the 'identity project'.[27] An identity project builds on what we think we are now in the light of our past and present circumstances together with what we think we would like to be, to form a trajectory of our hoped-for-future.[28] By reflecting on what it is they value, and 'about how matters of value are shared and disputed in the world

19 Cramton (1978) p 262 quoted in Economides and Webb (2000) p 9.

20 Huber et al (2013) p 213, quoting Clandinin and Connelly (1998).

21 Barker (2004) p 180.

22 As a story of the self, 'one's identity refers to points of temporary emotional attachment to the subject position which discursive practices construct for us': Barker (2004) p 180.

23 This is an anti-essentialist position, but it 'does not mean that we cannot speak of identity, rather it points us to the political nature of identity production and to the possibility of multiple and shifting identities': Barker (2000) p 66.

24 Blevins (2007) p 253 citing Holstine and Gubrium (2000).

25 Blevins (2007) p 253.

26 See Giddens (1991) p 75.

27 A student's identity project is therefore an attempt by the individual to form what Giddens has referred to as a continuous 'trajectory of development from the past to an anticipated future': Giddens (1991) p 75.

28 Barker (2000) p 167.

we inhabit with others',[29] students will be pushed to evaluate, defend, and sometimes reconstruct their self-identity in relation to the way they view the world of law. The identity project is therefore inextricably linked with the transforming work of law school, which should be seen not simply as a place where a legal curriculum is offered, but as a very powerful social environment in which transformation takes place. As Pommersheim argued many years ago, law schools should be places where 'students not only learn but also change. Change not only their ways of thinking but also their understanding of their values, their sense of what is meaningful, and the social obstacles that limit what is possible'.[30]

Importantly, it is through stories that self-identity builds up a consistent feeling of biographical continuity.[31] This makes sense because life is lived through stories—they are enormously commonplace, yet at the same time they can be unique. They can entertain and inform, they can involve and motivate us, and they can challenge us to reflect on the lives we lead. Yet, what is the place for stories within legal education? Can a story truly be used to affect change in the affective realm, on the way students feel; in the behavioural realm, the way students act or behave; and in the cognitive realm, on the way students think? Can story have an effect on a student's identity development and help them to be biopolitically aware and engaged? In my experience of teaching students over the last two decades, the answer to each of these questions is categorically affirmative.

In recognising that stories are the medium through which persuasion is enacted, and through which critique of societal practices and processes occur, my research has consistently sought to demonstrate that individuals use stories to frame and contextualise normative expectations of the legal system, and in so doing, they concomitantly participate in a transformation of meaning about law.[32] Examined through a legal lens, stories enable us to reflect on, question, and shape foundational legal assumptions upon which our legal system has been legitimised and authorised.[33] Stories therefore have enormous potential to shape experience,[34] and provoke, animate, and unmask biopolitics at work. In legal education, when students are invited to discuss stories, whether contemporary or historical, popular or disfavoured, they are prompted to imaginatively assess and reflect upon not only the various dimensions of life, but also upon the greater ethical, emotional, spiritual, and practical impacts of the world in which they live. As I have previously argued, students not only utilise the transformative power of stories

29 Elkins (2000) pp 127–9.
30 Pommersheim (1988) p 480.
31 Barker (2004) p 181.
32 Sharp (2011) p 33; Sharp (2005).
33 Olson (2015) p 43.
34 Presser (2010) p 434.

to construct identity and grapple with ethics,[35] but also, by discussing their views on the stories of law that are portrayed in popular culture and media, law students share and challenge each other's interpretations of law.[36] It is my contention that this process should be harnessed for the purposes of shaping biopolitical awareness. That is, to deploy stories in legal education towards biopolitical engagement is to value and yearn for diverse conversations about cultural, social, and political perspectives that are brought to bear on the law; and importantly to disrupt and strip bare dominant assumptions that regulate our collective existence.

This is the power of stories for shaping biopolitical awareness and engagement in the study of law. Of course, the use of stories in legal education is not new. The increasing prevalence of using stories to supplement traditional case teaching and analysis since the late 1980s to early 1990s,[37] is a result of a burgeoning recognition that storytelling is a form of active learning where the student listens to the story, absorbs the story at an emotional level, participates in the telling of the story, and then takes 'responsibility for his or her own learning by connecting it to what is familiar'.[38] Yet, it is by no means common place to adopt a story-based curriculum framework; nor is it prototypical that stories be deployed to develop biopolitical awareness or critical self-identity. This should be a cause for regret because there is much to be gained from incorporating storytelling and conversation into a curriculum. When students share their stories with one another and seek to jointly make sense of what is being learned and experienced, they are quite literally, 'talking' their self-identity into existence. It is in the referential circulation, transformation, and (re)production of stories the students tell one another that opens up a relational space to comfortably question and challenge ideas of oppression, injustice, and dehumanisation perpetuated through the law.

Given that stories connect us with the world beyond ourselves, and help us to work through big problems of human existence, when prompted to articulate our position, we are forced to think through not only our own ethical, spiritual, and biopolitical position on key societal issues, but also on how our bodies are positioned, disciplined, and controlled in this world. Such reflection has the resultant effect of character transformation, and refinement of self-identity. When we better understand who we have been through the past and in the present, we increase our capacity for imagining, explaining, and assessing who we are becoming in relation to this lived reality; and understanding the

35 Sharp (2005).

36 Sharp (2004).

37 Steslow and Gardner (2011) pp 252–6.

38 Steslow and Gardner (2011) p 252. See also Meyer (1992a) p 132 (discussing legal films as a pedagogical tool to reacquaint law students with the 'discontinuity and inexplicability of the lives they will encounter as lawyers'); Meyer (1992b) (discussing Meyer's experimental course entitled Law and Popular Storytelling).

subjective experience of others. The deliberate use of stories and storytelling towards a biopolitically aware legal education is so that students can be empowered to share this burgeoning (and ongoing) narrative of self with others, and in turn, to listen, engage, and reflect on the stories of others. As they read, interpret, and pursue the narratives around them, students begin a story production of their own, thus enabling them to begin addressing (and critiquing) biopolitical questions of character, human nature, and power relations.

Conversation as Pedagogy

As the previous sections have demonstrated, stories are fundamental to the way we learn, to the way we communicate,[39] and to the way we construct identity. As individuals tell stories of their experiences, they actively engage in a sense-making activity; as they narrate, they give meaning to their experiences and make sense of what is happening in their lives. It is therefore of central importance to facilitate for students the space in which to have meaningful dialogue and conversation. It is argued that in order for students to construct and understand their personal identity, it is incumbent on legal education to facilitate story-telling and story-listening. Through conversation, much can be explored by students about the conditions that affect life.

Interestingly, Rorty views a 'conversation' as a metaphor for culture. To him, an individual's ethical justifications are made within conversation and are bounded by community warrants. The words, opinions, and ideas we use in conversation to tell the 'story of our lives' is what Rorty terms our 'final vocabulary'.[40] In this sense, the interconnectedness of story and identity cannot be ignored.[41] As students learn how to use their ever-developing skills of critical reflection and analysis to interpret law's activity, they will also actively and consciously contribute to their reflexive project of the self.[42] In valuing the dialogue of students, legal education has the potential to empower student awareness of their own final vocabulary and to help them grow by developing and expanding it.

A story approach to engaging biopolitical awareness within student identity formation facilitates student reconceptualisation of their 'relationships among themselves, the profession, the law, its users, and the broader social and moral order'.[43] This provides a counter-balance to the danger that law students will learn to separate their professional and personal lives to the point

39 Steslow and Gardner (2011).

40 Rorty (1989) p 73: 'All human beings carry about a set of words which they employ to justify their actions, their beliefs, and their lives ... I shall call these words a person's "final vocabulary"'.

41 The 'final vocabulary of any person is that in which long-term projects are formulated, deep hopes and fears are expressed, and the story of one's life is told' Macintyre (1990) p 709.

42 Giddens (1991) p 75.

43 Kandel (1993) p 19.

of 'unreflective complacence and compliance'.[44] Such a permutation of student development must be avoided if the facilitation of biopolitical awareness and engagement is to be achieved. Elsewhere I have discussed my own deployment of stories in dedicated subject curricula at my institution.[45] Rather than simply treating popular fiction as legal and cultural texts to evaluate critical legal issues, practices, and institutions, I have developed two distinct subjects that *use* popular stories as an avenue for contextual learning and student exploration of ethics and identity.[46] My experience in teaching these subjects is that by allowing the communal generation and reproduction of meaning about life, love, and the community through conversation, students are enabled to actively engage in a transformation of stories. As they participate in classroom discussions, conduct informal conversations with friends, and engage in writing tasks, students are caused to re-evaluate and shape their lives and responsively adjust their ideals and paradigms. In this last section of the chapter, I wish to reflect on two particular interventions in my classroom pedagogy that rely on conversation to help shape biopolitical engagement: (i) student led 'roundtable' conversations using popular stories; and (ii) igniting reflexivity.

Conversation by Roundtable

Encouraging students to discuss and evaluate their perceptions and responses to stories engages them 'in the spoken, everyday world of connective, communal, constitutive talk'.[47] It enables students to explore the ways in which various values might be shared and disputed within their cultural community 'when we act by speaking, the dimension of our character "shows through"'[48] and we can explore the ways in which various values might be shared and disputed within our cultural communities. The pedagogical frameworks in my teaching are squarely based on providing opportunities for mutual discussion and growth along these lines. The aim is to regularly expose students to stories of law from a variety of non-traditional contexts[49] and to ask them to use 'conversation' to tell the 'story of their lives' in response to the stimulus material. The selection of stories for each class is based on the potential of each to challenge and explore the constructed nature of both law and culture, to highlight diverse cultural and political perspectives, and to provoke student reflection on

44 Kandel (1993) p 20.

45 Sharp (2019).

46 These two subjects are *Law and Popular Stories* (an elective for upper year students) and *Foundations of Law B* (a compulsory subject for first year students to introduce them to principles, theories, and concepts fundamental to the study and practice of law).

47 Elkins (1985) p 128.

48 Elkins (1985) p 127.

49 This includes the legal stories found in media, fictional literature, and the law (official and non-official, primary and secondary sources).

their own perspectives. Practically, this meant for example, developing curricula and class programmes that would provoke discussion about not only the dramatic ingredients in a particular text, but also a reflection about how these ingredients contribute to student responses and interpretation of legal stories. This 'pragmatic awareness' by students' cognitive, affective, and social selves[50] encapsulates another key objective for my teaching, and it became the stimulus for the roundtable experience.

Students are encouraged in each class to first critique a narrative strategy they can identify in the assigned text. The class begins with a plenary discussion critical of the chosen text/story/topic itself, where students are then prompted to reflect on how these strategies might have contributed to the stories occupying their imagination and/or transforming their understanding of law and its practice. By using popular topics and stories as stimulus, the emphasis is placed not on the students' responses to the stories per se, but instead on *how* those responses are constructed and then challenged by each other. The lesson then moves to student-led roundtables where students in small groups of 3–4 take turns in presenting prepared responses to stimulus questions within the theme of the week. Students are encouraged to humbly and compassionately engage in dialogue which would provoke their classmate to make sense of their emotional and intellectual experience of a text, 'to draw conclusions about the value of that experience, and then to communicate that value to others'.[51] As such, these focused roundtables are designed to direct the critical gaze to the ways in which these texts inform and transform ideas, values, and attitudes towards the norms that govern our collective existence.

The concept of roundtables in the small seminar mode is modelled on key aspects of focus group methodology, which recognises that perspectives are not static, but are instead discursively generated in the moment and as part of an ongoing process.[52] This means that built into the curriculum is the expectation that students will share their own responses to the prescribed stories, share speculations of the ways meanings are transformed in relation to those stories, and discuss the implications of those constructed meanings. By having an opportunity to express their responses to various legal issues as presented in stories, the benefits for students are twofold. First, students learn to take responsibility for their own thought processes, so that as they articulate their response or argument, they are taking a stand for their developing identity (even perhaps in the face of disagreement or conflict). Second, in being encouraged to hear and consider before responding, they are learning to actively listen to their

50 Liebes and Katz (1993) p 115.

51 Elkins (2004) p 866.

52 Sherwin advocates this approach too: Sherwin (2011). Our 'sense of self is distributed by the stories that circulate around and through us' p 141.

peers and humbly provoke each other to challenge assumptions and provide justifications for their stance on a given issue.

As a dynamic point of access to student identity development, the idea of roundtables produces an environment that is mutually stimulative and encourages the expression of views in a spontaneous and reactive manner. Although each student *will* have a varied interpretation of the meaning they create about a particular story,[53] Hall's theory of culture would recognise that a group of law students within the institutional context of law school, would at least be able to express their ideas in ways that would be understood by each other.[54] For this reason, class roundtables provide an opportunity to communally confront and critique these shared meanings and to expose the interpretive framework within which the students transform their individual expectations of life within the law. In my experience delivering these subjects, the benefit of conducting classes in this dynamic way enables exploration of the motivations and values *behind* student perspectives and expectations, and this is crucial for encouraging biopolitical awareness and engagement. As educators, we must allow space for students to question and reflect on the kinds of subjects that are constituted by discourses in law, including those of legal education. We should yearn for the re-assessing of dominant narratives through attention to 'relationships and lives in the making, understandings of telling … if we want a different future'.[55] This is a critical pedagogical framework that trades in honesty, transparency, and authenticity about the learning process that both teacher and student must participate in. That is why igniting the capacity for reflexivity is key.

Reflexivity

As the students articulate their storied responses to popular narratives, they participate in learning through reflection: 'to narrate a story is already to reflect upon the event narrated'.[56] Indeed, as referenced earlier, self-identity is constituted not by the possession of traits but rather as a reflexively sustained narrative of the self.[57] But what does it mean to be reflexive? Giddens argues that reflexivity involves a continual monitoring of an individual's activities and purposefully enabling oneself to constantly revise social activity in the light

53 Barker (2000) p 271. Barker argues that the reader will not merely reproduce textual meaning but will produce new meaning which is the result of the 'oscillations between the text and imagination of the reader'.

54 Hall (1997).

55 Huber et al (2013) p 213.

56 Ricoeur (1986) p 61 quoted in Tappan and Brown (1989) p 192.

57 See Giddens (1991) p 53: 'Self-identity is not a distinctive trait, or even a collection of traits, possessed by the individual. It is the self as reflexively understood by the person in terms of her or his biography'.

of new knowledge.[58] This means that reflexive law students would reflect on their own experiences, as well as those of around them, and actively construct identity in light of those reflections.

Given that education itself is a 'manifestation of power relations, co-extensive with the production of subjectivities',[59] law students will be active in the process of taking up subjective positions that help to constitute their subconscious and unconscious dimensions of the self. Indeed, the 'degree to which individuals can "choose" forms of identity is circumscribed by social power relations',[60] and students will be using sometimes complementary, sometimes conflicting discourses as contributors to their identity projects. On this basis, it is reasonable to expect that there may be contradictions in what the students say as they articulate the construction of identity while it is occurring, because 'identities shift according to how subjects are addressed or represented'.[61] This shifting, dislocation, and merging of identities is an exciting and integral part of the transformative process of law school and is a process that lays the foundation for developing biopolitical awareness. In turn, this requires significant training in reflexivity.

Encouraging reflexivity involves commitment from both the teacher and student to work together to produce alternative ways of thinking (and being) in a life lived with the law.[62] It involves commitment, willingness, and courage to confront oppressions inherent within the law; to expose the heavy-laden political nature of terms and concepts that often embody political positions but have been obscured by the context; and to fundamentally question political subjectification processes and activities. A classroom that seeks to expose the inequitable access, practices, and technologies that control and dominate our existence is one that pursues biopolitical awareness.

Emphasising reflexivity in the classroom means requiring students to produce evidence of that reflection. As I have described in this chapter, by assigning tasks that require students to question their assumptions, understandings, and ethical awareness, students are drawn one step closer to being aware of their personal identity construction, and to becoming biopolitically engaged.

58 Giddens (1991) p 35.

59 Bazzul (2017) p 45.

60 'In racist societies, for example, the subject positions open to Black people are often those defined by White institutions and it tends to be extremely difficult to escape hegemonic definitions of what it means to be "Black"': Jordan and Weedon (1995) pp 17–18.

61 Barker (2000) pp 66–7. Butler (1997) also recognises that the subject is always already a constituted subject that is disciplined and regulated by objects, institutions, others, and oneself: 'the subject produced and the subject regulated or subordinated are one, and that compulsory production is its own form of regulation', p 84.

62 Galloway and Jones (2014) argue that pursuing and harnessing transformation within legal education requires commitment from the academic as much as the student. They suggest that significant perspectives changes must 'call into question the very underlying assumptions upon which current value and practices are based', p 25.

Apart from the benefit of encouraging students to engage actively in self-reflection which enhances understandings, challenges perceptions, and maps emotions; reflexivity that is provoked through the pedagogical strategies outlined above, validates the notion of reflection and critical awareness within the context of formal legal education. Doing so facilitates student modulation and synthesis of the wide range of influences and resources that are informing their understanding of the law and legal culture.

Law school can (and should) explicitly nurture biopolitical engagement within student construction of identity. When students actively recognise and engage in the re(construction) of stories within their own realities, they are catalysed to stimulate critical reflexivity and subjective attentiveness. Pedagogical innovation can and should be developed to allow students to examine the practices that constitute subjectivities, and in so doing, develop their own biopolitically aware sensibilities.

References

Chris Barker (2000) *Cultural Studies: Theory and Practice*, SAGE Publications.

Chris Barker (2004) *The SAGE Dictionary of Cultural Studies*, SAGE Publications.

Jesse Bazzul (2017) 'Biopolitics and the "Subject" of Labor in Science Education' 12 *Cultural Studies of Science Education* 873–87.

Dean Blevins (2007) 'Story Telling or Storied Telling? Media's Pedagogical Ability to Shape Narrative as Form of Knowing' 102(3) *Religious Education* 250.

Gregory Bourassa (2011) 'Rethinking the Curricular Imagination: Curriculum and Biopolitics in the Age of Neoliberalism' 41 *Curriculum Inquiry* 5–16.

Judith Butler (1997) *The Psychic Life of Power: Theories in Subjection*, Stanford University Press.

Lyn Carter, Matthew Weinstein and Larry Bencze (2017) 'Biopolitics and Science Education' 12 *Cultural Studies of Science Education* 761–67.

D Jean Clandinin and F Michael Connelly (1998) 'Asking Questions about Telling Stories' in Craig Kridel (ed) *Writing Educational Biography: Explorations in Qualitative Research*, Garland Publishing.

Roger C Cramton (1978) 'The Ordinary Religion of the Law School Classroom' 29 *Journal of Legal Education* 247–63.

Geoff Danaher, Tony Schirato and Jen Webb (2000) *Understanding Foucault*, Allen & Unwin.

Kim Economides and Julian Webb (2000) 'Do Law Schools Care about Law Students and Legal Values?' 3(1) *Legal Ethics* 1–9.

James R Elkins (1985) 'On the Emergence of Narrative Jurisprudence: The Humanistic Perspective Finds a New Path' 9 *Legal Studies Forum* 123–55.

James R Elkins (2000) 'Lawyer Ethics: A Pedagogical Mosaic' 14 *Notre Dame Journal of Law, Ethics & Public Policy* 117–222.

James R Elkins (2004) 'Reading/Teaching Lawyer Films' 28 *Vermont Law Review* 813.

Francois Ewald (1986) *"Bio-Power" History of the Present*.

Stanley Fish (1980) *Is There a Text in This Class? The Authority of Interpretive Communities*, Harvard University Press.

Michel Foucault (1980) *The History of Sexuality*, Volume 1, Vintage Books.

Kate Galloway and Peter Jones (2014) 'Guarding our Identities: The Dilemma of Transformation in The Legal Academy' 14(1) *QUT Law Review* 15.

Anthony Giddens (1991) *Modernity and Self-Identity*, Polity.

Andrew Goldsmith (1995) 'Warning: Law School Can Endanger Your Health!' 21(2) *Monash University Law Review* 272–304.

Steve Greenfield, Guy Osborn and Peter Robson (2001) *Film and The Law*, Cavendish Publishing.

Stuart Hall (ed) (1997) *Representation: Cultural Representations and Signifying Practices*, SAGE.

JA Holstein and JF Gubrium (2000) *The Self we Live By: Narrative Identity in a Postmodern world* Oxford University Press.

Janice Huber, et al. (2013) 'Narrative Inquiry as Pedagogy in Education: The Extraordinary Potential of Living, Telling, Retelling, and Reliving Stories of Experience' 37(1) *Review of Research in Education* 212–42.

Glenn Jordan and Chris Weedon (1995) *Cultural Politics: Class, Gender, Race and the Postmodern World*, Oxford Press.

Randy Frances Kandel (1993) 'Whither the Legal Whale: Interdisciplinarity and the Socialization of Professional Identity' 27 *Loyola of Los Angeles Law Review* 9–24.

Tamar Liebes and Elihu Katz (1993) *The Export of Meaning: Cross-Cultural Readings of Dallas*, Polity Press.

Alasdair Macintyre (1990) 'Book Review: Contingency, Irony and Solidarity' 87 *The Journal of Philosophy* 708.

Philip N Meyer (1992a) 'Convicts, Criminals, Prisoners and Outlaws: A Course in Popular Storytelling' 42 *Journal of Legal Education* 129–38.

Philip N Meyer (1992b) 'Law Students Go to the Movies' 24 *Connecticut Law Review* 893.

Philip N Meyer and Steven Cusick (2004) 'Using Non-Fiction Films as Visual Texts in the First Year Criminal Law Course' 28(4) *Vermont Law Review* 895–914.

Greta Olson (2015) 'Futures of Law and Literature: A Preliminary Overview from a Culturalist Perspective' in Christian Hiebaum, Susanne Knaller and Doris Pichler (eds) *Law and Literature In-Between: Contemporary Inter- and Transdisciplinary Approaches*, Transcript Verlag.

John Jay Osborn Jr (1990) 'UFOs in the Law School Curriculum: The Popularity and Value of Law and Literature Courses' 14(1) *Legal Studies Forum* 53–61.

Timothy Peters and Karen Crawley (eds) (2018), *Envisioning Legality: Law, Culture and Representation*, Routledge.

Frank Pommersheim (1988) 'Voice, Values, and Community: Some Reflections on Legal Writing' 12(4) *Legal Studies Forum* 477–88.

Lois Presser (2010) 'Collecting and Analysing the Stories of Offenders' 21 *Journal of Criminal Justice Education* 431–46.

Paul Ricoeur (1986) *Time and Narrative*, University of Chicago Press.

Richard Rorty (1989) *Contingency, Irony and Solidarity*, Cambridge University Press.

Cassandra Sharp (2004) 'Changing the Channel: What to do With the Critical Abilities of Law Students as Viewers?' 13(2) *Griffith Law Review* 185–99.

Cassandra Sharp (2005) 'The "Extreme Makeover" Effect of Law School: Students being Transformed by Stories' 12(1) *Texas Wesleyan Law Review* 233–50.

Cassandra Sharp (2011) '"Represent a Murderer … I'd Never do That!" How Students use Stories to Link Ethical Development and Identity Construction' in Michael Robertson et al. (eds) *The Ethics Project in Legal Education*, Routledge.

Cassandra Sharp (2019) 'Why Law Students Should Watch More TV … Reflections on the Deliberate Use of Popular Stories in Training Future Lawyers' in Christine Corcos (ed) *Teaching Law and Popular Culture* (CAP, 2019).

Cassandra Sharp and Marett Leiboff (eds), *Cultural Legal Studies: Law's Popular Cultures and the Metamorphosis of Law* (Routledge 2016)

Richard K Sherwin (2011) 'Visual Jurisprudence' 56 *New York Law School Law Review* 137–65.

DM Steslow and C Gardner (2011) 'More than One Way to Tell a Story: Integrating Storytelling into Your Law Course' 28 *Journal of Legal Studies Education* 249–71.

Mark B Tappan and Lyn Mikel Brown (1989) 'Stories Told and Lessons Learned: Toward a Narrative Approach to Moral Development and Moral Education' 59(2) *Harvard Educational Review* 182–206.

John Wittman (2006) 'Biopower and Pedagogy: Local Spaces and Institutional Technologies', Spring, *Composition Forum* 15.

Part III

Posthuman Resistance

Chapter 11

Rosi Braidotti's Posthuman Knowledge and Legal Education

A Critical Appraisal

Luca Siliquini-Cinelli

Introduction

This chapter offers a critical contextualisation of Rosi Braidotti's ethical call for posthuman knowledge from the perspective of the crisis which legal education has been witnessing over the past few decades. I have been writing on legal education's malaise for some time now. At present, I am also working on a new monograph which explores it in relation to how law has been studied and practised in both the Civil and Common law traditions since the Late Roman Republic.[1] The following reflections are not aimed at reproducing, in a shorter format, the thoughts developed in my past works and the new book. Rather, they focus on a very specific, and narrower, question: whether Braidotti's argument for posthuman knowledge can be of any assistance in overcoming legal education's crisis. The chapter answers this interrogative by critically engaging with the two much-acclaimed books where Braidotti outlined her posthuman programme: *The Posthuman* and *Posthuman Knowledge*.[2]

As with my other works on the status of legal education, what follows starts from the premise that law appears to be witnessing an existential paradox in Western and Western-oriented jurisdictions, with two apparently opposing trends taking place. On the one hand, human existence and interaction are more regulated (that is, monitored and controlled) than ever before. Legal theorists and empiricists increasingly hold that that of our time is an uncertain and liquid normative architecture characterised by a growing regulatory density, intricacy, and uncertainty of which the global and transnational emergence and spread of processes of legal diversification, fragmentation, and transformation (i.e., de-formalisation) are they key protagonists.

Yet, on the other hand, scholars and practitioners in Western and Western-oriented jurisdictions have also been claiming that legal education is experiencing profound difficulties for a variety of reasons. These include the inability of teachers to efficiently educate their students for the highly contested market

1 Under contract.
2 Braidotti (2013, 2019), respectively.

DOI: 10.4324/9781003179283-15

environments; the failure of the teaching curricula and law degrees more generally to meet the legal professions' entry level requirements and real-life demands; the increasing difficulty for graduates to enter the legal services world; the incapacity of the modern legal infrastructure to cope with the pace of innovation and change on the global and transnational scales; and the growing reliance on technological means to teach legal subjects and perform legal tasks.

For my own part, I believe these two trends to be complementary, rather than antithetical. More specifically, they are part of a broader phenomenon regarding law's theoretical and practical categorisation as a cognitivist enterprise revolving around rational techniques of ontological abstraction and as opposed to an act of experience. What both trends signal is the increasing inability of law's juridical component to embrace the reality of contemporary (and future) forms of regulation. In short, they are signalling the vanishing of the jurist[3] (specifically, of her experiential intermediation) rather than of (the) law as such, as is often too easily assumed. If knowledge is a metaphysical end result of intellectual processes of ontological abstraction;[4] if knowing (i.e., the cognitive process broadly understood), as the Humanist Giacomo Zabarella believed, is an impersonal function;[5] and if all that law needs to perform its regulatory function is knowledge, then we do not need the experiential figure of the jurist to act as an ontological medium between law and life. Nor do we need legal education to embrace, protect, and nourish education's individualising (i.e., other-regarding) ethos. All we need is a form of education that focuses on bare, constructivist learning. And, whenever possible, either let us do the job by one-right answer problem-solving assessments (such as the multiple-choice test of the Solicitors Qualifying Examination), or computational, algorithm-based modes of legal reasoning and argument (as is increasingly being done).[6]

Now, when asking whether Braidotti's posthuman knowledge can offer any solution to this, one is faced with the difficulty that due to its interdisciplinary nature, her thought can be approached from various perspectives of inquiry. For the purposes of this chapter, I propose to explore it from the perspective of what distinguishes knowledge from experience *philosophically*. Adopting this angle, this chapter welcomes Braidotti's ethical proposal to the extent that, in moving beyond 'Humanism and anthropocentrism',[7] it draws attention to what legal education has been avoiding since its inception—namely, the facticity, finitude, and relationality of life. However, it also shows that Braidotti

3 Or 'lawyer', in Common law jurisdictions.

4 I return to this below, Section 3.

5 Randall Jr. (1956) pp 262, 264.

6 I develop this argument in full in the above-mentioned new monograph. On the spread of artificial intelligence in the legal domain, see Ashley (2017).

7 Braidotti (2019) p 69. See further below, Section 2.

fails to appreciate that as long as (any) ethics remains confined within the realm of knowledge, as hers does, it cannot assist teachers in overcoming legal education's existential crisis. What is required is, rather, a form of experiential, biopolitically-charged thinking which is freed from epistemic ambitions. Only such thinking, I submit, can accommodate the facticity of otherness *qua* immanent and unique diversity and alterity.

To show this, I first outline the tenets of Braidotti's posthuman knowledge (Section 2), to then expound some critical reflections on it in relation to legal education's crisis (Section 3). Concluding remarks follow.

Braidotti's Posthuman Knowledge

A leading philosopher and biopolitical thinker worldwide, Braidotti's scholarship has inspired, and will no doubt continue to inspire, generations of thinkers who tackle established narratives of the West and its culture(s) broadly understood. Braidotti's work has proved capable of dismantling orthodox assumptions regarding who we are and what we do, thereby setting the stage for new directions of thought both within and outside the humanities. As such, it deserves proper consideration, particularly in a project, like the one this chapter is part of, which intends to fill an important void in the literature on legal education by examining the latter's biopolitical nature, aims, dynamics, and implications.

Before proceeding with my analysis, however, I ought to clarify why Braidotti's views are worth considering in an essay which is, ultimately, concerned with jurisprudential issues. Reflecting biopolitically on the status and future of *legal* education simply means embarking upon a type of inquiry which is, inevitably, of a jurisprudential tenor. This should be obvious, especially if one considers, first, that law is a human artefact whose job is to regulate human conduct (and thus, life, human and non-human, more generally); and second, that the training of future lawyers is based on the assumption that to be able to know *what* a norm states and prescribes, one ought to know *how* to extract and apply the rule(s) it contains. Once combined, these considerations help us appreciate why, in the Western legal tradition, jurisprudence is conceived as the epistemic *prudentia*[8] of legal reasoning and argumentation culminating in the *contextual* pointing of *ius* (*iuris-dictio*)—a categorisation which legal education validates, nourishes, and pushes further.[9]

Braidotti's thought fits the threshold where legal education and jurisprudence meet well. This is clear from two considerations which open and guide her posthuman philosophy. First, Braidotti rejects the 'social constructivist

8 Cf. *Dig*., 1.1.10.2.

9 For space constraints, I cannot delve into these themes at length here. I discuss them in detail, with supporting sources, in my forthcoming monograph, mentioned earlier.

approach'.[10] The latter Braidotti understands as a complex web of instrumentalist techniques which falsify what (human) life really is and entails. Braidotti replaces constructivism with the 'nature-culture continuum'[11]—that is to say, with 'a non-dualistic understanding of nature-culture interaction'[12] that emphasises the 'self-organizing (or auto-poietic) force of living matter'.[13] The nature-culture continuum is the 'starting point'[14] of Braidotti's posthuman philosophy of 'life beyond theory'.[15] Now, what is of interest for our discussion is that in calling for a dialectic between nature and culture, Braidotti reproduces and pushes further within biopolitical discourse the very foundational paradigm of Western jurisprudence (and social thought more generally)[16]—i.e., the *physis-nomos* relationship. While nature and convention have been conceptualised as separate realms since ancient times,[17] throughout Western jurisprudence they kept interacting consistently, with one (nature) serving as an inspiration for the other (convention) more often than not.[18] The fact that Braidotti has not considered this theme reveals a great deal about the limits of her posthuman argument, especially in light of the heavy jurisprudential terminology (i.e., subject, justice, freedom, resistance, etc.) and lines of thought she employs in her work.[19]

The other preliminary consideration Braidotti makes which confirms the appropriateness of contextualising her thought from the perspective of the teaching and learning of law concerns her 'dream'[20] to be part of 'communities of learning'[21] and 'produc[e] socially relevant knowledge'.[22] Braidotti's posthuman project is not a theoretical or abstract one. It is, rather, very much practical and concrete—it is, in short, a *praxis* (on which more shortly). As she writes, posthuman knowledge

> shapes [her] vision of what a university should look like – a *universum* that serves the world of today, not only as the epistemological site of scientific production, but also of epistemophilic yearning for the empowerment that comes with knowledge and sustains our subjectivity.[23]

10 Braidotti (2013) p 2.
11 Ibid., p 2.
12 Ibid., p 3.
13 Ibid., p 3.
14 Ibid., pp 2, 82. See also Ibid., p 103.
15 Ibid., ch 4.
16 Kelley (1990).
17 Ibid., pp 16–17.
18 See e.g., ibid., pp xii, 1, 19, 24–8, 38, 45, 49, 58, 116ff, 137–44, 168ff, 213ff, 234ff, ch 15.
19 see e.g., Braidotti (2019) pp 128–30.
20 Braidotti (2013) p 11.
21 Ibid., p 11.
22 Ibid., p 11.
23 Ibid., p 11. See also ibid., ch 4; Braidotti (2019) pp 91, 145–52, ch 4.

With these words, Braidotti asks that she be considered as an educator prior than a philosopher. Accordingly, one cannot but wonder whether the posthuman knowledge she crafts can also shed new light on *legal* education's problems and how to solve them.

So, then, how does Braidotti conceive of posthuman knowledge? Assuming I have understood her correctly, posthuman knowledge is Braidotti's preferred epistemic tool to frame a relational, inclusive, pluralist, and affirmative ethics.[24] Posthuman knowledge is the epistemic referent for the crafting of an analytical framework which, on Braidotti's view, accommodates life's alterity by dismantling humanistic and anthropomorphic ideologies and power structures,[25] among which stand exclusionary, polarised logics and related cultures and practices of governance. Crucially, while Braidotti argues for such an epistemic framework, she clearly states that the posthuman, including posthuman knowledge, is not something to be awaited. Rather, it is 'already happening'[26]—or 'circulating'.[27] Accordingly, Braidotti's posthuman knowledge should be seen as conducive to the emergence of an ethically-charged, affirmative 'space of encounter'[28] where posthuman phenomena can intelligibly appear (and be valued) for what they truly are and entail: 'The posthuman convergence', Braidotti affirms, 'is an analytical tool for understanding the grounded, perspectival, and accountable nature of the affective, social and epistemic processes *we are currently involved in*'.[29]

Stated otherwise, to the extent that the 'posthuman times'[30] we find ourselves in 'call for and are sustained by posthuman subjects of knowledge constituted within them across a number of rather exhausting contradictions and paradoxes',[31] a whole new set of notions, concepts, and theories where life's immanent plurality can be adequately understood and communicated are needed. Rejecting 'unilateral or universal'[32] conceptualisations,[33] 'disciplinary purity',[34] and 'flat ontolog[ies]',[35] what Braidotti seeks to establish is, then, 'an [epistemic] workable framework',[36] or 'plane of encounter for multiple

24 Braidotti (2019) pp 3, 11, 13, 17, 19, 27f, 34f, 41, 52, 61–74, 72, 79, 90, 115, 132, 123, 132, chs 6–7.
25 See e.g., ibid., pp 11, 43, 69, 84, 177; Braidotti (2013), chs 1–2.
26 Ibid., p 90.
27 Braidotti (2013) p 5.
28 Braidotti (2019) p 36.
29 Ibid., p 17. Emphasis added.
See also ibid., pp 12, 28, 40.
30 Ibid., p 39.
31 Ibid., p 39.
32 Ibid., p 38.
33 Such as 'the people': ibid., pp 23, 11, 46, 52ff, 175.
34 Braidotti (2013) p 145.
35 Braidotti (2019) p 50.
36 Ibid., p 17.

differential positions which acknowledge[s] their situated and hence partial perspective'.[37]

Braidotti's challenge is clear: it is 'how to re-define the subject of knowledge and power without reference to that unitary, humanistic, Eurocentric and masculinist subject'[38]—the famous 'Man of Reason'[39]—that has come to define our socio-political, socio-economic, and socio-legal existence. Given the pervasiveness of established modes of thinking and practices which for centuries (if not millennia) have nourished what is also known as the 'man *qua* Man' (or '*quid est Homo*'[40]) construct, it comes as no surprise that 'posthumanizing subjectivity'[41] will take some doing. A crucial part of this endeavour is admitting that inherited, 'dominant systems of thought'[42] ought to be openly rejected: '[W]e need … an enlarged, distributed and transversal concept of what a subject is and of how it deploys its relational capacities'.[43] Braidotti makes this point throughout her posthuman scholarship. Already in *The Posthuman*, she affirmed that:

> Instead of falling back on the sedimented habits of thought that the humanist past has institutionalized, the posthuman predicament encourages us to undertake a lead forward into the complexities and paradoxes of our time. To meet this task, new conceptual creativity is needed.[44]

Only by taking this much-needed leap into the unknown we can 'find adequate theoretical and imaginary representations for our lived conditions'.[45] This explains why, as mentioned above, the move Braidotti advocates is inherently ethical: our posthuman existence calls for a new 'ethical bond of an altogether different sort from the self-interests of an individual subject'.[46] And it could not be otherwise given that, as was seen, the defining characteristic of our posthuman condition is that it is *relational*. In this sense, and as one might expect, limiting posthumanisation to the realm of theory is not enough. If we are to epistemically *actualise* the rich potential which posthuman subjectivities carry, then a 'practical',[47] destabilising turn is also required. Accordingly, a defining

37 Ibid., p 39. See also ibid., pp 12, 175; Braidotti (2013) p 5.
38 Ibid., p 43.
39 Ibid., p 46. See also ibid., pp 3, 85, 105, 175; Braidotti (2013) pp 169ff.
40 Cacciari (2019) p 42.
41 Braidotti (2019) p 41.
42 Ibid., p 124.
43 Ibid., p 40. See also above (nn 24–5).
44 Braidotti (2013) p 54.
45 Ibid., p 187.
46 Ibid., p 190.
47 Braidotti (2019) p 74.

feature of Braidotti's posthuman project is that it 'bases the [new] ethical relation on positive grounds of joint projects and activities'.[48]

While the basic elements of this venture are laid out in *The Posthuman*,[49] it is in her later work *Posthuman Knowledge* that Braidotti outlines it in detail while also qualifying some of its requirements. There, the need for 'new concepts'[50] is re-affirmed, as is that for bringing to the surface posthumanism's ethical nature. 'We are indeed becoming posthuman ethical subjects',[51] Braidotti affirms. 'We do so by overcoming hierarchical dichotomies and cultivating instead our multiple capacities for relations and modes of communication if a multi-directional manner'.[52] We are, in short, *experimenting*: posthumanism is a continuous 'experimentation'[53] that gives voice and space to, while also constantly adapting, our creative and multi-faced 'becoming'.[54] This is why Braidotti repeatedly qualifies the posthuman, including posthuman knowledge, as a '*praxis*'[55]—or 'grounded shared project'.[56] In fact, ethics and *praxis* are for Braidotti one and the same: 'ethics is a *praxis* that begins with the production of adequate knowledge in the sense of providing qualitative differentiations between different instances, ideas and relations'.[57]

Braidotti's ambitious 'recipe'[58] deserves extended treatment, certainly more than can be provided here. Due to the biopolitical focus of the present chapter and collection of essays, an element which I would like to draw the reader's attention to is that the move away from the 'binary',[59] exclusionary logics of the '*Homo Universalis* of Humanism [and] the other-than-the *Anthropos* of anthropocentrism'[60] Braidotti envisages demands recognising that life, *zoe*, 'exceed[es] anthropocentric perspectives and humanistic expectations'.[61] We are 'members of a species, and not just of a culture or polity',[62] Braidotti notes. Thus '*bios*'—

48 Braidotti (2013) p 190.
49 See especially chs 1 and 2.
50 Braidotti (2019) p 123. See also ibid., pp 34, 76.
51 Ibid., p 63.
52 Ibid., p 63.
53 Ibid., p 63. See also ibid., p 9.
54 Ibid., p 63.
55 See e.g., ibid., pp 63, 68.
56 Braidotti (2013) p 92. See also ibid., p 100; and above (nn 23–4).
57 Braidotti (2019) p 92. Emphasis added.
See also ibid., p 132:

> [T]he quest for adequate understanding is both epistemological and ethical. Epistemologically, understanding requires critical elucidation of one's conditions. Ethically, the posthuman subject needs to stay in tune with one's innermost essence. Combining them expresses a fundamental freedom, which is experienced as a joyful passion.

58 Ibid., p 55.
59 Ibid., p 54.
60 Ibid., pp 54–5.
61 Ibid., p 177.
62 Ibid., p 10.

'the life of humans organized in society … regulated by sovereign powers and rules'[63]—is an insufficient, if not misleading, category of thought. Yet, at the same time, Braidotti rejects the *zoe-bios* 'opposition'[64] as it has been conceived and promoted in the Humanities to date. The category of thought which better fits our posthuman times is, instead, that of '*zoe*/geo/techno assemblage'.[65] The latter is a phrase which aims at preserving life's immanent priority (its being 'inexhaustible'[66]) while also recognising and giving validation to 'the geological and technological aspects of [our posthuman] transformation'.[67] It is, then, a fundamental, 'neo-materialist'[68] step towards the epistemic and ethical (and thus, strictly 'non-profit'[69]) experimentation Braidotti calls for to actualise, via the 'nature-culture continuum',[70] mentioned earlier, the subjectivising potential(s) which the posthuman constellation expresses and which the contemporary 'capitalization of living'[71] suffocates.

In this sense, it is worth pointing out that contrary to what is argued by Giorgio Agamben, Braidotti is of the idea that an affirmative, posthuman ethics of *zoe* 'cannot be reduced to devalued and dehumanized life'.[72] Rather, the posthuman, including its knowledge, is the expression of an extraordinary potential, whose actualisation is precisely what Braidotti aims to contribute to. 'Politics', we read in a key-passage of *Posthuman Knowledge*, 'requires not resistance, but the effort to activate the generative force of virtual possibilities'.[73] What Agamben has not understood, according to Braidotti, is that conceptualised as 'bare life[, *zoe*] is devalued life, assigned to the status of disposable scapegoat'.[74] Once we instead realise that '[l]ife is a generative force beneath, below and beyond what we humans have made of it',[75] we can consequently appreciate that '[*z*]*oe*/geo/techno perspectives at the core of [it] … provide multiple alternatives'[76] through which the posthuman can finally appear and be nourished. This is why, to Braidotti, '[e]thics starts with the composition of transversal subject assemblages – "we, posthuman subject" – that actualize the unrealized or virtual potential of what "we" are capable of becoming'.[77]

63 Ibid., p 10.
64 Ibid., p 10.
65 Ibid., p 44.
66 Ibid., ch 7.
67 Ibid., p 44. See also ibid., pp 45, 52.
68 Ibid., pp 45, 50, 64, 66.
69 Braidotti (2013) p 61.
70 Ibid., p 61.
71 Ibid., p 61.
72 Braidotti (2019) p 177.
73 Ibid., p 177.
74 Ibid., p 177.
75 Ibid., p 177.
76 Ibid., p 177. See also ibid., pp 44–63, 111–12.
77 Ibid., p 54. See also ibid., pp 50, 79, 166–8, 177.

A Critique

I have been arguing for some time now that since its inception, legal education has been voiding the facticity, finitude, and relationality of life. This is due to the constructivism which animates legal education's nature, aims, and operations. Legal education is indeed a matter of knowledge revolving around rational techniques of world-disposition that metaphysically measure, organise, *structure* and ultimately, void experience. This categorisation is not confined to the theoretical (i.e., notionistic) study of legal norms only: as the latter are not (yet) self-applying, it also involves their learned actualisation through juristic practice.[78]

In its own way, Braidotti's thought draws much-needed attention to this phenomenon. However, insightful though they are, Braidotti's views are, I contend, ultimately incapable of assisting legal education overcoming its malaise. This is due to a simple consideration: namely, that experience is not, and cannot be, knowledge. This is because, philosophically, or so at least I submit, experience is factical, imperfect, and self-defining, whereas knowledge is ethereal, perfect, and self-dissolving. Accordingly, whenever we try to decode experience epistemically, or try to craft an epistemic framework through which experience can be known, as Braidotti does, we inevitably fall prey to analytical techniques of world-disposition that void what makes our experiential finitude such.

The very claims Braidotti makes, as well as by the overall trajectory of her thought confirm that appraising her posthuman project from the perspective of what distinguishes knowledge from experience philosophically is all the more appropriate. Ultimately, indeed, Braidotti's is an ethics of relationality, whose protagonist is the situatedness, as she calls it, of posthuman subjects. Rejecting the relativism of universalist logics of subsumption, Braidotti's interest lies in what makes us who we are in our own experiential facticity. Her very purpose is to free the latter from instrumentalist practices of labelling so that it can appear for what it really is. True, Braidotti clearly states that posthuman relationality 'is not to be confused with individualized emotions … [or] individualism'.[79] Rather, it is made by a 'thick and dynamic web of connections … that defy our collective and singular powers of perception and understanding'.[80] This is not surprising: self-referential individualism is the very source of the (man-centred, other-disregarding, capitalist, etc.) appropriation (i.e., destruction) of life that Braidotti opposes. Yet, in opposing the individualist stance, Braidotti is not rejecting experience. In fact, she places it at the very centre of her posthuman proposition.

78 With the caveat that not all law is jurist-made or jurist-dependent.

79 Braidotti (2019) p 45.

80 Ibid., p 45.

Now, the reader might observe that making experience the focal point of a relational ethics is not that surprising: for relationality to occur, an experiential encounter needs to take place. Relationality, we may say, *is* (a matter of) experience. Yet what makes Braidotti's thought interesting for our purposes is that she does not limit herself at recognising this factual circumstance. Rather, she assigns experience a prominent role *analytically*, continually referring to the '*immanence* of relations'[81]—or their situatedness, as already mentioned. We need, she writes, a 'politics of location or of immanence, and of perspectivism as multi-layered and multi-directional account of what is already happening'.[82] It is precisely this *active*, experiential element of 'specification [and] actualization'[83] that makes Braidotti's posthuman philosophy a *praxis*—that is, a 'practical',[84] relational ethics of affirmation.

Let us consider a few remarks that show this clearly: '[T]he posthuman convergence points to … a multi-directional opening that allows for multiple possibilities and calls for experimental forms of mobilization, discussion and at times even resistance. The keyword of posthuman scholarship is multiplicity';[85] '[p]osthuman knowledge is fuelled by transversality and heterogeneity … multiplicity and complexity';[86] 'heterogeneity and complexity allow us to think about the production of multiple actualized life-forms that are irreducibly differentiated. When posthuman subjects become individuated, they will become embodied and embedded in the process of actualization'.[87]

Yet, at the same time, Braidotti is unequivocal that the posthuman can only be made appear *epistemically*—it calls, she argues, for new knowledge capable of 'constructing sustainable alternatives'.[88] Hence the title of her second book discussed in this chapter, *Posthuman Knowledge*, where she speaks of 'posthuman knowledge production'.[89] Referring once again to the 'posthuman convergence'—that is, to the '*zoe*/geo/techno assemblage' discussed earlier—Braidotti writes that the latter is the 'coming into focus of new conditions for knowledge production and consequently relational encounters'.[90] Thus, relationality does not precedes knowledge; rather, it is knowledge that makes relationality possible. This is why, as anticipated above, Braidotti 'propose[s] to deal with [the posthuman] conceptually',[91] arguing for a new analytical framework.

81 Braidotti (2013) p 82.
82 Braidotti (2019) p 90.
83 Ibid., p 68.
84 Ibid., p 42.
85 Ibid., p 9.
86 Ibid., pp 18–19.
87 Ibid., p 53
88 Ibid., p 64.
89 Ibid., p 3, ch 3.
90 Ibid., p 68.
91 Ibid., p 84.

This leads me to what I perceive as the main philosophical inconsistency of Braidotti's thought—namely, that she blurs what distinguishes experience from knowledge and replaces the former with the latter. As I have argued elsewhere,[92] knowledge is a metaphysical end-result of intellectual processes of ontological abstraction that transcend life's finitude by objectifying beings as phenomena (and thus human existence and relations). To put it differently, knowledge phenomenologically equalises the targets of its reach for regulative and structuralising purposes, thus emptying their constituting properties as well as the unpredictability of their interaction. This also explains why, despite being 'organized and articulated',[93] experience is unique and imperfect, while knowledge looks for certainty and truth[94] through a logic that prompts objectification, and thus nullification.

In my earlier work, I substantiated my argument regarding what separates experience from knowledge philosophically through a philosophical-archaeological contextualisation of Emanuele Severino's scholarship on Aeschylus' *Prometheus Bound*. The latter offers invaluable philosophical insights into the origins of the 'the radical intellectualization of … life'[95] in the Western tradition by means of a theatrical representation of the replacement of experience's traumaticity with the reassuring, epistemic (i.e., rational) reading of life.[96]

More specifically, *Prometheus Bound* narrates, through the tragedy suffered by the father of all *téchnai*, how the making-sense act was turned from an illogical wandering into a normative quest for ultimate truths *qua* causal relations attainable through reason.[97] It displays the 'tragedy of … the civilizing genius[']'[98] desire to reach existential quietness through a causal decoding of life. For it is the causal reading and management of life that enable us to understand phenomena and predict the future, thereby liberating our existence from chaos, anxiety, and pain.[99]

Severino magisterially showed this through a philological analysis of the tragedy's text. For present purposes, the terms 'Prometheus' and '*epistḗmē*' are of particular interest. As his name reveals, Prometheus is the god that knows everything in advance ('*pro-mētheús*', '*pro-mathḗs*') and whose thinking moves

92 Most recently, see Siliquini-Cinelli (2020).

93 Cassirer (1944) p 208.

94 See e.g., Russell (1962) p 19: '… [K]nowledge must be defined in terms of "truth"'; and Nagel (2014) p 8: '… [A]s soon as we recognize the falsity [of what we thought we knew], we have to retract the claim that it was ever known'.

95 Cassirer (1946) p 171.

96 Severino (1989). All translations are mine.

97 See especially *Prometheus Bound*, 101–3, 436ff, 506.

98 Jaeger (1965) p 262.

99 Severino (1989), (2010), ch 5. This is most evident in the case mathematics (see Rovelli (2017) p 30), the science which already in its name points to its Promethean origins. Not incidentally, Prometheus' main gifts to humankind are numbers—primary among the skills, or sciences ('*èxochon sofismaton*'): *Prometheus Bound*, 459.

on a rectilinear plane on which all that exists is effectually commeasured (*'pánt' epistathmṓmenos'*, *'pro-ex-epístasthai'*) for epistemic purposes.[100] *'Epistḗmē'*, a noun to which a whole family of terms (i.e., epistemic, epistemological, etc.) is related, literally means knowledge that is certain, absolute, unshakable (*epi-hístēmi*[101]) knowledge[102]—or, to use Aristotle's terminology, 'non-accidental'.[103] Epistemic knowledge is the type of causal, salvific knowledge which defines Prometheus' commeasuring analysis of phenomena and which the titan donates to humankind.[104]

Thus, *Prometheus Bounds* shows that epistemic knowledge is obtained through reason's methodological effectuality—i.e., the cognitive process is propelled by a calculating reason whose effectuality is expressed through an intellectual *act of measurement* whereby any given data is *causally made sense of* for ordering, guiding (and thus, normative) purposes.[105]

Now, epistemic knowledge was first sought with the inception of philosophical thinking in the cultural climate of the ancient Greek world, where it was conceived as scientific knowledge. Philosophical thinking emerged as *analytical* thinking, i.e., as myth-dispelling and truth-seeking thinking founded on discovery of causal relations *qua* universal truths.[106] Since its inception, philosophical inquiry has never stopped concerning itself with what causes the existence of the manifold as alterity be, and with the related issue of the orderability of particulars (to which philosophers oppose universals or similar constructs, such as concepts). The possibility, trajectories, and outcomes of these sorts of inquiries depend on our ability to *make sense* of the world—that is to say, it depends on our ability to intelligibly understand and communicate it. While this was first realised in antiquity, things have not changed to date: as David Owens writes, 'the *making sense* relation is the basic normative relation'.[107]

This might sound puzzling given that the present-day understanding of scientific knowledge is altogether different from its ancient counterpart. As Karl Popper, Bertrand Russell, Severino, Massimo Cacciari, Giorgio Agamben, Naomi Oreskes, Carlo Rovelli, David Wootton and other philosophers, historians, and scientists say, modern (i.e. post-Scientific Revolution) scientific

100 Severino (1989) pp 27–31, 179–207. See also Jaeger (1965) pp 253, 265.

101 Severino (1979) p 17; (1989) pp 28–9; (2010) p 29.

102 Severino (1979) pp 13ff; (1989) pp 27–9; (2010) pp 21–3, 29, ch 5, p 310.

103 *Post. Anal.*, I 71^{b}10, 71^{b}28; *Metaphysics*, 1026^b.

104 Severino (1989) pp 21–31, 79–80, 185, 187–96, 198, 205–7, 346, 352.

105 See Severino (1989) p 28: '*Epistathmṓmenos*' (meaning 'to measure' and which is the 'verbal mode through which *epistēmē* presents itself') derives from the substantive '*státhmē*', which was the rope used to measure and work stone and wood in Ancient Greece and which means 'norm' or 'rule'.

106 *Post. Anal.*, I 71^{b}9–15, II 89^{b}23–90^{a}34, II 94^{a}20; *Physics*, 184^{a}10–11, 188^{a}30–188^{b}2, 194^{b}16–22, 197^{a}19, 198^{a}14–^{b}9; *Metaphysics*, 981^{a}15–16, 1028^{a}36ff.

In literature, see Cassirer (1946), 54; Severino (2010), ch 1; (2013a) p 17; (2013b) pp 10–11; Jaeger (1965) pp 150–84; Rovelli (2011) pp 38, 68, 181; (2017) pp 4–5; Bronstein (2016) pp 31, 81.

107 Owens (2012) p 12.

knowledge does not aim at ultimate, definitive truths. Rather, scientific knowledge is relative and imperfect. Were it otherwise, it would not be *progressive*. Yet, however correct these considerations may be, we should not forget that truth, even if momentary, continues to be science's objective.[108] Moreover, while science's *télos* might have changed (from certain to probable truth), the underlying belief that how one progresses towards truth matters a great deal has not. Accordingly, it is believed that what distinguishes the scientific production of knowledge from other cognitivist enterprises lies in in the systematisation of the various end results (theoretical knowledge) as well as in the further sophistication of the methodologies deployed by the analyst, among which stand the 'systematic observation and experimentation, inductive and deductive reasoning, and the formation and testing of hypotheses and theories'[109] (experimental knowledge). Thus, Wootton correctly observes, 'scientific enquiry is path-dependent'.[110] A path which, if followed, safely leads us out of the woods (even if for a while).

What can be gathered from the foregoing discussion is that, as the possession of that which 'is intellectually known (*ipsum intellectum*)',[111] knowledge is a metaphysical end-result of intellectual processes of ontological abstraction that, through reason's methodological effectuality, objectify life for ordering purposes. Accordingly, the distinction between knowledge as such (or regular, ordinary knowledge) and scientific knowledge should not be over-emphasised: being today understood as a 'specific practice of rationalization',[112] the type of knowledge science produces (scientific knowledge) is but a *refined variant* of the cognitivist, objectifying approach to (and management of) life which informs the cognitive process generally.

In this sense, that there is an ontological continuum between the ancient and contemporary understanding of (scientific) knowledge can be further proved by considering the philosophical origins of concepts. In Western philosophy, it was Socrates who, in his search for truth *as* 'stabilization'[113] of life, found in concepts the solution to efficiently mediate between reason (*lógos*) and experience. Socrates' search for truth was both political and epistemic: he was after an 'eternal moral truth'[114] that could guide our actions, of which the naturalistic,[115] causal understanding of the world was a constitutive part. More specifically, according to Socrates, our experiences are inevitably limited and contradictory and cannot lead to safe knowledge. The latter is of universals

108 See e.g., Russell (2001) p xxviii.
109 Andersen and Hepburn (2015), (unpaged).
110 Wootton (2016) pp 527, 539.
111 Gilson (2016) p 190. Emphasis in original.
112 Mau (2019) p 11. Cf. Tagliapietra (2017) p 101.
113 Cassirer (1946) p 57.
114 Jaeger (1986) p 89. See also ibid., p 64; Severino (2010), pp 114–6.
115 Rovelli (2011) p 41.

only—it is, and can only be, of something's '*eidòs*'.[116] This *true* knowledge is to be pursued through the dialectical crafting of conceptual definitions capable of delving into what makes any given subject (including virtue, justice, and all related ethical notions) what it is *universally*, i.e., 'as a whole'.[117] Thus, Socrates' approach transcended life's immanency and laid the foundations on which to solve the linguistic-ontological puzzle concerning our ability to make sense of life which had kept philosophers busy until his day—that is, the 'problem of how to reconcile experience with reason'.[118] Not coincidentally, from Socrates' thought there sprang Platonic dialectic and *epistḗmē*, and Aristotelian analytics, logic, and *epistḗmē*.[119] There, finally, experience and reason could meet fully.

Given the heavy use that Braidotti makes of concepts to frame her experience-sensitive epistemology, it is a real pity that she never defines experience and knowledge, nor distinguishes between the two for the purposes of her posthuman project, philosophically or in any other way. Or, perhaps, the fact that Braidotti overlooks what experience and knowledge are, and thus, what separates them, reveals more than what might be thought at first glance.

Conclusion

Immanency is a matter of experience, not knowledge. In fact, and as argued, knowledge transcends the experience of immanency. While Braidotti ought to be praised for wanting to preserve experience, her project to do so by crafting an epistemology of situatedness conceals an ontological oxymoron. For present purposes, this means that, insightful though it is, Braidotti's ethical vision cannot be of assistance in trying to solve legal education's existential crisis. What is required is, rather, a form of experiential, biopolitically-charged thinking which is freed from epistemic ambitions—however sensitive these might be.

The reader might object that this type of thinking cannot be achieved. Specifically, it could be pointed out that to the extent that law is both an ethereal entity and artefact to be used for ordering purposes, it cannot but be studied, and thus, *known*. From a cognitive science point of view, it could be further objected that rational and epistemic constructivism in the study (and practice) of law might well just be an inexorable feature of brain activity.[120] In turn, this would mean that law's *experience* is, and will always be taking place within, its very 'epistemological foundation'[121]—or to say it differently, that law's instrumentality is inevitably dependent upon the epistemological (i.e. linguistic-ontological) mechanisms which we employ to metaphysically

116 Jaeger (1986) p 164.
117 Ibid., p 163. See also ibid., pp 62ff, 102, 163–6; Severino (2010) pp 112–4, 183.
118 Severino (2010) p 109.
119 Ibid., pp 121, 181ff.
120 Cf. Brożek (2019) pp 7, 46, 49, 121.
121 Kelley (1990) p 9.

synthesise (i.e. normatively make sense of) life. Whence one would have to conclude that there is no solution to legal education's malaise.

Acknowledgements

I wish to thank Kimberley Brayson for helpful conversations and exchanges as well as the reviewer for constructive feedback on an earlier draft. Errors are mine only.

References

Hanne Andersen and Brian Hepburn (2015) 'Scientific Method' in *Stanford Encyclopedia of Philosophy*, https://plato.stanford.edu/entries/scientific-method/, 17 March 2019.

Rosi Braidotti (2013) *The Posthuman*, Polity.

Rosi Braidotti (2019) *Posthuman Knowledge*, Polity.

David Bronstein (2016) *Aristotle on Knowledge and Learning: The Posterior Analytics*, Oxford University Press.

Bartosz Brożek (2019) *The Legal Mind: A New Introduction to Legal Epistemology*, Cambridge University Press.

Massimo Cacciari (2019) *La Mente Inquieta. Saggio sull'Umanesimo*, Einaudi.

Ernst Cassirer (1944) *An Essay on Man*, Yale University Press.

Ernst Cassirer (1946) *The Myth of the State*, Yale University Press.

Étienne Gilson ([1949, 1952] 2016) *Being and Some Philosophers*, 2nd Edition, Pontifical Institute of Mediaeval Studies.

Werner Jaeger ([1939, 1945, 1967] 1965) *Paideia: The Ideals of Greek Culture, Volume I. Archaic Greece: The Mind of Athens*, trans. Gilbert Highet, Oxford University Press.

Werner Jaeger ([1943, 1971] 1986) *Paideia: The Ideals of Greek Culture, Volume II. In Search of the Divine Centre*, trans. Gilbert Highet, Oxford University Press.

David R Kelley (1990) *The Human Measure. Social Thought in the Western Legal Tradition*, Harvard University Press.

Steffen Mau ([2017] 2019) *The Metric Society: On the Quantification of the Social*, trans. Sharon Howe, Polity Press.

Jennifer Nagel (2014) *Knowledge: A Very Short Introduction*, Oxford University Press.

David Owens (2012) *Shaping the Normative Landscape*, Oxford University Press.

John Herman Randall Jr. ([1948] 1956) 'Pietro Pompanazzi: Introduction' in E Cassirer, PO Kristeller and JH Randall Jr. (eds) *The Renaissance Philosophy of Man*, The University of Chicago Press 257–79.

Carlo Rovelli ([2009] 2011) *Anaximander*, trans. Marion Lignana Rosenberg, Westholme Publishing LLC.

Carlo Rovelli ([2014] 2017) *Reality is Not What it Seems: The Journey to Quantum Gravity*, trans. Simone Carnell and Erica Segre, Penguin Books.

Bertrand Russell ([1931] 2001) *The Scientific Outlook*, Routledge.

Bertrand Russell ([1940] 1962) *An Inquiry into Meaning and Truth*, Penguin Books.

Emanuele Severino (1989) *Il Giogo. Alle Origini della Ragione: Eschilo*, Adelphi.

Emanuele Severino (1979) *La Legge e il Caso*, Adelphi.

Emanuele Severino ([1996] 2010) *La Filosofia dai Greci al Nostro Tempo. La Filosofia Antica e Medievale*, BUR.

Emanuele Severino ([1996] 2013a) *La Filosofia dai Greci al Nostro Tempo. La Filosofia Moderna*, BUR.

Emanuele Severino ([1996] 2013b) *La Filosofia dai Greci al Nostro Tempo. La Filosofia Contemporanea*, BUR.

Luca Siliquini-Cinelli (2020) 'Experience vs. Knowledge in Comparative Law: Critical Notes on Pierre Legrand's "Sensitive Epistemology"' 16(4) *International Journal of Law in Context* 443–58.

Andrea Tagliapietra (2017) *Esperienza. Filosofia e Storia di Un'idea*, Raffaello Cortina Editore.

David Wootton ([2015] 2016) *The Invention of Science: A New History of the Scientific Revolution*, Penguin Books.

Chapter 12

Posthumanist Legal Education

Learning to Entangle Human Law with Its More-Than-Human World

Kate Galloway

Introduction

That we live amidst a global ecological crisis is now beyond debate.[1] Yet it is no abstract or isolated activity that is generating the crisis. Economy, society, politics, and environment exist as dynamic parts of a complex adaptive system. Law, too, plays its part both creating and reinforcing the preconditions for environmental disaster. While situated within these broader contexts, the peculiarly human endeavour of law contributes to the degradation of the biosphere including through a feedback loop comprising its text, its performance by legal actors, and its study. Beyond its self-referential logic, the human-centredness of the law—and the objectification of the more-than-human—is its biopolitical tell. Because the law is implicated in the subjugation of the more-than-human to the imperatives of capital and economy, the anthropocentrism of its mirror, legal education, is inherently political. To the extent that legal education privileges a humanist discourse in which humans are agents not only of their own fortunes, but those of the non-human world, legal education is biopolitical.

This chapter first outlines the premise of posthumanism as more-than-human and the relationship of this standpoint to biopolitics, before suggesting that the law's anthropocentrism is biopolitical. Advancing this argument, the chapter examines how legal education supports law as written and practised, and the anthroparchic imperatives of the discipline in the neoliberal university[2] shared by the profession in private practice. Assertions that legal education is not human enough[3] ignore the absence in law of the more-than-human, thus revealing a biopolitical standpoint.

The chapter turns then to the critique of law and of legal education in highlighting the law's biopolitical stand as inherently human. Law has been imbricated with critical perspectives for decades. However, both the legal education

1 Graham (2021a).

2 Thornton (2013); Thornton (2008).

3 See, e.g., Westaby and Jones (2018); Skead et al. (2020); Field and Duffy (2012); Jones (2018); Heath et al. (2017).

DOI: 10.4324/9781003179283-16

literature and the law curriculum remain anchored in the human because critical method is itself largely enmeshed within anthropocentric concerns. While offering a useful and important counterpoint to the destructive tendencies of patriarchal colonialism,[4] critique in general is insufficient to grapple with the underlying issues facing the planet.

As one part of a framework of interlocking systemic influences, so long as legal education is situated within the academy as well as adjacent to the profession, the institution of the university and its practices might usefully inform a structural and intellectual shift in lawyers' learning. Consequently, the final part draws on the concept of the 'ecological university'[5] to comprehend how legal education might extricate itself from the biopolitics of the human and embrace the posthuman.

Posthumanism, the More-Than-Human, and Biopolitics

The discourse of posthumanism encompasses a broad base.[6] In general terms, '[p]osthumanism rejects the premise that humans are the only species capable of producing knowledge and instead creates openings for other forms/things/objects/beings/phenomenon to know. It also problematizes distinctions that are drawn between and among species'.[7] This chapter argues that the human is not the sole measure of all things[8] adopting Whatmore's analysis that 'post' refers to the greater world 'beyond' the human.[9] It incorporates into law's curriculum the missing 'matter' of landscape.[10] More than mere biological matter, it extends to the more-than-human world embracing the whole of 'nature'.

'The posthuman subject is located within its environment in deep relationality to its fellow nonhuman species and entities. This relationality is exactly where the transformative potential of the posthuman subject lies'.[11] Adopting this framing of posthumanism engages this chapter in a biopolitical analysis of legal education and law. In the first place, the anthropocentrism of the law, echoed in legal education, is itself literally the mechanism of governmentality of humans, that is, of biopolitics. Where government of human life is the foundation of politics and of law, nature—the more-than-human—'depends on the practices of government itself'.[12]

4 Graham (2011); Watson (2014).
5 Barnett (2017).
6 Braun (2004) p 1352.
7 Ulmer (2017) p 834.
8 Badmington (2010); Lemke (2011).
9 Whatmore (2004) p 1361.
10 Whatmore (2006) p 603.
11 van der Zaag (2016) p 333.
12 Lemke (2011) p 6.

This construction of biopolitics has developed since environmental crises of the 1960s and 70s, resulting in a literature of ecological biopolitics.[13] The realm of that which was considered biopolitically governable expanded from humans to humans' natural world. Facing the existential threat posed by environmental catastrophe[14] demanded a political solution to stop environmental destruction, and ecological biopolitics evolved in response. Gunst observes that 'this political arena in its comprehensive form is comparatively new and takes into consideration the fact that questions about life and survival are increasingly relevant'.[15]

Despite this apparently hopeful engagement between ecological biopolitics and posthumanism, Lemke[16] and Gough[17] note the effect of technocentrism on the biopolitical turn. Ecological biopolitics originally saw the need for human society to adapt to uphold the integrity of the more-than-human to save human life itself. However, technological advancement in the decades since seeks to 'modify and transform' the environment.[18] Thus technologies have 'transformed the richness of this planet into a strategic raw material for industrial production … Biodiversity conservation then becomes merely conservation of "raw material" rather than conservation of "means of production" of life itself'.[19]

Whether adopting ecological biopolitics as originally conceived, or its technocentric overlay, neither conception extends far enough to embrace the necessary entanglements[20] between the human and the more-than-human world. Adapting to the environment fails to comprehend more-than-human for its own intrinsic worth. And technocentrism is an impoverished example of the very problem critiqued here. For these reasons, the posthumanist approach proposed in this chapter is directed at resolving the biopolitical orientation of the law and legal education.

Humans at the Centre of Law: Legal Education as Biopolitics

The history of the legal profession is entrenched within State governance. As proctors of the court and the pool from which the judiciary is drawn, lawyers in the common law tradition serve the interests of the State and the powerful. Where the overarching purpose of both has been the exploitation of the

13 Lemke (2011); Gough (2017).
14 Head (2016).
15 Gunst (1978) p 9, cited in Lemke (2011) p 23.
16 Lemke (2011).
17 Gough (2017).
18 Gough (2017) p 895.
19 Shiva (1991) p 44.
20 A term used in the work of Haraway (2008).

Earth as a resource, the law's implication in the apparatus of the State and the corporation is biopolitical.

Despite the evolution of the common law, Blackstone's *Commentaries*[21] continues to reflect the benchmark of anthropocentrism including the Biblical invocation for man (*sic*) to dominate the natural world. Enlightenment philosophy of economics and politics interacted with law to support and promote industrialisation, capitalism, and atomistic individualism that together generated modernity, continuing the law's central concern with exploitation of the more-than-human. Thus, as Grasso points out, '[c]ontemporary Western culture … is characterized by a spiritual orientation whose most striking characteristics are its anthropocentrism and immanentism, and whose roots are in the vast intellectual and spiritual movement known to us as the Enlightenment'.[22]

The Industrial Revolution[23] brought capitalism, a new class of wealth, and new calls on the law and on lawyers. Lawyers developed classical contract law, the law of the market,[24] and principles of property and company law to promote the interests of the growing middle class and the national economy. The growing preoccupation with the individual and his (*sic*) rights were closely bound with his wealth. Property in particular, distinguished rights from the physical landscape[25] leaving little tangible connection between an interest in land and the consequences for the landscape inherent in it.[26] The compartmentalisation of the more-than-human into marketable commodities has implications, now widely perceived, not only for the 'environment' per se but also for the economy and indeed for humanity itself.[27]

During its evolution in service to industry, the structure of the law also refined its formerly divine hierarchy. Law was the exercise of state power over the human world: human institutions exercised power over humans and provided for humans to exercise power over the more-than-human. The law, as did politics and social life, focused on 'the relief of the human estate by way of the conquest of nature'[28] and it continues to do so. The more-than-human has no place as subject within the legal order, relegated instead as the object of human endeavour.

The role of the legal profession and the lawyers comprising it is therefore to uphold the legal order. To do so implicitly engages a positivist approach whereby the ethical constraints on the lawyer are themselves embedded within the structures upheld by the profession as part of the third arm of government.

21 (1765).
22 Grasso (1999) p 239.
23 Malm (2016).
24 Atiyah (1979).
25 Graham (2011); Graham (2021b).
26 Graham (2011); Galloway (2012).
27 Graham (2021a).
28 Grasso (1999) p 240.

Despite professing the justice and ethics of legal practice[29] the traditional approach of the law of professional ethics is itself predisposed towards a rule-based rather than a values approach to legal practice. Consequently, '[t]he contemporary West's loss of a "transcendental anchor" … helps create the cultural soil from which the phenomenon of "the Victorious Lawyer" grows'.[30]

Given its governmental, social, and economic focus, the law and its practitioners contribute to anthroparchy by failing to engage meaningfully with the Earth—a disposition that starts in law school. Thus, legal education, overseen by the legal profession,[31] serving the profession as stakeholders,[32] captured by the employability discourse of the contemporary university,[33] and imbued with centuries of imprinting of human concerns,[34] features a compulsory suite of private law subjects dealing with matters of commercial importance[35] to the exclusion of the more-than-human. Beholden to those who drive it, its very purpose is to reproduce the existing normative framing of the law and legal practice: one dominated by the human.

Further, the primacy of doctrine, necessarily anthropocentric,[36] of appellate decisions[37] and 'thinking like a lawyer',[38] together reinforce the anthropocentrism of the law curriculum. The humanist curriculum is then upheld, enacted, reinforced, and modelled by practitioner academics who are themselves of the mould of the traditions of the law.[39] Although the more-than-human shapes the human experience and is radically transformed by it, the law fails to give expression to its being and this failure is reproduced within the way that law is taught and learned.

Given the climate crisis and the threat it poses to organised society, and the absence of the more-than-human sphere from the law and legal practice, there is an imperative for a transformed legal education designed to equip lawyers with skills to practise law that embraces the more than human within its fabric—a posthuman legal education. Despite critique of the law and of legal education designed to embrace alternative ways of knowing, doing, and being,[40]

29 See, e.g., Pepper (1999).
30 Grasso (1999) p 240.
31 Exemplified by the educational requirements for admission to the state Supreme Courts in Australia. See, e.g., *Admission Guidelines No 1 of 2016* issued under Rule 9AA of the *Supreme Court (Admission) Rules 2004* (Qld).
32 See, e.g., Peden and Riley (2005); Boon and Webb (2010).
33 Bridgstock (2017); Rees (2021).
34 Embodied in the idea of law as social science: see Berard (2009); Jones and Galloway (2015).
35 Of the 11 subjects mandated for admission to practice in Australia, almost half deal in commercially oriented private law: contact, property, equity and trusts, corporations, and civil procedure.
36 Given the centrality of rights vested in human actors.
37 Duffy and Field (2014); Field and Duffy (2012).
38 See, e.g., James (2012); Burton (2017).
39 Galloway and Jones (2014); Jones and Galloway (2015).
40 Nussbaum (2003); Rhode (2012).

just as ecological biopolitics appeared to embrace the more-than-human so too has the critique of the law been constrained by the anthroparchic constraints of the legal system itself.

The Limits of Critique (More of the Same)

The relationship between the text and practice of the law, and the discipline identity of the legal profession, also reflects the relationship between humans and the more-than-human. Together, law and society 'mirror the reality in which they are born and in which they grow'.[41] Even so, there has been some effort to address the failure of law and legal education to engage with the more-than-human. A growing body of practice and scholarship focuses on this aspect of the law and how it is reproduced in the next generation, including critical legal education generally, socio-legal approaches to legal education, and sustainability education.[42] However, each framework necessarily functions within the bounds of the law as it is and they are therefore limited in their capacity to usher in transformative posthuman change.

A critical legal education, for example, recognises the capitalism and even the anthropocentrism of the law and its priorities, and challenges the primacy of these assumptions. Hunt observes:

> Advocates of critical legal studies may not all share the same rank ordering of dissatisfactions but are all reacting against features of the prevailing orthodoxies in legal scholarship, against the conservatism of the law schools and against many features of the role played by law and legal institutions in modern society.[43]

Reinforcing the human-centred nature of legal education, Kennedy affirms law school as 'ideological training for willing service in the hierarchies of the corporate welfare state'[44] even as he proposes a radical and utopian turn for its transformation. He identifies the adoption of critical perspectives according to identities of those 'other than mainstream'[45] and observes that 'if you are invisible on the other side, you are likely to be a humanist'.[46] For 'resisters', he describes the study of law as a potential 'long-term life project that works against loss and injury and oppression'.[47]

41 Zamboni (2008) p 63.
42 Jones and Galloway (2015); Galloway (2015); Kennedy (1982); Hunt (1987); Collier (2004).
43 Hunt (1987) p 5.
44 Kennedy (1982) p 591.
45 Kennedy (2007) pp 2–3.
46 Kennedy (2007) p 5.
47 Kennedy (2007) p 6.

Similarly, Heath and Burdon[48] describe a mode of resistance to the neoliberal university as the 'humanisation of law schools'.[49] In advocating for activist law academics, they identify recognising the humanity of students and colleagues as resistance: a concern engaged with the human rather than the more-than-human. In observing the importance of student engagement with the law's role in 'socio-economic and political arrangements',[50] Appleby et al. offer strategies to promote independent thinking in elective and core units. Yet these appear, still, to fall within the human-centredness of the law and its engagements.

More directly engaging with environmental threat is the sustainability education movement. The Talloires Declaration,[51] for example, commits signatory universities to deliver education that promotes sustainability. While an internationally adopted, multi-disciplinary framework, sustainability education has received little attention in the law.[52] Comprehending higher education as a means of transforming the effects of untrammelled growth on the more-than-human, nevertheless the very concept of sustainability reflects a largely human concern: sustaining human life on Earth. Subsequent critiques of sustainability generally, reflect the same pathway as ecological biopolitics: a preoccupation with the adaptation of existing anthropocentric activity to maintain the status quo.[53]

There has, however, been some exploration of the connections between the discipline of law, with its traditional anthropocentric concerns, and issues emerging from an increasing understanding of the nature and extent of the unfolding ecological crisis. This interest manifests in attempts to discover both philosophical and theoretical alternatives to traditional legal approaches and to explore practical initiatives, in both education and in practice, through innovative litigation occurring worldwide.

However, given the urgency of the climate crisis, progress within both the profession and legal education seems slow and patchy.[54] Additionally, the integration of perspectives of the more-than-human, to the extent that this is taking place, appears to be an add-on to the core list of the law's concerns alongside conventional elective topics. If the profession is to make significant and meaningful contributions to realising a sustainable and just future, and if it is to move beyond reacting to or ameliorating the impacts of climate change, then a more radical and transformative approach is required. One dimension

48 Heath and Burdon (2013).

49 Heath and Burdon (2013) p 381.

50 Appleby et al. (2013) p 363.

51 University Leaders for a Sustainable Future Talloires Declaration (1990), http://ulsf.org/talloires-declaration/.

52 Though see Galloway (2015); Galloway et al. (2012); Graham (2014).

53 Barnett (2017) p 43.

54 Jones and Galloway (2015).

of such a shift is to move from seeing the environment as the setting within which social issues and questions of justice arise, instead re-conceptualising the necessary interrelationship between humans and their world: a posthuman orientation.

More-Than-Human Legal Education and the Ecological University

Given the shortcomings of the law and legal education in terms of a posthuman turn, this part considers the possibilities for transformation within the framing of what Barnett describes as the 'ecological university'.[55]

Barnett writes not of the crisis of the university itself, 'but rather that the university is falling woefully short of its responsibilities and its possibilities in the world'.[56] His work explains how the university's operations and functions might be informed by an 'ecological perspective' and how the university's involvement in various ecosystems, both internal and external, might be deployed. He concludes with the conceptualisation of an 'ecological' university. In Barnett's analysis, 'ecology' is a 'thick' concept[57] and he draws together facets of what ecology might represent—'fact and values ... past, present, and future ...' hope, and vision yet to be realised.[58]

The network aspects of the science of ecology apply to the metaphor of the ecological university. Multiple ecosystems work together within the institution, as well as between the institution and external influences. Barnett describes seven ecosystems, or the more permeable-sounding 'ecological zones' within which the university is implicated: the knowledge society, social institutions, persons, the economy, learning, culture, and the natural environment.[59] These ecosystems mesh, generating their own machinations and effects that cannot always be predicted. The university is *ecological* in that it navigates within, through and between these zones, comprehending their necessary interrelationship in all aspects of its operation and its very existence.

Barnett observes also, the relationships between 'time, space, movement and geography'[60] and the need for the university to 'be open to the whole reality of its time. It must be in the midst of real life, and saturated by it'.[61] While Barnett does not prefer an orientation towards the more-than-human, 'natural environment' appears to equate to the more-than-human. Its inclusion within

55 Barnett (2017).
56 Barnett (2017) p 1.
57 Barnett (2017) p 17, citing Williams (1985).
58 Barnett (2017) p 17.
59 Barnett (2017) p 56.
60 Barnett (2017) p 20.
61 Barnett (2017), citing Ortega y Gasset (1946) p 76.

the university as an institution helps frame a future-focused and transformative legal education suited to the supercomplexity of our times.

The characterisation of the climate crisis, for example, as supercomplex, identifies that it demands solutions beyond the capability of traditional problem solving. Supercomplexity is the state of diverse and proliferating competing conceptual frames of reference for comprehending the world.[62] Traditional methods involve a focus on the human and siloed, linear accounts of the nature of problems and their solutions. However, those methods cannot succeed in a complex adaptive system. Where time, space, movement, geography, and the more-than-human are implicated in the supercomplex, humans called upon to analyse and find solutions for the ensuing problems must themselves engage all domains—drawing on cognitive, metacognitive, emotional, and physical skills.

While the ecological university is an institutional environment that might support a legal education that meets these needs, more specifically the ecological curriculum[63] and ecological professionalism[64] might inform the teaching, and thus the practice, of law for the Anthropocene. The following sections interpret Barnett's framing of professionalism and curriculum to draw out a meaning of posthuman legal education. It starts with the concept of professionalism.

Professionalism

The goal of legal education is to educate students in the discipline of the law. Regardless of graduates' career destinations, the law is a professional discipline and graduates are generally destined to be professionals. Indeed, this critique of the anthropocentric nature of legal education is closely tied with the exclusively human orientation of the legal profession, and reorientation of both requires comprehending professionalism.

The 'ecological professional' engages in five ecological 'registers': the professional self, the client, the knowledge economy, the professional environment, and the profession's discursive ecology.[65] Through their knowledge, dispositions, and qualities, the ecological professional evinces a 'worldly responsibility'[66] towards these registers, and a concern for the fate of the world.[67] They '[voyage] across knowledges'[68] to 'discern the world in all its complexity'[69]

62 Barnett (2020).
63 Barnett (2017) pp 113–24.
64 Barnett (2017) pp 126–39.
65 Barnett (2017) pp 129–30.
66 Barnett (2017) p 134.
67 Barnett (2017) p 138.
68 Barnett (2017) p 134.
69 Barnett (2017) p 135.

where through critical and creative thinking, they meet the challenges wrought by supercomplexity.[70]

Barnett's professional's worldly responsibility is reflected also in other frames of thought. Integral theory, for example, contemplates an expanded identity within ecological thinking, beyond the self to one's group and country, thence to all of us, all beings and ultimately to 'all of reality'.[71] Practising as an ecological professional—engaging in ecological thinking, or integral theory—demands comprehending the very notion of a lawyer's professional identity and their praxis in a vastly enhanced way. This is an ecological consciousness[72] that might shift the existing 'discursive ecology of the profession'[73] to destabilise the law's traditional oppositional categories of human subjects as masters of the natural object. As Grasso points out, '[t]he renewal of our legal culture … presupposes the articulation of a new public philosophy embodying decisively richer conceptions of human nature and social life than those which inform today's liberalism of the sovereign self'.[74]

Similarly, the concept of inter- or multi-disciplinarity attendant on 'voyaging across knowledges' is encapsulated by Tynjälä and Gijbels' observation that the future of the professions is one of collaborative and multi-disciplinary networks.[75] Their work on integrative pedagogy, related to integral theory, envisages graduate professionals who have expertise—a broader conceptualisation of graduate competencies than simply traditional lawyerly knowledge and skills. Thus, the professional for our times requires the skills and attributes to generate multidisciplinary knowledge from seamless collaboration between professionals from multiple disciplines.[76]

For the lawyer to contribute to the problem of climate change and the attendant devolution of organised human society demands a posthuman orientation—in Barnett's terms, an ecological professional, with the expertise to identify, analyse, and solve problems from a standpoint entirely altered from that of the anthropocentric lawyer. Ecological consciousness, integrative thinking, and a broader conception of expertise, situate the posthuman lawyer within multiple networks where the more-than-human is integral to the lawyer's worldly responsibility, expressed not simply by 'interest in and care towards' that ecosystem, but through a willingness to 'play their part'.[77] Educating the posthuman lawyer is the contemporary challenge for legal education.

70 Barnett (2017) p 135; Barnett 2000.
71 Esbjörn-Hargens, 2010 p 42.
72 Panov (2013) p 380.
73 Barnett 2017 p 130.
74 Grasso (1999) p 252.
75 Tynjälä and Gijbels (2012).
76 Graham (2014); Matsuda (2014); Rousell (2016); Galloway and Graham (2023)
77 Barnett (2017) p 138.

Curriculum

Barnett writes about professional education as well as specifically about the ecological curriculum. This section draws on his framing of an ecological curriculum to outline some possibilities for a posthuman legal education.

Given the diverse registers of the ecological professional, Barnett identifies the need to stretch the student into 'zones of professional extension' into and across those ecosystems.[78] This is an education in the 'interconnectedness of the three moments of action, understanding, and sheer being' in which the student, as a future professional, is 'willed to play their part ... concerned about the fate of the world'.[79] The ecological curriculum brings the ecological professional into being. Features of such a learning environment include co-mingling and integration of heterogeneous elements[80] to generate a 'sense of connectedness with all things'[81] including connection to 'the wider world, to place, to Nature, to other peoples'.[82]

This type of curriculum resonates with other approaches to educate for the Anthropocene, and grapples with the biopolitical reality of the deeply human orientation of traditional legal education. It describes a posthumanist legal education entangling with the more-than-human as the foundation for problem solving in conditions of supercomplexity.

Networks of, between, within multiple ecologies of knowledge, skills, people, environments, discourses, and so on, across space and time[83] constitute the worldwide domain of learning in the ecological curriculum. As professional collaborators, the law student in an ecological curriculum will connect with teachers and other learners, consciously developing the skills of an expert collaborator. Collaboration grounds an integrative approach to curriculum and pedagogy, bringing together learners, teachers, disciplines, and skills for novel understanding of complex problems beyond the bounds of any single discipline[84] and as Barnett points out, beyond the constraints of learning outcomes and other bureaucratic tools[85] that narrow learners' outlook and potential.

The 'wide learning repertoire' of the ecological curriculum[86] demands that legal educators themselves engage with their discipline through an ecological consciousness. Advancing Barnett's argument and drawing on integral theory[87]

78 Barnett (2017) p 137.
79 Barnett (2017) p 137.
80 Barnett (2017) pp 115, 117.
81 Barnett (2017) p 119.
82 Barnett (2017) p 121.
83 Barnett (2017) pp 126–7.
84 Ong (2016).
85 Barnett (2017) p 115.
86 Barnett (2017) p 121.
87 Tynjälä and Gijbels (2012).

and even Earth jurisprudence,[88] legal education becomes reformist in nature, engaging with the Earth's systems beyond its current preoccupation with the solely human jurisdiction. A curriculum enmeshed with the world at large is freed from the constructed barriers of knowledge, skill, and disposition that are also barriers to a sustainable future for all.

Given the crisis unfolding, an ecological, or a posthuman, legal education takes the form of an emancipatory pedagogy.[89] This approach to the teaching and learning of law will equip law students and graduates—the legal actors of the future—to act outside the feedback loop of law and its entrenched human-centric norms, to solve problems by including the more-than-human in their calculation.

Conclusion

The law and legal education are mutually reinforcing systems concerned almost exclusively with the human world. In failing to acknowledge and accommodate the more-than-human, they are implicated in the wider systems that are generating a global crisis for the Earth. The political orientation of this anthropocentric endeavour is inherently biopolitical, even as its functioning necessarily contributes to the problems generating the crisis.

There is no simple solution to the law's traditional orientation. However, legal education—the institutional production of lawyers for the future—is one of the levers crucial to generate the necessary posthuman turn. Importantly, to achieve the desired skillset for graduates demands more than a simply critical approach to legal education as such approaches are themselves mired within the same biopolitical framing as the position they seek to criticise.

Barnett's conceptualisation of the 'ecological university' provides a starting point for imagining a posthuman legal education. The networked knowledges, disciplines, institutions, and actors envisaged in his concept represent aspects of an educational approach that will support moving beyond the human. The ecological professional is thus the integrative thinker—a collaborator and co-constructor of knowledge—who engages with the more-than-human at a global scale, following an internalised motivation to bring change. They are served by an ecological curriculum that traverses different disciplines and knowledges, to embrace a whole-of-world viewpoint. The conception of this global, whole-of-world context is, of course, a posthuman one.

88 Cullinan (2002); Rogers and Maloney (2017).
89 Freire (1972); Dewey (2011).

Acknowledgements

My thanks to my colleague Professor Nicole Graham for her comments on an earlier draft.

References

Gabrielle Appleby et al (2013) 'Critical Thinking in Legal Education: Our Journey' 23 *Legal Education Review* 345.

PS Atiyah (1979) *The Rise & Fall of Freedom of Contract*, Clarendon Press.

Neil Badmington (2010) 'Posthumanism' in *Cultural Theory, Volume III: A–Z*, Wiley, https://doi.org/10.1002/9781444337839.wbelctv3p003.

Ronald Barnett (2000) *Realizing the University in an Age of Supercomplexity*, Open University Press.

Ronald Barnett (2017) *The Ecological University: A Feasible Utopia*, Routledge.

Ronald Barnett (2020) 'Supercomplexity and Education Research: Six Scholarships' in Lorraine Ling and Peter Ling (eds) *Emerging Methods and Paradigms in Scholarship and Education Research*, IGI Global.

Timothy J Berard (2009) 'The Relevance of the Social Sciences for Legal Education' 19(1) *Legal Education Review* 189.

William Blackstone (1765–1769) *Commentaries on the Laws of England.*

Andrew Boon and Julian Webb (2010) 'The Legal Professions as Stakeholders in the Academy in England And Wales' in Fiona Cownie (ed) *Stakeholders in the Law School*, Hart.

Bruce Braun (2004) 'Modalities of Posthumanism' 36 *Environment and Planning A* 1352.

Ruth Bridgstock (2017) 'The University and the Knowledge Network: A New Educational Model for Twenty-First Century Learning and Employability' in Michael Tomlinson and Leonard Holmes (eds) *Graduate Employability in Context*, Palgrave Macmillan.

Kelley Burton (2017) '"Think Like a Lawyer" Using a Legal Reasoning Grid and Criterion-Referenced Assessment Rubric on IRAC (Issue, Rule, Application, Conclusion)' 10(2) *Journal of Learning Design* 57.

Richard Collier (2004) '"We're All Socio-Legal Now?": Legal Education, Scholarship and the "Global Knowledge Economy": Reflections on the UK Experience' 26(4) *Sydney Law Review* 503.

Cormac Cullinan (2002) *Wild Law*, Siber Ink.

John Dewey (2011) *Democracy and Education*, Simon and Brown.

James Duffy and Rachael Field (2014) 'Why ADR Must be a Mandatory Subject in the Law Degree: A Cheat Sheet for the Willing and a Primer for the Non-Believer' 25(1) *Australasian Dispute Resolution Journal* 9.

Sean Esbjörn-Hargens (2010) 'An Overview of Integral Theory: An All-Inclusive Framework for the Twenty-First Century' in Sean Esbjörn-Hargens (ed) *Integral Theory in Action, Applied, Theoretical, and Constructive Perspectives on the AQAL Model*, SUNY Press.

Rachael Field and James Duffy (2012) 'Better to Light a Single Candle than to Curse the Darkness: Promoting Law Student Well-Being Through a First Year Law Subject' 12(1) *Law and Justice Journal* 133.

Paolo Freire (1972) *Pedagogy of the Oppressed (Myra Bergman Ramos Trans)*, Penguin.

Kate Galloway et al (2012) 'Using Sustainability to Inform Renewal of the LLB Foundation Curriculum: Knowledge Skills and Attitudes for the Future' 12(1) *QUT Law and Justice Journal* 1.

Kate Galloway (2012) 'Landowners' vs Miners' Property Interests: The Unsustainability of Property as Dominion' 37(2) *Alternative Law Journal* 77.

Kate Galloway and Peter Jones (2014) 'Guarding Our Identities: The Dilemma of Transformation in the Legal Academy' 14(1) *QUT Law Review* 15.

Kate Galloway (2015) 'Sustainability in the Real Property Law Curriculum: Why and How' 8(2) *Journal of Learning Design* 31.

Kate Galloway and Nicole Graham (2023) 'Learning Ecological Law: Innovating Legal Curriculum and Pedagogy' in Peter D Burdon and James Martel (eds) *The Routledge Handbook of Law and the Anthropocene*, Routledge.

A Gough (2017) 'Searching for a Crack to Let Environment Light in: Ecological Biopolitics and Education for Sustainable Development Discourses' 12(4) *Cultural Studies of Science Education* 889.

Nicole Graham (2011) *Lawscape: Property, Environment, Law*, Routledge.

Nicole Graham (2014) 'This is not a Thing: Land, Sustainability and Legal Education' 26(3) *Journal of Environmental Law* 395.

Nicole Graham (2021a) 'Learning Sacrifice: Legal Education in the Anthropocene' in Kirsten Anker et al (eds) *From Environmental to Ecological Law*, Routledge.

Nicole Graham (2021b) 'Dephysicalised Property and Shadow Places' in Robyn Bartel and Jennifer Carter (eds) *Handbook of Space, Place and Law*, Edward Elgar.

KL Grasso (1999) 'The Decline of Liberalism and the Rise of the Victorious Lawyer' 40(1) *South Texas Law Review* 233.

Dietrich Gunst (1978) *Biopolitik zwischen Macht und Recht*, Hase und Köhler Verlag.

Donna Haraway (2008) *When Species Meet*, University of Minnesota Press.

Lesley Head (2016) *Hope and Grief in the Anthropocene*, Routledge.

Mary Heath et al (2017) 'Learning to Feel Like a Lawyer: Law Teachers, Sessional Teaching and Emotional Labour in Legal Education' 26(3) *Griffith Law Review* 430.

Mary Heath and Peter Burdon (2013) 'Academic Resistance to the Neoliberal University' 23(1) *Legal Education Review* 379.

Alan Hunt (1987) 'The Critique of Law: What Is "Critical" about Critical Legal Theory?' 14(1) *Journal of Law and Society* 5.

Nick James (2012) 'Logical, Critical and Creative: Teaching "Thinking Skills" to Law Students' 12(1) *QUT Law and Justice Journal* 66.

Emma Jones (2018) 'Transforming Legal Education Through Emotions' 38(3) *Legal Studies* 450.

Peter Jones and Kate Galloway (2015) 'Academic and Discipline Identities as Obstacles to Engaging with Education for Sustainability: Lessons from Law and Social Work' 11 *International Journal of Sustainability Education* 1.

Duncan Kennedy (1982) 'Legal Education and the Reproduction of Hierarchy' 32(4) *Journal of Legal Education* 591.

Duncan Kennedy (2007) *Legal Education and the Reproduction of Hierarchy: A Polemic Against the System*, NYU Press.

Thomas Lemke (2011) *Biopolitics: An Advanced Introduction*, New York University Press.

Andreas Malm (2016) *Fossil Capital: The Rise of Steam Power and the Roots of Global Warming*, Verso Books.

MJ Matsuda (2014) 'Admit that the Waters Around You Have Grown: Change and Legal Education' 89(4) *Indiana Law Journal* 1381.

Martha C Nussbaum (2003) 'Cultivating Humanity in Legal Education' 70 *University of Chicago Law Review* 265.

David Ong (2016) 'Prospects for Integrating an Environmental Sustainability Perspective within the University Law Curriculum in England' 50(3) *Law Teacher* 276.

Jose Ortega y Gasset (1946) *Mission of the University*, Kegan Paul, Trench, Trubner and Co.

VI Panov (2013) 'Ecological Thinking, Consciousness, Responsibility' 86 *Procedia-Social and Behavioral Sciences* 379.

Elisabeth Peden and Joellen Riley (2005) 'Law Graduates' skills—A Pilot Study into Employers' Perspectives' 15 *Legal Education Review* 87.

Stephen L Pepper (1999) 'Resisting the Current' 52 *Vanderbilt Law Review* 1015.

Sian Rees (2021) 'Re-imagining Employability: An Ontology of Employability Best Practice in Higher Education Institutions' 26(5) *Teaching in Higher Education* 663.

Deborah L Rhode (2012) 'Access to Justice: An Agenda for Legal Education and Research' 62 *Journal of Legal Education* 531.

Nicole Rogers and Michelle Maloney (eds) (2017) *Law as if Earth Really Mattered: The Wild Law Judgment Project*, Routledge.

David Rousell (2016) 'Dwelling in the Anthropocene: Reimagining University Learning Environments in Response to Social and Ecological Change' 32(2) *Australian Journal of Environmental Education* 137.

V Shiva (1991) 'Biodiversity, Biotechnology and Profits' in V Shiva (ed) *Biodiversity: Social and Ecological Perspectives*, Zed Books/World Rainforest Movement, https://doi.org/10.3917/rtm.188.0825.

Natalie Skead et al (2020) 'The Role of Place, People and Perception in Law Student Well-Being' 73 *International Journal of Law and Psychiatry* 101631.

Margaret Thornton (2008) 'The Law School, the Market and the New Knowledge Economy' 17(1&2) *Legal Education Review* 1.

Margaret Thornton (2013) 'Inhabiting the Neoliberal University' 38(2) *Alternative Law Journal* 2.

Paivi Tynjälä and David Gijbels (2012) 'Changing the World: Changing Pedagogy' in Paivi Tynjälä et al (eds) *Transitions and Transformations in Learning and Education*, Springer.

JB Ulmer (2017) 'Posthumanism as Research Methodology: Inquiry in the Anthropocene' 30(9) *International Journal of Qualitative Studies in Education* 832, https://doi.org/10.1080/09518398.2017.1336806.

Annette-Carina van der Zaag (2016) 'On Posthuman Subjectivity' 9(3) *Journal of Cultural Economy* 330, https://doi.org/10.1080/17530350.2015.1040436.

Irene Watson (2014) *Aboriginal Peoples, Colonialism and International Law: Raw Law*, Routledge.

Chalen Westaby and Emma Jones (2018) 'Empathy: An Essential Element of Legal Practice or "Never the Twain Shall Meet"?' 25(1) *International Journal of the Legal Profession* 107.

Sarah Whatmore (2004) 'Humanism's Excess: Some Thoughts on the "Post-human/ist" Agenda' 36 *Environment and Planning A* 1360.

Sarah Whatmore (2006) 'Materialist Returns: Practising Cultural Geography in and for a More-than-human World' 13 *Cultural Geographies* 600.

Bernard Williams (1985) *Ethics and the Limits of Philosophy*, Routledge.

Mauro Zamboni (2008) *Law and Politics A Dilemma for Contemporary Legal Theory*, Springer.

Chapter 13

Law as Relation and the Co-emergence of Beings

Towards a Paradigm Shift in Legal Education

Iván Darío Vargas Roncancio

Introduction

National and transnational legislations, court provisions, and governance models across the world increasingly recognise the legal subjectivity of animals, rivers, and forests, among other beings and relations[1]. The contested constitutional clause of the rights of nature,[2] for example, is a growing legal response to the 'inter-related global crises of climate, food, energy, poverty, and meaning'.[3] While the rights of nature express the interdependence between ecological and social systems, the legal discipline is still deeply informed by the mindsets, practices, and institutions casting nature a limitless source of goods and services to meet ever-expanding human needs.[4] To state it in terms of scholar Thomas Berry—considered one of the founding figures of the Earth jurisprudence movement—the discontinuity between humans and nonhumans, and the ensuing bestowal of all rights to humans alone is at the root of the socio-ecological devastation of our planet.[5] The task ahead, he insists, is that of reinventing the human while re-embedding our social and normative systems within the broader community of life. A radical transformation of legal education is part and parcel of this challenging task.[6]

Anishinaabe scholar Aaron Mills suggests that 'legal education harms when it fails to acknowledge and to begin to articulate the lifeworld beneath any

1 Acosta and Martínez (2011); Burdon (2010); Harris (2014); Youatt (2017).

2 In the Latin American context see: *Protective Action issued by the Provincial Court of Loja, Sentence* No. 1121-2011-001, 30 March 2011; *Constitution of the Republic of Ecuador 2008, Legislative Decree* No. 0, Official Registration 449 20 October 2008; *Colombian Constitutional Court, Sentence* C-035 2016; *Colombian Constitutional Court, Sentence* T-622 2016; *Justice Supreme Tribunal* STC 4390-2018.

3 Escobar (2016) p 13.

4 Mesa (2008).

5 Berry (1999) p 4.

6 Brown and Erickson (2016).

DOI: 10.4324/9781003179283-17

system of law it aims to impart'.[7] Guided by this material legal principle,[8] this chapter asks how legal education may incorporate the living and knowledge systems where the law is embedded by identifying some important preanalytical assumptions of Western law.[9] How does the transformation of legal education may contribute to a larger paradigm shift from reductionist and growth-oriented legal orders to systems-based and life-enhancing jurisprudence?[10] This challenging transformation is part of a larger legal and political agenda for what Thomas Berry and Brian Swimme call the Ecozoic, namely an epoch of 'mutually enhancing human-earth relationships'.[11]

One crucial response to the senseless economic growth and socio-ecological injustice of our time, this chapter will argue, is the critical re-*vision* of Legal Systems of the Anthropocene such as environmental law.[12] I consider this to be a crucial step towards a larger paradigm shift within law and governance systems in modern societies. As an example of how Legal Systems of the Anthropocene operate, the first section summarises the main ontological, epistemological, ethical, and pedagogical assumptions of a standard comparative law textbook, while the second section puts forward an altogether different vision. It focuses on models of Indigenous jurisprudence[13] and ecological law[14] as compelling sources of an emergent legal ontology that I tentatively call Relational Legal Systems based on the principle of radical interdependence between all that exists.[15] The second section draws attention to the earthly co-emergence and interdependence between humans, animals, plants, and spirits, among other beings and relations.[16] The concluding part outlines some research topics to further leverage ongoing transitions into Relational Legal Systems.

Legal Systems of the Anthropocene: A Critical Review of a Legal Textbook

Comparative law, broadly speaking, is the systematic study of the similarities and differences between legal traditions. *Comparative Legal Traditions*[17] offers an overview into the history, theories, and methods of this legal sub-discipline

7 Aaron Mills (2016) p 847. Mills defines 'lifeworld' as '...the ontological, epistemological, and cosmological framework through which the world appears to a people'. He argues that 'lifeworlds begins with creations stories'. Mills (2016) p 850, note 6.
8 Borrows (2016).
9 Burdon (2012).
10 See Capra and Mattei (2015); Winter (2001).
11 Berry and Swimme (1992).
12 On the Anthropocene see Crutzen and Stoemer (2000).
13 Anker (2017); Borrows (2016); Mills (2016).
14 Garver (2013) (2019).
15 Escobar (2018).
16 Kimmerer (2013).
17 Glendon et al. (1982).

in the Western canon by comparing the traditions of civil law and common law.[18] The following section is organised around a set of general pre-analytical dimensions of legal education in the Anthropocene as depicted by *Comparative Legal Traditions.* While such dimensions are deeply entangled, I'll treat them as separate domains for analytical purposes only. For example, ontology is defined here as a set of claims and practices around the nature of the 'real',[19] while epistemology stands for how different agents (human and not) represent this 'real' through language, behaviour, and practice.[20] Consequently, the way agents learn and teach what they render as real pertains to pedagogy, and the kinds of things they do with knowledge refers to politics. Politics thus signals the power-laden relationships between agents, as they negotiate (and produce) their positions within the social field. Finally, an ethics, in the context of this analysis, refers to the normative dimensions of power (politics), knowledge (epistemology), and being (ontology) in a particular discursive field.[21] I now turn to discuss this pre-analytical framework in some detail.[22]

Ontology of separation: In most Western legal narratives of the Anthropocene[23], nonhumans are confined to the realm of things that can be appropriated and/ or protected by the law. Humans, on the other hand, are considered persons with legal rights and responsibilities in relation to these things[24]. Both the traditions of common law and civil law, as *Comparative Legal Traditions* exemplifies, rest on the overarching assumption that, when it comes to the law, the 'real' encompasses two separate domains. On the one hand, external objects of rights such as cattle, land, forests, water, and minerals, and on the other, legal persons such as humans, civil organisations, and corporations exerting rights over these objects.[25]

Epistemology of expert knowledge: Along with this dualistic worldview, the legal narratives of the Anthropocene, as depicted in *Comparative Legal Traditions*, generally defend a historiography tracing legal institutions back to the Roman Empire.[26] Such accounts offer neither a broader connection to a deeper past, nor an analysis of the socio-material conditions involved in the making of legal systems—which are therefore separated from their underlying

18 For CTL authors the word tradition generally evokes the image of a frozen and static past. However, with this term they denote a 'vital, dynamic, and ongoing system' of principles and norms (14). In this sense, the Anglo-American common law and the Romano-Germanic civil law are both examples of living traditions.

19 Escobar (2018).

20 Kohn (2013).

21 Van Dijk (1993).

22 For the development of this analytical framework, I drew from Vargas Roncancio et al. 2019.

23 On 'Western Modernity' see Mignolo (2011).

24 Anker (2017).

25 See Glendon et al. (1982) chapters 1 and 2.

26 Glendon et al. (1982) pp 1–16.

socio-ecological relations, or lifeworlds.[27] This division between disembodied legal historiographies and theories, and peripheral place-based legal 'stories' and 'beliefs', informs an epistemology of expert knowledge at the expense of local theoretical practices. Furthermore, this division renders invisible non-Western legal practices at the root of concepts such as 'patrimony', 'debt', and 'responsibility'.[28]

A politics of colonial asymmetry: Along with this dualistic framework, the legalities of the Anthropocene tend to undermine the role Eastern law and culture played in the creation of a 'Western' legal canon.[29] Additionally, pre-Columbian normative systems occupy the position of the 'Other'[30] and are either subsumed within a universal Western-self represented by the idea of the 'State',[31] or made absent from the official legal canon. The state is then considered the main law-producing unit, while collective subjects such as indigenous communities only produce local customs. This targets a fundamental pre-supposition that places political subjectivities along a civilisational trajectory whose pinnacles are Western-modernity, and the state-form.[32]

An ethics of professionalisation: This commitment to 'othering' is further echoed by the professionalisation ideal of legal education in LS-A:[33] 'Comparative analysis (and legal education more broadly) begins by working out a topic: Your client poses a problem. Or your government wishes to formulate and implement a policy. Or, in the course of your studies, you encounter a puzzle'.[34] This ideal informs the ends of legal education for the most part. Legal fields such as property law or environmental law remain oblivious of local struggles for collective rights (including the rights of nature) thus reinforcing the enclosure of life-relations within silo regimes.[35]

Teaching 'development': While comparing 'societies (and legal traditions) at comparable stages of social and economic development [...]',[36] most legalities of the Anthropocene run parallel with narratives of development (Escobar 2008). This commitment to the development script couples non-growth oriented legal traditions with 'backwards' modes of production and being. Whereas many Legal Systems of the Anthropocene might recognise the dynamism of legal traditions[37]—common law being a case in point—they tend to foster an

27 Ingold (2011); Mills (2016).
28 Monateri (2006); Lopez-Medina (2018) (2004).
29 Dussell (1998).
30 Smith (2012).
31 Hegel 2001 (1820).
32 Mignolo (2011).
33 Evetts (2012).
34 Glendon et al. (1982) p 9.
35 Graham (2011).
36 Glendon et al. (1982) p 7.
37 Glenn (2014).

image of society as a machine whose parts can be scientifically reduced for analysis, and improved time and again. The law, then, is made into a tool to 'develop' societies.

As exemplified by *Comparative Legal Traditions*, Legal Systems of the Anthropocene are mostly characterised by an ontology of separation between humans and the larger community of life;[38] an epistemology of expert knowledge that either invalidates non-modern legal systems, or renders them invisible and/or non-scientific local beliefs;[39] a politics of coloniality reinforcing power asymmetries between social groups;[40] an ethics of professionalisation that reproduce a liberal view of the legal practice;[41] and finally, a development and growth-oriented legal pedagogy that renders invisibles or less valuable local practices of economic and cultural difference.[42]

Through a partial review of ecological and Indigenous legal proposals, the next section puts forward an altogether different vision. The underlying assumption is that distinct lifeworlds, namely 'the ontological, epistemological, and cosmological framework through which the world appears to a people', produce legal meaning and practice in different ways.[43] Legal education, therefore, can either incorporate methodologies from larger socio-ecological systems, or further contribute to the separation between law and life in theory and practice.

Relational Legal Systems

Legal Systems of the Anthropocene such as environmental law are framed as independent sets of norms and procedures to regulate social systems and the 'natural resources' they depend upon. However, these systems are often grounded in a 'one-world ontology' paradigm as suggested in the previous section.[44] From the perspective of the Western experience and its colonial legacies,[45] the 'one-world ontology' insists that humans and nature occupy one single real made up of discrete and separate entities.[46] The vision of Relational Legal Systems, on the other hand, is committed to a relational understanding of the real,[47] as well as the socio-ecological processes where the law is embedded. I organise this vision around three important aspects of the multi-dimensional framework developed in section 1, as follows:

38 Berry (1999).
39 De la Cadena (2010); Dussel (1998)
40 Mignolo (2011).
41 Evett (2012).
42 Quijano Valencia (2016).
43 Mills (2016) p 850.
44 Law (2007).
45 Mignolo (2011); Dussel (1998)
46 Escobar (2016).
47 Escobar (2018).

A relational ontology: Broadly speaking, the law deals with a universe of relations between individuals, communities (human and not), states, and 'elementary groupings themselves'.[48] Usually depicted as the interpretation of legal doctrine, however, legal education tends to overlook the relational and material dimensions of legal systems.[49] Relational Legal Systems suggest a framework of interdependency and co-emergence of beings,[50] that is, 'a vision of the world that echoes the autopoietic dynamics and creativity of the Earth and the fact that no living being exists independently of the Earth', and each other[51]. To state it in terms of Nuu-chah-nulth scholar Umeek ER Atleo, the principle of interdependence—'(l)iving in balance and harmony with diverse life forms'—is applied to every dimension of existence through the development of human-nonhuman protocols.[52] This relational approach to life then seeks to de-centre the human in legal systems, while attending to the world-making potentials of legal orders.[53] The prescriptive attributes of legal systems are maintained in a Relational Legal Systems framework, yet the law is not reduced to this regulatory function only; rather, legal systems are defined according to their imagistic and world-making properties as well (Kohn 2018).

An epistemology of symmetry: A non-anthropocentric stance to knowledge making brings the principle of interdependence into legal theory, education, and normative systems. A vision for Relational Legal Systems underlines an epistemological symmetry between human and other-than-human beings,[54] the human does not have a monopoly over the world of meaning (social or otherwise) for meaning also emerge from a non-representational source, namely the diversity of corporeal dispositions, affects, and modes of being between different kinds of beings.[55] Rights-bearing agents in national legislations today, other-than-humans are also active law-making selves in that they represent the world in other than symbolic forms. Anthropologist Eduardo Kohn's work with the Runa of the Ecuadorian Amazon offers unique ethnographic evidence on the intrinsic sign-producing capacities of other-than-humans such as plants, animals, and spirits.[56] As the polyphonic Earth jurisprudence movement suggests, the law emerges from a thinking Earth.[57] Thus, a vision for a Relational Legal Systems framework expands the notion of human representa-

48 Graham (2011) p 15 cited in Burdon (2010) p 28.

49 Vermeylen (2017).

50 Haraway (2007).

51 Escobar (2015) p 14. See also Atleo (2011); Berry (1999); Cullinan (2011); Margulis and Sagan (2002).

52 Atleo (2011) p 36.

53 Grear (2017); Vermeylen (2017); Philippopoulos-Mihalopoulos (2017); Pottage (2016).

54 De la Cadena (2015).

55 Viveiros de Castro (1998); Descola (2013); Kohn (2013).

56 Kohn (2013).

57 Anker (2017); Berry (1999); Borrows (2016); Burdon (2012); Cullinan (2011); Garver (2011); Zuni Cruz (2009).

tion to include other-than-human sentient and intelligent beings as law-making selves in their own right.[58]

An ethics of care and socio-ecological justice: Attention to the situated character of inter-being relations, Relational Legal Systems challenge liberal understandings of justice as the distribution of individual rights and responsibilities. A more comprehensive notion of socio-ecological justice,[59] for example, is rooted in indigenous *Ley de Origen* (Law of Origin) and *Derecho Mayor* (Earth Law) across the Andean–Amazonian region.[60] Indigenous Earth Law are neither an abstract notion actualised in positive law as rules and procedures, nor a normative system expressed through customary law only. These systems encompass a set of practices of situated justice and responsibility embedded in material labour, family care, communal nurturing, plant sowing, commensality, ritual, among other practices and social institutions. At the same time, such practices are non-future oriented in that they strive for a situated, actual, and material world beyond a legal command that guides action for an abstract time and space (Ingold 2011). Indigenous Earth Law propose embodied justice, rather than justice as an act of judicial adjudication alone; justice through material practices of living together, rather than abstract ethical principles that only a few can relate to. Justice in a Relational Legal Systems approach is incarnated, actual, and place-based.

Indeed, other legal concepts will be radically re-*visioned* as we attend to their underlying lifeworlds.[61] In summary, this alternative proposal suggests a relational ontology based on the principle of radical interdependence of all that exist;[62] an epistemology of symmetry, that is, a non-anthropocentric stance to knowledge making that brings this ontological principle of interdependence into legal theory, education, and normative systems; and finally, and ethics of care and justice that challenges liberal understandings towards a more comprehensive notion of socio-ecological justice and responsibility embedded in material labour, family care, and ritual, among other practices.

Concluding Remarks: Transitions into Relational Legal Systems

Living in balance and harmony with multiple, sentient, and intelligent life forms can compromise every dimension of existence: from nourishment and social relations to knowledge making and legal protocols.[63] A non-anthropocentric

58 For the case of plants see Gagliano (2013); Gagliano et al (2014), (2017); Mancuso and Viola (2015); Marder (2013), (2016); Pelizzon and Gagliano (2015); Trewavas (2016).

59 Temper (2019).

60 Muelas (2000).

61 Mills (2016); Ingold (2011).

62 Escobar (2018); Mills (2016).

63 Atleo (2011); Kimmerer (2013); Trosper (2009); Brown and Timmerman (2015).

stance to life and knowledge ought to take this principle of interdependence seriously. If the human is already embedded within a shifting assemblage of cosmic matter, solar energy, water, soil nutrients, cultivation technologies, and social systems, among other agencies, the human shall not have the monopoly over the world of meaning, knowledge, and value.[64] Other-than-human beings, then, are not to be described, controlled, or protected through the law as discrete parts of an external reality, but partnered with as agential beings in their own right: every*thing*, or better yet, every*one*, co-emerge, thrive in mutuality, and even decay relationally—as the foliage decomposes back into the soil from where it came from as a living tree.

As suggested in this chapter, a Relational Legal Systems framework is characterised by a relational ontology that foregrounds the radical interdependence between humans and other-than-humans;[65] an epistemology of symmetry that integrates non-modern and modern legal ontologies, while recognising the inherent sign-making capacities of living (and non-living) nonhumans;[66] a politics of care that fosters harmonious relations between human groups, and between humans and the territories they are part of;[67] a de-professionalised ethics pledging for post-liberal views of legal practice that seriously engage with the imagistic and world-making properties of the law; and finally a post-development and degrowth[68] oriented legal pedagogy respectful of local practices of cultural, legal, and economic difference.[69]

An emergent legal education agenda for relational futures joins long-standing traditions of indigenous resurgence movements across the world.[70] This resurgence opens up a cross-cultural research agenda of interest for the transformation of legal education towards the Ecozoic: 1) the relationship between indigenous legal traditions and science-based ecological law approaches; 2) how decolonial research re-visions official legal historiographies; 3) how to effectively integrate nonhuman selves into decision-making models beyond the framework of the rights of nature; and 4) how to link ontological approaches to the law (what is the law?) with socio-political realities on the ground, among other topics (See table 13.1).

64 Kohn (2013); Viveiros de Castro (2016).
65 Kimmerer (2013); Borrows (2016).
66 Kohn (2013).
67 Muelas (2000).
68 Kallis et al. (2018).
69 Escobar (2008); Quijano Valencia (2016).
70 Mignolo and Walsh (2018). Over the last few decades, indigenous organisations and social movements around the world have faced the interrelated crises of extractivism, climate change, socio-ecological injustice, and epistemic violence using different strategies. These strategies range from political mobilisations on the ground to various forms of legal activism, and from practices of cultural resistance and autonomy at the local level to international advocacy efforts.

Table 13.1 Relational Legal Systems: a paradigm shift in legal education

Dimensions of Legal Change	Epochal Change *From Human Driven Planetary Change to Human–Earth Radical Interdependence and Co-emergence*		Legal Change *From Legal Systems of the Anthropocene to Relational Legal Systems*	
	Main Features		*Main Features*	
	Anthropocene (Predominant)	Relational futures (Emergent)	Anthropocene (Predominant)	Relational futures (Emergent)
Worldview (ontology)	One-world world Separation	Pluriverse Relationality	One-world world Separation of things/persons	Relational ontology Interdepen./human- nonhuman legal protocol
Ethics	Individualism	Co-responsibility	Professionalisation Allocation of rights	Care for territories Socio-ecological justice
Power relations	Top-down Asymmetrical	Dispersed Symmetrical	Universalism Western self	Pluriversality Decolonial/resurgence
Knowledge-making practices (epistemology)	Science (mainly) Expert knowledge	Co-prod. of know. Other narratives	Official legal narratives	Legal pluralism Rights of Nature Nonhuman as legal agents and sources of the law
Agents of knowledge	Some humans	Subalternised humans Other-than-humans	Some humans	Subalternised humans Other-than-humans
Pedagogy	Development-oriented Growth-oriented	Post-development Degrowth-oriented	Development-oriented Growth-oriented	Post-development Degrowth-oriented

Acknowledgements

Special thanks to Hermann Greene and Meybeth Alayón Velasquez; to Thomas Giddens and Luca Siliquini-Cinelli, editors of this volume; to the Leadership for the Ecozoic and the Centre for Indigenous Conservation and Development Alternatives (CICADA) at McGill University and COLCIENCIAS in Colombia.

References

Primary Sources

Colombian Constitutional Court, Sentence C-035 2016.

Colombian Constitutional Court, Sentence T-622 2016.

Constitution of the Republic of Ecuador 2008, Legislative Decree No. 0, Official Registration 449 20 October 20 2008.

Justice Supreme Tribunal STC 4390-2018.

Protective Action issued by the Provincial Court of Loja, Sentence No. 1121-2011-001, 30 March 2011.

Secondary Sources

Alberto Acosta and Esperanza Martínez (2011) *Naturaleza Con Derechos: De La Filosofía a La Política*, 1st Edition, Ediciones Abya-Yala.

Kirsten Anker (2017) 'Law As...Forest: Eco-logic, Stories and Spirits in Indigenous Jurisprudence' 21 *Law Text Culture* 191.

Richard (Umeek) Atleo (2011) *Principles of Tsawalk: An Indigenous Approach to Global Crisis*, University of British Columbia.

Thomas Berry (1999) *The Great Work: Our way into the Future*, Bell Tower.

Thomas Berry and Brian Swimme (1992) *The Universe Story: From the Primordial Flaring to the Ecozoic Era—A Celebration of the Unfolding of the Cosmos*, Harper.

Peter Brown and Peter Timmerman (2015) *Ecological Economics for the Anthropocene*, Columbia University Press.

John Borrows (2016) *Freedom and Indigenous Constitutionalism*, University of Toronto Press.

Peter Burdon (2010) 'The Rights of Nature: Reconsidered' 49 *Australian Humanities Review* 69.

Peter Burdon (2012) 'A Theory of Earth Jurisprudence' 37 *Australian Journal of Legal Philosophy* 28.

Frijoft Capra and Ugo Mattei (2015) *The Ecology of Law: Towards a Legal System in Tune with Nature and Community*, Berrett-Koehler Publishers.

PJ Crutzen and EF Stoermer (2000) 'The "Anthropocene"' 41 *Global Change Newsletter* 17.

Cormac Cullinan (2011) *Wild Law: A Manifesto for Earth Justice*, 2nd Edition, Chesea Green Publishing.

Marisol De la Cadena (2015) *Earth Beings: Ecologies of Practice*, Duke University Press.

Marisol de la Cadena (2010) 'Indigenous Cosmopolitics in the Andes: Conceptual reflections beyond "politics"' 24 *Cultural Anthropology* 334–70.

Philippe Descola (2013) *Beyond Nature and Culture*, University of Chicago Press.

Enrique Dussel (1998) *Ética de la liberación: en la edad de la globalización y de la exclusión*, Editorial Trotta and Universidad Autónoma de México.
Arturo Escobar (2008) *Territories of Difference: Place, Movements, Life, Redes. New Ecologies for the Twenty-First Century*, Duke University Press.
Arturo Escobar (2016) 'Sentipensar con la Tierra: Las Luchas Territoriales y la Dimensión Ontológica de las Epistemologías del Sur' 11(1) *Revista de Antropologia Iberoamericana* 11.
Arturo Escobar (2015) 'Transiciones: A Space for Research and Design for Transitions to the Pluriverse' 13 *Design Philosophy Papers* 13.
Julia Evetts (2012) 'Professionalism: Value and Ideology' in *Sociopedia.isa*, DOI: 10.1177/205684601231.
Monica Gagliano (2013) 'Persons as Plants: Ecopsychology and the Return to the Dream of Nature' 5(2) *Landscapes: The Journal of the International Centre for Landscape and Language* 1.
Monica Gagliano, Mayra Grimonprez, Martial Depczynski and Michael Renton (2017) 'Turn In: Plant Roots Use Sound to Locate Water' 184(1) *Oecologia* 151.
M Gagliano, M Renton, M Depczynski and S Mancuso (2014) 'Experience Teaches Plants to Learn Faster and Forget Slower in Environments Where It Matters' 175 *Oecologia* 63.
Geoffrey Garver (2011) 'A Systems-based Tool for Transitioning to Law for a Mutually Enhancing Human-Earth Relationship' 157 *Ecological Economics* 165.
Geoffrey Garver (2013) 'The Rule of Ecological Law: The Legal Complement to Degrowth Economics' 5 *Sustainability* 316.
Nicole Graham (2011) *Lawscape: Property, Environment, Law*, Routledge.
Anna Grear (2017) '"Anthropocene, Capitalocene, Chthulucene": (2017) Re-encountering Environmental Law and its "Subject" with Haraway and New Materialism' in Louis Kotzé (ed) *Environmental Law and Governance for the Anthropocene*, Hart Publishing.
Mary Ann Glendon, Paolo G Carozza and Colin Picker (1982) *Comparative Legal Traditions*, Thomsom/West. Ed 2008.
Patrick Glenn (2014) *Legal Traditions of the World*, 3rd Edition, Oxford University Press. 2007.
Angela P Harris (2014) 'Vulnerability and Power in the Age of the Anthropocene' in *Washington and Lee Journal of Energy, Climate, and the Environment*. Research Chapter No. 370.
Donna Haraway (2007) *When Species Meet*, University of Minnesota Press.
GWF Hegel (trans. SW Dyde) (2001) *The Philosophy of Right*, Batoche Books/Kitchener.
Tim Ingold (2011) *Being Alive: Essays on Movement, Knowledge, and Description*, Routledge.
Giorgos Kallis, Vasilis Kostakis, Steffen Lange, Barbara Muraca, Susan Paulson and Matthias Schmelzer (2018) 'Research On Degrowth' 43 *Annual Review of Environment and Resources* 291.
Robin Wall Kimmerer (2013) *Braiding Sweetgrass. Indigenous Wisdom, Scientific Knowledge and the Teching of Plants*, Milkweed Editors.
Eduardo Kohn (2013) *How Forests Think*, University of California Press.
Eduardo Kohn (2018) 'Forest for the Trees: Spirit, Psychedelic Science, and the Politics of Ecologizing thought as a Planetary Ethics' *Living Earth Workshop* Chapter. 26 October.
Law, John. 2007. 'Actor Network Theory and Material Semiotics' Version of 25th April 2007. http://hwww.heterogeneities.net/publications/Law2007ANTandMaterialSemiotics.pdf.
Lopez Medina and Diego Eduardo (2004) *Teoría Impura del Derecho. La Transformacion de la Cultura jurídiica latinoamericana*, Legis 2018.

Stephano Mancuso and Viola Brilliant Green. (2015). *The Surprising History and Science of Plant Intelligence*, Island Press.
Michel Marder (2013) *Plant-thinking. A philosophy of Vegetal life*, Columbia University Press.
Michel Marder (2016) *Grafts*, University of Minnesota Press.
Lynn Margulis and Dorian Sagan (2002) *Acquiring Genomes: A Theory of the Origins of Species*, Basic Books.
Gregorio Mesa Cuadros (2008) 'De la ética del consume a la ética del cuidado: De cómo otro mundo sí es posible desde otra manera de producir y consumer' 22 *Pensamiento Juridico* 333.
Aaron Mills (2016) 'The Lifeworlds of Law: On Revitalizing Indigenous Legal Orders Today' 61(4) *McGill Law Journal* 847.
Walter Mignolo (2011) *The Darker Side of Western Modernity. Global futures, Decolonial Options*, Duke University Press.
Walter Mignolo and Catherine Walsh (2018) *On Decoloniality: Concpets, Analytics, Praxis*, Duke University Press.
Gioussepi Gayo El Negro Monatery (2006) 'En busqueda de los origenes multiculturales de la tradicion juridical occidental', *La Invencion del Dercho Privado*, Siglo del Hombre.
Lorenzo Muelas (2000) 'El Derecho Mayor no Prescribe' 19 *Ecología Política* 99.
Alessandro Pelizzon and Monica Gagliano (2015) 'The Sentience of Plants: Animal Rights and Rights of Nature Intersecting?' 11 *Australian Animal Protection Law Journal* 5.
Andreas Philippopoulos-Mihalopoulos (2017) 'Critical Environmental Law in the Anthropocene' in Louis Kotzé (ed) *Environmental Law and Governance for the Anthropocene*, Hart Publishing.
Alain Pottage (2016) 'The Materiality of What?' Social Science Research.
Olver Quijano-Valencia (2016) *Ecosimias. Visiones y practicas de diferencia economica/cultural en contextos de multiplicidad*, Universidad del Cauca.
Leah Temper (2019) 'Blocking Pipelines, Unsettling Environmental Justice: from Rights of Nature to Responsibilities to Territory' 24(2) *Local Environment: The International Journal of Justice and Sustainability* 94.
Anthony Trewavas (2016) 'Plant Intelligence: An overview' 66(7) *BioScience* 542.
Ronald Trosper (2009) *Resilience, Reciprocity and Ecological Economics*, Northwest Coast Sustainability.
Linda Tuhiwai Smith (2012) *Decolonizing Methodologies: Research and Indigenous Peoples*, Zed Books.
Teun Van Dijk (1993) 'Principles of Critical Discourse Analysis' 4(2) *Discourse and Society* 249.
I Vargas Roncancio, L Temper, J Sterlin, NL Smolyar, S Sellers, M Moore, R Melgar-Melgar, J Larson, C Horner, JD Erickson, M Egler, PG Brown, E Boulot, T Beigi and M Babcock (2019) 'From the Anthropocene to Mutual Thriving: An Agenda for Higher Education in the Ecozoic' 11 *Sustainability* 3312.
Saskia Vermeylen (2017) 'Materiality and the Ontological Turn in the Anthropocene: Establishing a Dialogue between Law, Anthropology, and Eco-philosphy' in Louis Kotzé (ed) *Environmental Law and Governance for the Anthropocene*, Hart Publishing.
Eduardo Vivieros de Castro (1998) 'Cosmological *Diexis and* Amerindian Perspectivism' 4(3) *Journal of the Royal Anthropological Institute* 469.

Steven Winter (2001) *A Clearing in the Forest: Law, Life, and Mind*, The University of Chicago Press.

Rafi Youatt (2017) 'Personhood and the Rights of Nature: The New Subjects of Contemporary Earth Politics' 11 *International political Sociology* 39.

Christine Zuni Cruz (2009) 'Law of the Land - Recognition and Resurgence in Indigenous Law and Justice Systems' in Benjamin J Richardson, Shin Imai and Kent McNeil (eds) *Indigenous Peoples and the Law: Comparative and Critical Perspectives*, Hart Publishing.

Chapter 14

Study of Law Without Ends

Francesco Forzani

Introduction

This chapter develops a critique of the *governmentality* of the *learning society* through the lens of Giorgio Agamben's problematisation of the *function of instrumentality* in different thematic areas, including *sociality*, *study*, and *law*. This problematisation is used here to advocate for a particular kind of (legal) criticism that could be described as a *study (of law) without ends*. In the first section, I draw a theoretical distinction between learning and study through a re-interpretation of the literature on the governmentality of learning grounded on Agamben's critique of sociality. As a result, study is interpreted as a form of *permanent criticism* of the *governmental logic* or *function* organising learning and sociality in general, namely, *instrumentality*. In the second section, some remarks from Benjamin's *Kritik der Gewalt* are used to question critically the *pseudo-instrumental logic* which shapes the *canon* of legal knowledge and, to this purpose, some examples of how this logic plays out in legal theory are examined. This brief overview should be intended as a practical *exemplification* of the *potentiality of study* (as criticism) *in action*. In the third section, the canon of instrumentality is reinterpreted through Agamben's notion of *law as a (biopolitical) signatura* which constructs society as a space in which life is *made governable* (i.e., life used as a means to the ends of *governability*) through an *ambiguous* articulation of *form* and *force* (of *both* law and life). To conclude, it is suggested that the *(dis)function* of the student could be *not* to disrupt the law but rather to *problematise* the whole *legal tradition* (which includes but is not limited to legal theory) as a field in which *life is rendered governable through instrumental reasoning*. Whereas learners can only endlessly *presuppose* this *signatura* in all the juridical operations they learn about, the student can make of this presupposition the object of a permanent criticism.

DOI: 10.4324/9781003179283-18

Learning, Study, Criticism

Some critics have suggested that modern universities embody the logic of what has been generally described as the *learning society*, namely, the idea[1] of the necessity of 'the productive involvement of individuals in education throughout their lives, to the benefit of themselves, their employing organisations and society'.[2] On one side, these critics warn us about the *conflation of society and productivity*—which in turn is defined by 'individual earnings, organisational productivity and national economic performance'[3]—and, on the other, about the full *instrumentalisation of education for the purposes of productivity*.[4]

The life of the student appears therefore transformed into an endless process of self-adaptation in which the act of study itself becomes an economic asset and a means of production.[5] Through market economy, school and life become indistinguishable, in the sense that the life itself of the student is turned into a zero-degree of economic productivity, a 'force to produce added value' in a sort of 'permanent state of learning' named 'lifelong education'.[6] According to its critics, within the learning society, study has a *biopolitical function*, meaning that it represents 'a natural force to live … life'[7] which, in turn, becomes conflated with employability.[8]

The *subjugation* of life as such to a process of capitalist production[9] is what, at the same time, allows the student to constitute themself as a subject, i.e., a *learner*. To learn becomes, at the same time, an imperative (an ought) and a form of liberation (a will)[10] and, from this perspective, the critics of the learning society speak of learning as a form of 'self-government' which 'renders … society as a whole governable'.[11] The learning society, in other words,

1 Hughes and Tight call it a 'myth', that is to say, 'an idea which may or may not have validity, but which many people believe in': (1995) p 290.
2 Hughes and Tight (1995) pp 292–3.
3 Hughes and Tight (1995) p 291.
4 Hughes and Tight speak, in this respect, of the 'productivity myth' ('the idea of a continuing need to increase productivity') being tied to education: (1995) p 291.
5 Simons and Masschelein (2008) pp 396–7.
6 Simons and Masschelein (2008) pp 397–8.
7 Simons and Masschelein (2006) p 417. Jarvis defines 'lifelong education' as '[t]he combination of processes throughout a life time whereby the whole person – body … and mind … – experiences social situations, the perceived content of which is … integrated into the individual person's biography resulting in a continually changing (or more experienced) person': (2006) p 134.
8 The 'lifelong learner today has to ask whether he or she possesses the necessary competencies or employable learning results in order to live a successful life': Simons and Masschelein (2008) p 402.
9 Simons (2006) p 528.
10 The student is thus described as a lifelong manager, driven by an 'educational imperative of self-empowerment': Jarvis (2006) p 134.
11 Simons & Masschelein (2008) p 393.

represents a form of *governmentality*, that is to say, a conceptual space[12] of *both* government and self-government[13] in which (presumably formless) students, to put it simply, constitute themselves as (*empowered*) subjects through a *subjection* to the logic of learning which, in turn, makes society as a whole governable.

Following Giorgio Agamben's *analogical* reinterpretation[14] of the two terms, it can be suggested that learning represents a (biopolitical) *function qua office*. The term '*officium*'—originally borrowed by Ambrose from Cicero to translate the Greek '*leitourgía*'—comes to designate in the Christian tradition the priestly function which in turn becomes, in Agamben's philosophical-historical interpretation, the paradigm of an ontological condition such that

> being and praxis, what a human does and what a human is, enter into a zone of indistinction in which being dissolves into its practical effects and, with a perfect circularity, it is what it has to be and has to be what it is.[15]

A priest *is*, more concretely, their particular *function*, namely, an *action* split into two, an '*opus operantis*'—the action of the celebrant which constitutes them as an 'animate instrument'—and the '*opus operato*'—'the sacramental effect in itself, which is unfailingly realized, whatever the condition of the celebrant may be'.[16]

Priestly office is thus divided into an 'instrumental being', the mere action, and the actualisation and perfection of this action, its powerful '*effectus*'.[17] A priest administering a sacrament is—*like*[18] a learner—a *functionary* because their action becomes a means for the exercise of an *end* (i.e., a *function*) which *exceeds* it, constituting specifically 'an alterity in whose name the "function" is carried

12 The concept was originally employed by Foucault (2009) to describe the multiple ways in which the State, since the 18th century turned itself into an apparatus for the conduct or government of a *population* of *individuals* (p 144) living 'side by side': Foucault (1990) p 82. As a conceptual tool then 'governmentality' allows to study modern subjectivity as a *process* (i.e., *subjectivation*, the process through which 'human beings are made subjects') and, more particularly, as a process of *conduct of conduct*: quote from Foucault (1982) p 777. Subjects, in this respect, are not merely controlled by external powers: they also produce power through their own self-knowledge (Foucault (1982) p 781), which means that the same governmentality which shaped, for example, the modern state produces also an 'individualising power' (Foucault (1990) p 60) that allows individuals to construct themselves as, precisely, modern subjects.

13 Simons and Masschelein (2008) p 391.

14 For an overview of Agamben's use of analogy see his work on method (2009a).

15 Agamben (2017) p 650.

16 Agamben (2017) p 1096.

17 Agamben (2017) p 715.

18 It should be noted that the juxtaposition of learner and priest should be treated as an *analogy*, which means that the two positions are *not* equivalent. The analogy makes sense in the context of this chapter's critico-theoretical reflection, but its concrete relevance (or irrelevance) in particular educational contexts can only be measured, in concrete, by the reader who operates in those contexts.

out'[19] and which makes the action *effective* in a given social context—namely, that of a 'hierocratic and institutionalised Church'[20] or that of a society of productive learners.[21] In both instances a particular action—respectively, the sacrament and the act of studying—becomes means of a higher function which produces a social institution—respectively, the Church and the many economised institutions of the learning society (including universities).

Crucially, the argument can be further expanded, in more abstract terms, into a critical account of the very possibility of inscription of human action into a general function of sociality. Agamben, in fact, suggests that—through what appears as an analogical extension of its semantic context,—the term *officium* (signifying also *duty*) was later used by Pufendorf to describe human action insofar as it conforms to the principle of '*socialitas*', which says that 'every man *ought to do* as much as he can to cultivate and preserve sociality'.[22] In philosophical terms, sociality turns being into functional action, into an '*efficere suum officium*', the exercise of a socially codified function. Human action is effective when it has the *force* to produce a social bond—namely, as the expression of a function (or duty) of sociality—and, *similarly*, one studies effectively only if such action is the performance of a social function, i.e., learning.

A modern social being is thus one who assumes an office, namely, one for whom action 'coincides with the effectuation of a function', meaning that this action has neither an end in itself (*praxis*), nor is simply defined by an external end or product which results from the action (*poiesis*): what makes it effective is rather the fact that it fulfils a function.[23] Moreover, Agamben's semantico-analogical inquiry suggests that this onto-social function is biopolitical or governmental from the start. Before its Christianisation, in fact, Cicero conceptualises '*officium*' as a translation of the Greek '*kathêkon*' (referring to an action 'whose appropriateness depends on the circumstances'[24]) charged with a particular institutional significance; '*officium*', Agamben stresses, refers here to 'the use of life as a whole', a form of 'instituting the common life [*vitam instituere*]' which allows humans to 'govern[] things [*rem gerere*]' and which, overall 'renders life *governable*' thus constituting what Seneca would later define its '*sociabilitas*'.[25]

From within this functional paradigm of *governability* the action becomes 'indifferent to the subject who carries it out and the subject becomes indifferent to the ethical quality of his action'[26] which means that being becomes

19 Agamben (2017) p 694.
20 Dean (2017) p 217.
21 See n 18.
22 Agamben (2017) p 738.
23 Agamben (2017) p 717.
24 Agamben (2017) p 705.
25 Agamben (2017) p 710.
26 Agamben (2017) p 694.

'indiscernible from its effects … functional to them'[27] and, therefore, absorbed by them. To *live* in society means, in this sense, to render life *governable*. This particular relation between subject and social function is described by Agamben as one of '*instrumental causality*', namely, the idea (originally developed by Thomas Aquinas to account, precisely, for the function of the liturgy) of an instrument which 'serves the end of another, only to the degree that it realizes its own end' and thus which, 'remaining in relationship with its own action, … [is] rendered autonomous with respect to it and can be referred to any extrinsic finality whatsoever',[28] i.e., an '*external final cause*'. The end of *the instrument life*—namely, *to live*—is *absorbed into the external finality of governability*.

This is also how the relation between studying and learning can be reconfigured. On this basis, a student's form of life tends to be increasingly absorbed—as a means to an end—into the function of learning, which represents the efficacious actualisation of its governmental potentiality. In the learning society studying has not an end in itself and is not merely productive of a separate end either. It is rather a function of sociality, that which makes the student a (social qua productive) subject.

Agamben's critique of sociality as a process dominated by a pseudo-instrumental functionality (instrumental causality), however, is *not* meant to provide new means or ends for the (post-)modern subject. The point is, more radically (and more simply), to *problematise* the function of social subjectification through (what appears to me as) a method (of study) which produces a suspension of the logic of instrumentality tout court: a re-conceptualisation of critique itself as a form of *interminable study without ends*. An account of this experience is provided by Agamben in *The Idea of Prose*, where he argues that

> those who are acquainted with long hours spent roaming among books where every fragment, every codex, every initial encounter seems to open a new path, immediately left aside at the next encounter … know that not only can study have no rightful end, but does not even desire one.[29]

The critic gesture of the student consists precisely in giving up the right to and the desire for an end and, in this sense, it undermines the logic of instrumentality through which sociality is *organised*.

This studious use of criticism, Agamben continues, is akin to 'the condition which Aristotle, contrasting it with the act, defines as potential'[30] and yet, from a philosophical perspective, it does not represent a potentiality separate from

27 Agamben (2017) p 701.

28 Agamben (2017) pp 1092–4. Aquinas' examples include an *axe*—which (thanks to its own ability, i.e., cutting) becomes the instrument for the carpenter's art—and *water*—which (thanks to its own ability, i.e., cleansing the body) becomes the instrument of God's power to cleanse the soul.

29 Agamben (1995) p 64.

30 Agamben (1995) p 64.

actuality (of, for example, learning): it is, instead, the very act of questioning the (instrumental) relation between potentiality and actuality and, in this sense, it can be argued that *it is always already actual* (end) *as a potentiality* (means)[31]. The *idea of study* consists, in other words, in questioning the idea of *power qua 'organisation of potentiality'*, power as 'the isolation of potentiality from its act'.[32] Power, Agamben continues, is grounded on '*forces*[found] everywhere—even within ourselves—which constrain potentiality to hang fire within itself'.[33] It is, in abstract terms, the use of *life's forces as instruments* for the constitution of an isolated potentiality, a governmental function which, to a certain extent, remains *indifferent* to the means of its realisation.[34]

Learning, in this respect, represents a form of (bio)power, the organisation of a studious life's force or potentiality, through its *pseudo-instrumental* inscription into the social function of 'lifelong learning'. The latter is thus to be firmly distinguished from study as a 'permanent condition' in which, according to Agamben, the desire for knowledge is so intense to become a 'form of life'.[35] While the student (permanently) *questions* the functional logic of instrumentality which commands (also permanently) the learner's self-production and, therefore, has always already found what they need in, precisely, the *medium of this questioning*, the learner constitutes and preserves themself and their sociality through the *external finality* of learning, an endless deferral of what they need to achieve.[36]

In a similar fashion, Lewis questioned 'the instrumentalization of potentiality' in education arguing, specifically, that the generic potentiality of the student is 'subjected to relentless actualization according to the necessities of market control and institutional capture'.[37] Following Agamben's account of study, Lewis opposes this (learning) logic of a 'not yet that must be'[38]—a potentiality that *must be* actualised so as to fulfil a particular function—so that, in governmental terms, the (studious) subject is endlessly 'commanded to self-

31 Study, as a means, 'has always already found its object' (author's translation) (Agamben (2017) 'Studenti', www.quodlibet.it/giorgio-agamben-studenti) and, in this sense, it desires no end.

32 Agamben (1995) p 71.

33 Agamben (1995) p 71.

34 This is why Agamben claims that power 'pervert[s] the strict link between means and ends' Agamben (1995) p 71.

35 Agamben (2017) 'Studenti', www.quodlibet.it/giorgio-agamben-studenti.

36 The capture of study into learning, in this respect, is realised precisely through its subjugation to the modern utilitarian paradigm which turns all human things and actions (including the most useless) into 'social needs'. As a result, Agamben suggests, study has now become even more worthy of protection precisely in so far as it is useless and, therefore, not reducible to a social need: Agamben (2017) 'Studenti', www.quodlibet.it/giorgio-agamben-studenti.

37 Lewis (2013) p 9.

38 Lewis (2013) speaks specifically of 'an ontology of generic potentiality as a "not yet" that "must be" made manifest in measurably determinate, socially useful, and economically manageable skill sets' (p 6).

actualise its latent potentiality'[39]—to the experience of *im-potentiality*, namely, of the 'capability not to be' which is also the capability 'to be otherwise, to think otherwise, to live otherwise'.[40]

Power, in fact, consists not only in the 'separation of humans from what they can do' but also 'from what they can not do'[41] and the modern subject of power is therefore being rendered 'blind not to his capacities but to his incapacities'.[42] Study then—the paradigm of 'being-otherwise'—refers to an experience of 'absolute impotence',[43] namely a potentiality which is not absorbed into an external finality, 'a potential that does not precede but follows its act'.[44] Concretely, the impotence of study rests on its always-already actualised ability to *expose* the pseudo-instrumental functioning of power.[45] *Otherwise-ness*, in fact, requires more (or less) than imagining a new manner of being, thinking and living: whatever *manner* is imagined has, in fact, to be *other* than the one(s) made possible under the current governmental horizon of possibility, which means that a reflection on the limits of governmentality (i.e., on its manners) is what is (end-lessly) needed. The notion of study then represents 'the zero-point for critically examining both the logic of necessity that characterizes the current age of biotechnological control and the proposed alternatives'[46] which means, in other words, that impotentiality stands for a *capability-not-to actualise* the existing biopolitical forms of subjectivity by, precisely, *exhibiting* in what terms these are made possible.

Arguably, this is also how Foucault understands his own critique, namely, as a form of 'permanent criticism' which 'point[s] out on what kind of assumptions, what kinds of familiar, unchallenged, unconsidered modes of thought the practices that we accept rest'.[47] The form of life of the student, as opposed to the learner, would then be that of a permanent criticism addressed to what Foucault called 'the contemporary limits of the necessary', that is to say, what historically has been represented as 'indispensable for the constitution of ourselves as autonomous subjects'.[48] Foucault's 'permanent critique of ourselves' consists in a 'philosophical ethos characterizable as a limit-attitude' which situates us 'at the frontiers of the outside-inside alternative' and turns 'what is given to us as universal, necessary, obligatory' into a 'possibility of transgression'.[49]

39 Lewis (2013) p 6.
40 Lewis (2013) p 9.
41 Agamben (2011) pp 43–4.
42 Agamben (2011) p 44.
43 Agamben (1995) pp 71–2.
44 Agamben (1995) p 65.
45 This is how I suggest one should or could interpret Agamben's notion of 'destituent power'.
46 Lewis (2013) p 12.
47 Foucault (1990) pp 154–5.
48 Foucault (1991a) p 43.
49 Foucault (1991a) p 45.

Transgression though coincides here with the exhibition of the limits that characterise the organisation of man's potential, which is why Foucault speaks of his critique as a 'historical ontology of ourselves' and, more precisely, as 'a historico-practical test of the limits that we may go beyond' which, nevertheless, should 'turn away from ... the claim to escape from the system of contemporary reality so as to produce the overall programs of another society'.[50]

To study is not to programme a society *beyond* the limits of the current society but, rather, to investigate under what circumstances a certain *beyondness* has become thinkable, which is to say, how human potentiality has been organised in *this* society.

Means and Ends in Law

The critics of the learning society investigate, among other things, how universities 'support state rationality by cultivating individuals whose lives foster the strength of the state' and the dynamics 'establishing the dominance of certain discourses ... and continually replenishing the technologies that connect knowledge to power'.[51] Within academia a certain 'canon' is produced, representing 'a standard against which all forms of knowledge are gauged' producing an official intellectual discourse which 'organizes and determines knowledge'.[52] The organisation of knowledge at university level is, in this respect, the organisation of potentiality (for thought and action) of the subject who is confronted with this knowledge, i.e., the student. The role of a law student involved in 'permanent criticism'—their social (dis)function—then is (or simply *can* be[53]) questioning the way in which a certain 'canon' of legal knowledge has been produced within the (legal) tradition they are confronted with.

Agamben's biopolitical study of law focuses, in this respect, on the *ontological* canon that defines the limits of law's potentiality.[54] This canon is ontological because its study provides, at the same time, also a critique of the function through which the very potentiality for sociality of the human subject is organised, in and through law, in pseudo-instrumental terms. To be criticised is not simply the constitution of the student as a learner, that is to say, their subjection to the market's logic but, more radically, *the social function of the law*, the *production of sociality by juridical means*. In this respect, criticism of governmentality concerns not only that which is directly linked to the marketisation of knowledge, its use as a means to economic ends, but the very constitution of a knowing subject endowed with a social function defined by a *juridified version of the logic of instrumentality*.

50 Foucault (1991a) p 46.
51 Howley and Hartnett (1992) p 264.
52 Howley and Hartnett (1992) p 276.
53 For a similar point see Zartaloudis (2018).
54 It is, in this sense, critique of law's *power*.

Study as a means without ends consists precisely in questioning law's instrumentality and is rooted in Walter Benjamin's 'philosophical-historical' critique of law's '*Gewalt*' (a term whose semantic complexity could be rendered as 'power-force-violence') which, in fact, begins with the acknowledgement that the (philosophico-historical) canon of Western law is *instrumentality, the ambiguous idea of law a means to an end*. Specifically, Benjamin stresses that the problem of *Gewalt*—i.e., the problem that the law *is* a certain use (i.e., monopoly) of violence—is somehow obscured by 'the ambiguous logic of means and ends' that ground law's functioning and which is reflected, for example, in the dialectical oscillation of the two main schools of legal thought, natural and positive theory of law. In his own words:

> [i]f natural law can judge all existing law only in criticizing its ends, then positive law can judge all evolving law only in criticizing its means. If justice is the criterion of ends, legality is that of means. Both schools however meet in their common basic dogma: just ends can be attained by justified means, justified means used for just ends. ... Natural law attempts, by the justness of the ends, to justify the means, positive law to guarantee the justness of the ends through the justification of the means.[55]

More recently, authors like Green and Tamanaha have, similarly, investigated the 'instrumental conception of law'—the idea that '[l]aw belongs to the meaningful world of ends and means'[56]—suggesting that no proper understanding of law is possible 'without reference to ends'.[57] This conception can be further articulated into two, seemingly, opposed views, namely: a) the 'instrumental thesis' (law as a *means* to an end)—i.e., the idea that 'law can only be identified by focusing on its (species-typical) means rather than on its ends'[58] and, therefore, that 'what makes the law special are the means by which it serves those ends',[59] including for example *legality*, *validity*, and *the rule of law*; b) The finalistic view of law (law as a means to an *end*), which considers law mainly from the perspective of the ends that it serves and which can be further articulated, based loosely on Tamanaha's own systematisation, into two almost opposite approaches: the first, 'non-instrumental', argues that law *as a whole* has a definite *end in itself*—e.g., the medieval idea of law as the right ordering of society or, in modernity, as expression of the public good[60]—whereas the second rests

55 Benjamin (1996) p 237.

56 Green (2009) p 5.

57 Green (2009) p 8. See also Tamanaha (2006) p 6.

58 Green (2009) p 7.

59 Green (2009) p 8.

60 Tamanaha (2006) speaks of the view of law as provided with a built-in integrity serving the public good (p 215), whose roots are to be found, according to him, in the medieval conception of law as custom 'emanating from below' (p 11).

on the assumption that society is a chaotic space comprised of opposing forces all striving inconsistently for the realisation of particular ends through legal means.[61]

In spite of their differences, these views are complementary and eventually can become *ambiguously indistinguishable*. For example, Green suggests that Tamanaha's criticism of the modern use of law as an instrument to be appropriated for whatever end[62]—its use as an 'empty vessel devoid of any inherent principle or binding content or integrity unto itself'[63]—is ambiguously similar to Kelsen's (one of the main advocates of the study of law from the perspective of its *means*) 'criptic remark that legal norms may have any kind of content'.[64] Kelsen's focus on the means of law, then, makes possible a reflection on the multiple ends that the law serves.[65] At the same time though, Tamanaha's interpretation of medieval law[66] as the expression of a finalistic view that conceived (natural) law as, among other things, 'perfection of reason', 'universal', 'embracing all cases and questions that can possibly arise', 'superior to all laws and regulations'[67]—shares equally some similarities with Kelsen's account of the validity of legal norms and the related idea of hierarchical structure of the legal order.[68] More generally, non-instrumental finalistic ideas of law as order provided the ideological foundation for the development of a judicial technique, that is to say, a rational *science of legal means* grounded on the logic of both induction and deduction whose function became precisely to *maintain* the order of which the law was said to be natural expression.[69] In spite of its focus on means, formalism played, and keeps playing, a crucial function in sustaining an ideology of social ordering as the end of law.[70] For example, MacCormick, working at the intersection between sociological jurisprudence and legal positivism, considers syllogism a fundamental *means* of decision making functional

61 This is the position criticised by Tamanaha (2006) as a form of corrupted instrumentality according to which the 'driving force behind legal development is continuous struggles among individuals and groups within society to have their interests reflected in and backed up by legal coercion' (p 3).

62 See n 61.

63 Tamanaha (2006) p 7.

64 Green (2009) p 8.

65 The fact that 'law aims to help a variety of people attain a variety of ends': Green (2009) p 25. Green speaks of the law, if considered from the perspective of means, as a 'Swiss-Army knife: a multi-purpose tool handy for lots of ends, but not necessarily an all-purpose tool' (p 26). This position is ambiguously similar, though slightly less radical, to the one enunciated by Tamanaha in his critique of instrumentalism (see n 61).

66 Tamanaha (2006) distinguishes between a Catholic tradition and a tradition of customary law, both considered by him as 'non-instrumental' traditions of law (p 11).

67 Tamanaha (2006) p 14.

68 The analogy here is between *Grundnorm* and Natural Law. For a reflection on this see Peterson (2017).

69 Tamanaha (2006) pp 15–18.

70 Tamanaha (2006) pp 48–9.

also to the universalisation of particular legal interpretations which are integrated into a coherent set of social values, i.e. *ends*, that the legal system sustains and reproduces.[71]

In general, these ambiguities take on a new meaning as soon as all the different views on law's instrumentality are interpreted as expressions of a general *canon of decidability* on the means and ends of life: 'guidance of human action'[72] to be made possible in terms of means and ends of *both* law and life. Benjamin, in this respect, distinguishes between natural and legal instrumentality and suggests that 'the legal system tries to erect, in all areas where individual [natural] ends could be usefully pursued by violence, legal ends that can be realized only by legal power'.[73] Law represents itself as *capable* of endlessly 'evaluating conduct'[74] and, from this perspective, its ultimate end is precisely to preserve this *power of evaluation* (*decidability*), i.e., *to avoid that it would become impossible.* In Benjamin's own terms, 'the law's interest in a monopoly of violence vis-a-vis individuals is explained not by the intention of preserving legal ends but, rather, by the intention of preserving the law itself'.[75] Different views on law's instrumentality share a fundamental presupposition, namely, *self-preservation* as *law's external final cause.*

Take, for example, MacCormick's account of legal rules. At first, he distinguishes between rules and 'operative facts' to which rules *deductively* apply (if fact-x occurs then rule-y applies), suggesting that the application of a rule *presupposes* the necessity of 'ascriptive decisions'—the necessary *relatability* of life and law, namely, treating a certain fact as, precisely, the (operative) fact *of* a rule;[76] second, he distinguishes between the content of rules (means) and the general social values (ends) that each rule, as expression of the legal system, sustains and further suggests that '*the coherence of law*' as a whole, namely 'treating [i.e., *deciding*] like cases alike and different cases differently', represents a 'grand-scale legal value'[77] in itself. Rules are therefore not just means for the ends (social values) of law but also instruments for the *preservation* of a *foundational* (ascriptive) *decision* which concerns the *relatability* of law and life.[78] The

71 MacCormick (2005), in this respect, argues that 'recourse to the legal syllogism is a necessary part of the rhetoric of legal justification, on the ground that respect for the Rule of Law requires respect for the rules of the law' (p 54).

72 Green (2009) p 23.

73 Benjamin (1996) p 238.

74 Green (2009) p 26.

75 Benjamin (1996) p 239.

76 MacCormick (2005) p 71.

77 MacCormick (2005) pp 207–8.

78 Implicitly Shapiro (2009) makes a similar argument when, reinterpreting Hart, he suggests that constitutional law represents 'the shared plan of a legal system', which 'determines goals and values [the] system should pursue and realise', and that, in turn, this organisation of goals and values represents a 'plan of governance' whose function is ultimately 'to guide and organize the shared activity of legal officials' (p 18).

function of legal rules and values is law's (coherent) self-preservation in and through endless decisions on the (legal) form of life, i.e., decisions on the relatability of law and life.

Benjamin's critique of the logic of instrumentality which grounds both positive and natural schools of law can be expanded further by suggesting that *the ultimate end of law is its own survival as a means, the preservation of its power to act as a means*. This power presupposes another (founding) power: the power to exercise an endless scrutiny on the ends of life, which is to say, the power to turn life as such into an instrumental cause, i.e., a force of the law.[79] In this respect, law's *external final cause* (i.e., self-preservation) presupposes, in ontological terms, the *indistinction of law and life*, which is to say, the possibility of their articulation by *means* of *decisions*: the production and preservation of a sphere of (law's) decidability (on life).

Signatura of Law and Life

It can therefore be suggested that the function of the subject who has *learnt* the law is to preserve—by presupposing it (that is to say, without questioning it)—the thinkability of its power to articulate law and life in pseudo-instrumental terms through actual formulations of their articulation. This applies *analogously* to decision-makers, legislators, administrators, theorists, and so forth, and in general it can be suggested that while a law-learning-student is not specifically trained to become any of these 'functionaries', the learner is nevertheless exposed (more or less uncritically) to this generic potentiality of the law. It is only in this sense that it is possible to claim that their actions are *analogous*: they all share what Agamben defines a '*signatura*' (of law), an 'analogical and immaterial model'[80] which 'signifies a force' (for signification) in a certain social context.[81]

The '*signatura*' represents, specifically, the *efficacy* or *power* of a certain language (including also legal language):

> [it] operates in signs, phrases and sentences, at the level of their simple existence as a bearer of efficacy, which each time allows us to decide

79 Zartaloudis (2015) speaks in the same terms of the logic of (law's) *Gewalt* when he claims that '[l]ife as a juridical institution (where life and law are collapsed into a zone of indistinction) becomes the enabling device through which the law can exceed itself and maintain its office intact' (p 172).

80 Agamben (2009a) p 36.

81 Agamben (2009a) makes a series of practical ordinary examples of this signifying force, including, among others, the insignia worn by couriers on their garment or by soldiers on the battlefield—signifying who they are and how they should be treated—the sign which indicates the value of a coin, the seal impressed on a letter and the signature of the author written in a lower edge of a painting (pp 36–7).

whether the act of language is efficacious, if the sentence is correct, or whether an aim is realised.[82]

Philosophically speaking, Agamben suggests, both language and law are *signaturae* that signify the efficacious relation between respectively, words and world, law and life.[83] Like language, law is not merely signification, '"*ius dicere*" (saying what is in conformity with the law)': it is always also a '"*vim dicere*" (saying the efficacious word)'[84] which constitutes the *legal order* as the sphere in which law *can* (i.e., has the power to) *refer to life* (like words refer to the world) in a stable and efficacious manner. This efficacious relation—which represents, with Agamben's words, an 'excess of efficacy over signification', 'a relation that exceeds and grounds every relation'[85]—is thus allowed to produce meaning (i.e., to signify) in accordance with the logic of instrumentality. Most importantly, the concrete instances (including theories, judicial and legislative decisions, administrative acts, juridical categories, and so forth) in which this relatability is expressed and articulated become *paradigms* of the *signatura* of law, examples of its power (i.e., organised potentiality).

Law's self-preservation coincides with the administration of the relatability of law and life and, from this perspective, it is biopolitical or governmental: it constitutes life itself as a *governable force* and, at the same time, produces the subject (of law) who will administer life's governability, the (law's) '*signator*',[86] *the subject who administers the signatura* (of law). This figure represents an '*enunciative function*', to be understood, with Foucault, as a 'vacant place' within a network of power relations that individuals must fill in order to produce intelligible meaning in a given historical moment.[87] This '*signatura*' produces a 'sanctioned mode of intelligibility'[88] through the institutions of 'subjective enunciative positions' that pre-determine the intention to signify of the individuals entering that framework of meaningful signification, thus allowing them to construct the objective world around them.[89]

82 Agamben (2009a) p 36.
83 Agamben (2009a) pp 75–6.
84 Agamben (2009a) p 75.
85 Agamben (2009a) p 50.
86 In the field of language, a paradigmatic '*signator*' (at least in the Western tradition) is Adam who, in fact, founds the relation between words and world 'giv[ing] its own proper name to everything': Agamben (2009a) p 35. Similarly, in Augustine, the priest or minister represents the '*signator*' of the sacrament, the 'active principle that animates it and makes it effective': Agamben (2009a) pp 46–7.
87 Foucault (1972) pp 92–6.
88 Watkin (2013) p 12.
89 Watkin (2013) p 33. From this perspective, the problem of the 'vanishing of the jurist's experiential mediation' discussed by Siliquini-Cinelli (this volume) can be interpreted as inscribed within the problematisation of law as a *signatura*: jurists themselves are always-already split into experience and knowledge because they are *signators*, an enunciative function which preserves the articulability of

In this sense, for example, when legal theorists speak of a fundamental norm (such as Kelsen's *Grundnorm* or Hart's *rule of recognition*) which allows to determine the criteria for identifying the law, they are implicitly dealing with the issue of law's *signatura*. My suggestion, specifically, is that the enunciative function presupposed by legal theory's fundamental norm(s) is to turn *life* into a 'zero-degree of law',[90] that is to say, *an instrument for the self-preservation of law*. Crucially, these 'master norms', which found the relation between law and life in terms of *decidability*, are shaped and sustained by various 'officials' and, ultimately, also by 'the man in the street',[91] that is to say, by society at large.[92] For example, as Atienza and Manero suggest, the fact that 'one could not use the law as a mechanism of foreseeing the consequences of one's own behaviour, if one would not expect norm-applying and norm-producing organs to follow one and the same rule of recognition',[93] implies that private citizens themselves enforce, through their thoughts and actions, law's decidability, and, in this respect, act as (quasi)officials who perform a social function. In similar terms, Lindhal has recently re-interpreted Kelsen's *Grundnorm* as an 'ought form' which provides subjects with social agency by, precisely, allowing them to understand 'something as something in law'.[94]

Law can thus be interpreted, with Agamben, as a process of 'desemanticisation and suspension of concrete praxis … custom and usage of individuals' (i.e., life) which produces ('isolates') a norm,[95] a 'generic proposition endowed with a merely virtual reference'[96] which, in turn, grounds a generalised ability to decide (decid-ability). In fact, the application of a norm—'the passage … from virtual reference to a concrete reference to a segment of reality'—is not merely a logical (deductive or inductive) operation and, in this sense, 'is in no way contained within the norm and cannot be derived from it; otherwise, there would have been no need to create the grand edifice of trial law'.[97] The application of the norm, Agamben continues, is the expression of an 'enunciative function', 'a trial that always involves a plurality of subjects and ultimately culminates in the pronunciation of a sentence, that is, an enunciation whose operative reference to reality is guaranteed by the institutional powers'.[98] The

the two spheres of life and law. Siliquini-Cinelli (this volume), in this respect, further suggests that 'whenever we try to decode experience epistemically … we inevitably fall pray of analytical techniques of world-disposition that void what makes our experiential finitude such': (p 179).

90 For a similar argument see Zartaloudis (2015).

91 Atienza and Manero (1998) p 150.

92 Hart claims so explicitly and while Kelsen was not willing to go that far, there is room to interpret his work accordingly: see for example Marmor (2021) and, particularly, Lindhal (2013).

93 Atienza and Manero (1998) p 150.

94 Lindhal (2013) p 119.

95 Agamben (2017) p 197.

96 Agamben (2017) p 199.

97 Agamben (2017) p 200.

98 Agamben (2017) p 199.

law, from this perspective, is split into two poles, namely, on one side, a 'pure form of law' 'reduced to the zero point of its significance',[99] (the idea of law's virtuality as the ultimate representation of law as *means*) and, on the other, a '*force-of-law*', a 'juridically formless ... *vis obligandi* or applicability'[100] (representing *the necessity of a decision* as the *external finality* of law).

In biopolitical terms, life itself is, at the same time, desemanticised and turned into a means for a decision on, precisely, life's governability (the ultimate end of bio-power).[101] The desemanticisation of life produces not only decidability but more generally life's governability, the idea that life as such is governable, or better, ungovernable (*an-archos*) and, for this very reason, something that *has to be governed*[102] through a praxis which will always demand, more or less directly, also a decision on the relationship between life and law. Any meaning biopolitics attributes to life will presuppose the '*signatura*' of life's governability, its constitution as a force-of-law, that is to say, *life normatively charged in order to ground a decision on its relationship with the law*—and, therefore, on law's self-preservation. *Life's governability is thus defined by its relationship with law's decidability.*

This is true even in situations in which the law seems to disappear. In this respect, even (Foucault's) *normalisation*, namely, processes through which all the aspects of life can become intelligible in terms of (deviation from) a norm—i.e., 'a new form of law, a mixture of legality and nature, prescription and constitution',[103] a 'natural rule', providing 'standards against which people are measured incessantly'[104]—is functionally (and thus instrumentally) related to *legalisation*. As Kelly observes, on one side, law is colonised by the norm and, on the other, the norm provides law 'with a new, indefinitely expanding

99 Agamben (2017) p 46.

100 Agamben (2017) p 198.

101 Siliquini-Cinelli (this volume) generally remarks that knowledge is 'a metaphysical end-result of intellectual processes of ontological abstraction that, through reason's methodological effectuality, objectify life for ordering purposes' are, in this sense, particularly instructive here (p 183). In this respect, I agree with his suggestion that 'law's experience is, and will always be taking place within, its very "epistemological foundation"' (p 184), (what I would describe as its *normative instrumentality of form and force*). If this implies, as he suggests, that 'law's instrumentality is inevitably dependent upon the epistemological (i.e., linguistic-ontological) mechanisms which we employ to metaphysically synthesise (i.e., normatively make sense of) life' (p 184) then study—as I theorised it here—is precisely the practice of remembering this fact without taking it for granted. Whereas law presupposes life as a normatively charged 'raw fact of existence' (Watkin (2013) p 184), the experience of studying the law—which is not law's experience—makes of this presupposing procedure a field of problematisation. This can be achieved, concretely, by exposing law's articulating logic (of both means and ends, form and force) through a constellation of paradigms of this articulating power (most of the remarks in sections two and three of this chapter can be interpreted in this sense).

102 See Agamben on 'apparatus' for a similar argument (2009b).

103 Foucault (1991b) p 304.

104 Kelly (2019) p 9.

scaffold'.[105] In other words, the norm stands for a representation of 'society itself in a perfected form'[106]—and, therefore, for the *end* of law (as a means) which gives it *force* (i.e., justifies its enforcement as a *formal means*)—but this constitution of norm as an end and a force (of law as means and form) stands ultimately, and again, for the constitution of a sphere of decidability on the ambiguous relation between law and life: society 'in a perfected form' is, in this sense, merely a virtual space in which 'everything is punishable',[107] the space of a never-ending trial.

Conclusion

All those who occupy the vacant place provided by law's biopolitical *signatura*, thus using and thinking the law as means to an end (and this certainly includes even all those who, at university, are trained to that purpose) partake in some way or another to the empowering of law itself, to the (biopolitical) function of its preservation. The student, if studying is considered as a means without ends, is the one who *questions* this framework by precisely gathering paradigmatic instances of law's *signatura*, examples of ambiguation and articulation of form and force, means and ends (of *both* life and law). By doing so the studious subject neither preserves nor destroys the law: more simply, in exhibiting its functioning—like Bartleby the scrivener who 'would prefer not to' write the law[108]—they *decide not to* reproduce law's *decidability*, thus exhibiting (without making it *effective*) their own power and, therefore, *actualising their own impotentiality*.

References

Giorgio Agamben (1995) *The Idea of Prose*, SUNY Press.
Giorgio Agamben (2009a) *The Signature of All Things: On Method*, Zone Books.
Giorgio Agamben (2009b) *What is an Apparatus?*, Stanford University Press.
Giorgio Agamben (2011) *Nudities*, Stanford University Press.
Giorgio Agamben (2017) *The Omnibus Homo Sacer*, Stanford University Press.
Manuel Atienza and Manero Ruiz (1998) *A Theory of Legal Sentences*, Springer.
Walter Benjamin (1996) 'The Critique of Violence' in Marcus Bullock and Michael W Jennings (eds) *Selected Writings: Vol. 1 (1913–1926)*, Harvard University Press.
Michel Foucault (1972) *The Archaeology of Knowledge and the Discourse on Language*, Pantheon Books.
Michel Foucault (1982) 'The Subject and Power' 8(4) *Critical Inquiry* 777.
Michel Foucault (1990) *Michel Foucault: Politics, Philosophy, Culture*, Routledge

105 Kelly (2019) p 21.
106 Kelly (2019) p 7.
107 Kelly (2019) p 18.
108 See Whyte (2009).

Michel Foucault (1991a) 'What is Enlightenment' in Rabinow Paul (ed) *The Foucault Reader*, Pantheon Books.

Michel Foucault (1991b) *Discipline and Punish*, Penguin Books

Michel Foucault (2009) *Security, Territory, Population*, Palgrave Macmillan

Leslie Green (2009) 'Law as a Means' in P Cane (ed) *Hart-Fuller Debate in the Twenty-First Century*, Hart Publishing.

Christina Hughes and Tight Malcolm (1995) 'The Myth of the Learning Society' 33 *British Journal of Educational Studies* 290.

Aimee Howley and Hartnett Richard (1992) 'Pastoral Power and the Contemporary University: A Foucaultian Analysis' 42(3) *Educational Theory* 271.

Peter Jarvis (2006) *Towards a Comprehensive Theory of Human Learning*, Routledge.

Mark Kelly (2019) 'What's in a Norm? Foucault's Conceptualisation and Genealogy of the Norm' 27 *Foucault Studies* 1–22.

Tyson Lewis (2013) *On Study: Giorgio Agamben and Educational Potentiality*, Routledge.

Hans Lindhal (2013) *Fault Lines of Globalization: Legal Order and the Politics of A-Legality*, Oxford University Press.

Neil MacCormick (2005) *Rhetoric and the Rule of Law*, Oxford University Press.

Andrei Marmor (2021) 'The Pure Theory of Law' in E Zalta (ed) *The Stanford Encyclopedia of Philosophy*, forthcoming, https://plato.stanford.edu/archives/fall2021/entries/lawphil-theory/.

Dean Mitchell (2017) 'Office and Agamben's Genealogy of Economy and Government' 4(2) *European Journal of Cultural and Political Sociology* 200.

Claes Peterson (2017) 'Natural Law Systematics: Is There a "Grundnorm" in Natural Law?' in P Langford, I Bryan and J McGarry (eds) *Kelsenian Legal Science and the Nature of Law*, Springer.

Scott Shapiro (2009) 'What is the Rule of Recognition (and Does it Exist)?' in M Adler and K Himma (eds) *The Rule of Recognition and the U.S. Constitution*, Oxford University Press.

Maarten Simons and Jan Masschelein (2006) 'The Learning Society and Governmentality: An Introduction' 38(4) *Educational Philosophy and Theory* 417.

Maarten Simons and Jan Masschelein (2008) 'The Governmentalization of Learning and the Assemblage of a Learning Apparatus' 58(4) *Educational Theory* 391.

Maarten Simons (2006) 'Learning as Investment: Notes on Governmentality and Biopolitics' 38(4) *Educational Philosophy and Theory* 523.

Brian Tamanaha (2006) *Law as a Means to an End*, Cambridge University Press.

William Watkin (2013) *Agamben and Indifference: A Critical Overview*, Rowman & Littlefield.

Jessica Whyte, '"I Would Prefer Not To": Giorgio Agamben, Bartleby and the Potentiality of the Law' 20 *Law and Critique* 309.

Thanos Zartaloudis (2015) 'Violence Without Law? On Pure Violence as a Destituent Power' in Brendan Moran and Carlo Salzani (eds) *Towards the Critique of Violence: Walter Benjamin and Giorgio Agamben*, Bloosmbury.

Thanos Zartaloudis (2018) 'An Introduction' in Zartaloudis Thanos (ed) *Law and Philosophical Theory: Critical Intersections*, Rowman & Littlefield.

Index